THE
ZULUS
AND
MATABELE

THE
ZULUS
AND
MATABELE

WARRIOR NATIONS

GLEN LYNDON DODDS

ARMS AND
ARMOUR

To the memory of my grandparents

Arms and Armour Press
An Imprint of the Cassell Group
Wellington House, 125 Strand, London WC2R 0BB

Distributed in the USA by Sterling Publishing Co. Inc.,
387 Park Avenue South, New York, NY 10016-8810.

British Library Cataloguing-in-Publication Data:
a catalogue record for this book is available from
the British Library

ISBN 1-85409-381-9

Designed and edited by DAG Publications Ltd.
Designed by David Gibbons; layout by Anthony A.
Evans; edited by John Gilbert; printed and bound
in Great Britain by Creative Print and Design Wales.

CONTENTS

PREFACE

In this book I have attempted to write lucid, authoritative and enjoyable accounts of the histories of the Zulu and Matabele nations, concentrating on their rise to power in the first half of the nineteenth century and their downfall at white hands as the century drew to a close.

My interest in both peoples stems back to my childhood in southern Africa. I can clearly recall seeing Zulus for the first time when I was on holiday in Durban. I was only three at the time and was taken by my parents to see traditional dancing by Zulu men dressed as warriors. The display they put on was awesome, and involved hitting their spears against their shields, stamping their feet on the ground, and alternately falling back and advancing in an ominous manner. It was too much for me. I got up and tried to make my escape.

Contact with the Matabele was also made at an early age, for my grandparents owned a farm at Filabusi in Matabeleland, Rhodesia, a place which featured in the Matabele Rebellion of 1896. On visits to the farm I was shown Matabele graves by my grandfather and also met a man named Fana (my grandfather's principal employee), a friendly Matabele. Fana had two young sons, named Robert and Tembo, with whom my brothers and I sometimes played cowboys and Indians.

I wish to thank relatives in southern Africa, Julie Edwards, Jack Crampton and Frank and Valerie Edmonstone, for either obtaining illustrations on my behalf or for sending me other material that I had requested. Thanks must also go to Philip Haythornthwaite for allowing me to use a number of photographs belonging to his collection, and to my brother, Gavin, for providing the maps which accompany the text. I also wish to thank Ashley Sutherland and other staff of Sunderland City Library for obtaining requested books and articles.

Finally, I wish to say something about the people to whom this book is dedicated, my grandparents Edward and Mary Crampton, affectionately known as Teddy and Tony. Though born in South Africa, they ended their days in what is now Zimbabwe after living on their farm through the bitter war which ended white minority rule in Rhodesia. Although staunchly right-wing, they did not have any animosity towards blacks in general, and were kind, decent people whom I remember with a great deal of affection. This is especially true of my grandfather, who loved history and one of whose favourite books was F. C. Selous's *Sunshine and Storm in Rhodesia*, a graphic account of the Matabele Rebellion. It is a source of pleasure to me to dedicate this book to their memory. *Glen Lyndon Dodds*

PART ONE

CHAPTER 1

IN THE BEGINNING WAS SHAKA

'In war he was an insatiable and exterminating savage, in peace an unrelenting and a ferocious despot....The world has heard of monsters – Rome had her Nero, the Huns their Attila, and Syracuse her Dionysius; the East has likewise produced her tyrants; but for ferocity, [Shaka] has exceeded them all.' *Nathaniel Isaacs*

'That man used to play around with people. A man would be killed though he had done nothing.' *Baleka kaMpitikazi*

In May 1824 a young English adventurer named Henry Francis Fynn was sitting on a beach in southern Africa gazing out over the Indian Ocean, hundreds of miles from civilisation. He was accompanied by three natives, one of whom was making coffee. Suddenly, they caught sight of an awesome spectacle. It sent Fynn's companions scurrying into the bush, but he remained where he was, as what appeared to be thousands of Zulu warriors approached, heading north up the beach homeward bound.

Fynn proceeded to communicate as best he could with the bemused Zulu commanders, principally using sign language, but repeating the name 'Shaka', which evidently struck a chord. The Zulus soon pressed on, leaving Fynn to follow in their wake. His hope was to meet the king whose name he had just mentioned: a hope that was initially to be frustrated, though in due course he was to become well acquainted with the Zulu monarch.

Shaka (whose name was formerly spelt 'Chaka') is one of the most celebrated and controversial figures in the history of southern Africa. To some, he was a cruel savage and bloodthirsty despot. Others maintain that he has been much maligned: his gruesome reputation is unwarranted and has come about as a result of a deliberate propaganda campaign by whites with selfish motives. What is undoubted is that Shaka was a man of great ability, who transformed the Zulu people into the most powerful African nation in southern Africa, and who is still widely revered as a potent symbol of Zulu nationhood.

He was born around 1787 in one of the most scenic parts of what is now South Africa, a well-watered and productive region situated between the majestic Drakensberg Mountains and the Indian Ocean to the east, inhabited by many clans belonging to the Nguni cultural and linguistic group. One such was the Zulus, a small group which traced its descent from a man named Zulu who is said to have settled beside the White Mfolozi River during the seventeenth century.

Shaka was the son of the Zulu chief, Senzangakhona, while his mother Nandi belonged to a neighbouring people, the Langeni. The circumstances surrounding Shaka's conception are often presented in a straightforward manner, but an examination of the relevant source material highlights a number of discrepancies.

In the early twentieth century, Jantshi kaNongila recounted one version of events to James Stuart, a fluent Zulu speaker and an avid recorder of Zulu testimony. Jantshi (whose father had been one of Shaka's principal spies), said that as an unmarried youth Senzangakhona had met Nandi when tending Zulu cattle with a number of colleagues near her home. The couple were mutually attracted and Shaka was conceived in one of several shelters which the young Zulu males had constructed to serve as temporary accommodation while they were in the neighbourhood.

Whether or not this version of events is correct, Shaka was certainly conceived while his mother was unmarried. To fall pregnant in such circumstances was viewed as a disgrace, and initially, according to some sources, including Jantshi, Nandi tried to conceal the cause of her condition. Rather than having succumbed to passion, she had been afflicted with an intestinal ailment, an *itshaka*. Others, however, maintain that when word of her pregnancy was sent to the Zulus, they responded by declaring that Nandi must had been affected in such a manner.

Either way, in due course Nandi gave birth to a son, who was consequently given the name 'Shaka'. It is generally maintained that shortly after his birth Nandi married Senzangakhona and went to live among the Zulus, though this view does not harmonise with all the evidence available. Jantshi, for instance, declared: 'Nandi never went at all to Senzangakhona to be his wife.' Instead, he believed that 'when Shaka had grown a little', Senzangakhona's mother brought him from the Langeni to grow up at her own homestead.

Whatever the truth, Shaka did not grow to manhood among the Zulus, for in about 1794 he returned with his mother to live among the Langeni, although the reason why this occurred is likewise uncertain. There he benefited from the affection of his maternal grandmother. In other respects, however, he was unhappy, for he was taunted and bullied by boys of his own age with whom he herded Langeni cattle. He had been tormented previously by young Zulus, and the consequent pain, both physical and mental, evidently left its mark. By nature Shaka appears to have been proud, and such experiences led him to become withdrawn, angry and vengeful.

In about 1802, Nandi and Shaka left the Langeni. One explanation for their departure is that they were expelled after Shaka stabbed an animal

10

belonging to the family of a boy who had infuriated him while they were playing a traditional game. Some suggest, though, that their departure was due to a food shortage caused by drought, and that this was an excuse for the Langeni to send the unpopular Nandi and her son packing.

In time, after residing among the Qwabe clan, Shaka placed himself under the protection of Chief Jobe of the Mthethwa people whose heartland lay between the lower reaches of the Mfolozi and the Mhlatuze Rivers south-east of Zulu territory. Shortly thereafter, in about 1807, Jobe died and was succeeded by a shrewd and capable individual named Dingiswayo. He placed Shaka under the special care of one of his principal advisers and chief military commander, Ngomane kaMqoboli, who effectively became Shaka's adoptive father.

Reportedly, Shaka was not a handsome young man. Baleka kaMpitikazi relates that, according to her father, he had 'a large nose, and was ugly' and that he had a speech impediment, probably a lisp or a stutter. She stated, moreover, that on one occasion in later years Shaka killed a 'pretty girl' for refusing to sleep with him. Baleka's unflattering description generally harmonises with other sources, though it is also generally agreed that Shaka had a fine muscular body.

During this period, conflict was on the increase in the region. One explanation offered as the reason for the rise in bloodshed was growing competition for land owing to population growth. Severe episodes of drought were evidently an additional factor. Ambition clearly played its part, too, for some chiefs were prepared to use force to enhance their wealth and power, notably by controlling local trade with a Portuguese settlement to the north at Delagoa Bay in Mozambique. This principally involved supplying the Europeans with ivory in exchange for goods such as brass and beads. Dingiswayo, for example, is said to have endeavoured to monopolise the whole of the Delagoa market, using violence to achieve this end.

Shaka distinguished himself whilst serving in Dingiswayo's army as a member of the iziCwe *ibutho* or regiment (which he came to command) and is said to have gained a reputation as a ferocious fighter. He considered that traditional Nguni warfare was too tame and inept, for instead of closing in for the kill and engaging in hand-to-hand fighting, warriors would merely stand some distance from each other and hurl throwing spears at their opponents – often with little result – while civilians looked on. The change to a more aggressive approach was probably already underway, in which case Shaka completed the process. Zulu tradition maintains that he developed a large-bladed stabbing spear set in a stout shaft, although as John Laband comments, Shaka's invention was 'probably a refinement on a weapon already in use by the Mthethwa and other people of the region'.

11

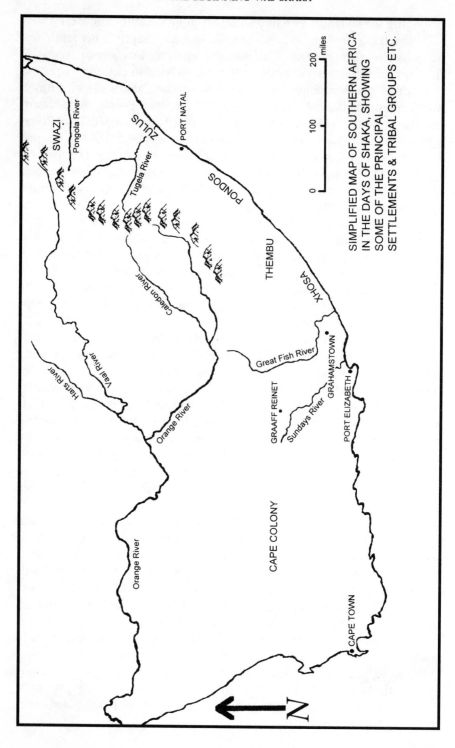

SIMPLIFIED MAP OF SOUTHERN AFRICA
IN THE DAYS OF SHAKA, SHOWING
SOME OF THE PRINCIPAL
SETTLEMENTS & TRIBAL GROUPS ETC.

In 1816 Senzangakhona died and Shaka became chief of the Zulus, with the backing of Dingiswayo, after murdering the rightful heir. Shaka then built himself a homestead which he called Bulawayo and organised the clan's manpower, perhaps about 400 men, into small regiments grouped according to age.

A programme of rigorous training ensued. The warriors were drilled and redrilled. The throwing spear was abandoned and the warriors instructed in the use of Shaka's new stabbing spear. They were to thrust the weapon underarm, and to employ it in conjunction with their shields. Shaka introduced a larger version of traditional oval shields, one that covered the warrior from shoulder to ankle. Each man was apparently instructed to hook the left edge of his shield over the edge of that of his adversary, and wrench the latter sheild to the left, dragging it across his opponent's body, thus throwing him off balance and rendering him vulnerable to the stabbing spear. Furthermore, to enhance manoeuvrability, Shaka is reported to have ordered his men to discard their cowhide sandals and fight barefoot. To toughen up the soles of their feet they were required to stamp on thorns, while to increase their fitness they were compelled to undertake lengthy marches. A dynamic little war machine was in the making.

Once prepared, Shaka took the offensive. Some sources say that the first people to suffer – understandably, in view of the treatment he had received – were the Langeni clan. He reportedly took them by surprise, singling out and putting to death individuals who had wronged himself or his mother, but sparing the majority of the people, who duly came under Shaka's rule.

Among other clans attacked in this period were the Buthelezi, who had been a tributary people of the Zulus but had gone their own way during the chieftainship of Shaka's father, and who were now sharply brought under Shaka's sway, as were other neighbouring clans. He was ruthless in his approach, prepared even to slaughter women and children. An old Zulu warrior was to recall: 'Women were not [previously] killed in war [nor] children....The practice of killing even women was one begun by Shaka. Chiefs are responsible for acts of madness.'

It seems probable that such brutality was calculated. Shaka evidently realised the value of terror – that it could intimidate actual and potential adversaries, who would either simply take to their heels or submit. Others no doubt understood this as well but were insufficiently ruthless to play by such rules. Shaka clearly had no such scruples.

The campaigns conducted by Shaka during this period were only several of many. Clans and confederations of clans were continually warring with one another, and the key players were Dingiswayo and his arch rival, Zwide, chief of the powerful Ndwandwe located to the north-west.

In 1817 the conflict between Dingiswayo and Zwide was bloodily resolved. The part Shaka played in the proceedings is uncertain. Henry

Fynn says that the Zulu chief accompanied Dingiswayo during the campaign and betrayed him to Zwide by informing the latter where Dingiswayo would position himself to watch the impending conflict, which led to Dingiswayo's capture. However, A. T. Bryant (a Catholic missionary who collected a wealth of oral tradition in Zululand late in the nineteenth century) states that after Dingiswayo arrived at an agreed rendezvous near the border, and before Shaka's arrival, he halted to await the rest of his forces. He then wandered off from his warriors accompanied by his handmaidens, and was seized by an enemy patrol. In any event, whether by fair means or foul, Dingiswayo fell into the hands of Zwide, who had him killed. It was an ignominious end for one of the most remarkable men of his generation, and following his death the Mthethwa confederacy began to collapse.

War with Zwide
To ensure that Shaka would not become as much of a threat as Dingiswayo had been, Zwide determined to deal with the growing power of the Zulu. In 1818, therefore, he sent an army south under his heir, Nomahlanjana, which may have been as many as 10,000 strong. Shaka is said to have deployed to oppose it on Gqokli Hill, a rocky knoll cresting a spur running northwards down to the White Mfolozi.

Little is definitely known about the ensuing battle, and Stephen Taylor has recently stated that 'the action was probably no more than a limited defence of high ground with an indecisive outcome'. It seems likely, however, that the encounter was bloody. Cetshwayo kaMpande (one of Shaka's nephews, and subsequently king, who was born in about 1832) comments that Shaka was attacked before he was ready and that 'a desperate fight ensued [with] great slaughter' in which the left wing of each army was victorious. Furthermore, Cetshwayo states that Shaka himself had a narrow escape when the part of the army with which he was stationed was surrounded, but that his warriors managed to break their way out. According to other sources, five of Zwide's sons, including Nomahlanjana, were killed.

Following the battle, the Ndwandwe laid waste much of the valley of the White Mfolozi as they headed home. For his part, Shaka retired and, after assembling his followers and cattle, temporarily withdrew towards the coast.

He continued subsequently to consolidate and strengthen his position through diplomacy and violence. Moreover, his strength was augmented by gaining the allegiance of a number of clans who deemed it expedient to throw in their lot with the Zulus. At some stage, too, Shaka killed the chief of the Qwabe clan and replaced him with a grateful tributary called Nqetho.

In 1819, after Shaka had beaten off a second Ndwandwe expedition near the Mhlatuze River, Zwide sent a powerful army under a formidable individual named Shoshangane to deal with the growing Zulu menace once and for all.

Instead of confronting his opponents in a pitched battle, Shaka fell back before them, deeper and deeper into Zululand towards the wooded terrain of the Nkandla range. The Ndwandwe had expected to forage for food – in line with traditional Nguni military practice – but Shaka had taken with him his cattle and grain. Hunger and exhaustion took their toll as the dispirited and increasingly famished Ndwandwe were led on a fruitless chase, much of it over rugged country. They were subjected, moreover, to the occasional hit-and-run action. Jantshi kaNongila relates that at night Zulu warriors infiltrated their camp and 'stabbed Zwide's people a good deal' before retreating 'to the forest and back to Shaka'. Matters finally came to a head when Shaka launched a full-scale attack and decisively defeated and scattered the enemy in a battle which, according to Cetshwayo, lasted from the early morning until past midday.

Shaka quickly followed up his victory by moving into the heart of his opponent's kingdom. It is said that as he approached Zwide's homestead, his warriors sang a Ndwandwe victory chant to lull the inhabitants of the royal kraal into a false sense of security; they emerged to greet their returning army only for many of them to be butchered. Zwide fled north-west across the Pongola River with some of his people into what is now southern Swaziland, leaving Shaka the dominant force south of the river, with the areas most firmly under his control extending from the Tugela River northward to the Mkhuze and as far west as the Mzinyathi (Buffalo) River. He had 'emerged from a grim war of survival a king indeed,' comments Laband. 'All at once he found himself ruling a larger territory, with a greater population, than had any chief in south-eastern Africa before him.'

Shaka did not allow his army to rest on its laurels. Other campaigns were now initiated, partly with the aim of seizing cattle to sustain the growing machinery of the Zulu state, especially in view of the renewed onset of severe drought which took its toll on Zulu livestock and crops. In particular, Shaka concentrated on an area to the south of the Tugela – Natal. This region was so named after the Portuguese explorer Vasco de Gama logged its existence on Christmas Day 1497, referring to it as *Terra Natalis*. The Zulu king now subjected its inhabitants to repeated and savage raids in a devastating period known as the *mfecane* (usually rendered 'the crushing'). Some of the Natal clans resisted and paid a heavy price; they were defeated and the survivors expelled. Many less powerful clans simply took to their heels and fled to inaccessible strongholds, leaving the Zulus to plunder at will. Hundreds of homesteads were destroyed and thousands of livestock

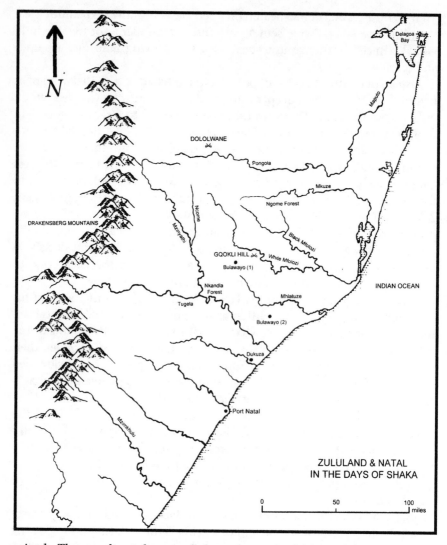

ZULULAND & NATAL
IN THE DAYS OF SHAKA

seized. The resultant hunger led to more death and despair as clans, desperate for food, began attacking one another. By 1824 much of the region was almost wholly depopulated. As Leonard Thompson states: 'In Natal organised community life virtually ceased.'

Furthermore, from the mid 1820s, Shaka exercised a loose control over the Tsonga kingdom of Maputo (or Mabhudu), which had formerly been under the sway of Zwide. Founded in the closing years of the eighteenth century in what is now southern Mozambique, the kingdom lay to the north-east of Zululand in the vicinity of Delagoa Bay, and through it the bulk of trade from the south to the bay was conducted. According to Alan Smith:

Shaka's envoys interacted peacefully, and concerned themselves almost exclusively with matters of trade and apparently only resorted to force in cases of disagreement over trade. While the other chiefdoms of the bay, especially Tembe [to the west] were being desolated, Maputo remained well cultivated, populous, and continued to do a brisk trade. The reason that the Maputo were granted virtual independence by Shaka was that they had gained a reputation for being shrewd traders.

Zululand – the state and its people

Zululand lies on the south-eastern coast of Africa between the beautiful and imposing Drakensberg Mountains and the Indian Ocean. Geographically, it is one of the most favoured areas in southern Africa. From frequently cool inland heights, it descends in a series of terraces to a subtropical coastal belt and is bisected by a number of rivers and streams which in some instances have cut impressive gorges.

In the nineteenth century, much of the high ground was heavily forested, while in the valleys and along the coastal belt thornbush grew profusely. There was moreover an abundance of game including antelope, elephant, lion and hippopotamus. Owing to a wide variety of grasses which matured throughout the year, and the comparative absence of the tsetse fly – the scourge of domestic livestock in much of Africa – Zululand was ideal cattle country. Indeed, cattle were central to the Zulu way of life, for in addition to providing meat, milk curds and hides, they were a major indicator of social standing and played a crucial role in marriage settlements. Such unions could only take place after an exchange of cattle.

The Zulus, as mentioned, belong to a cultural and linguistic group often referred to as the Nguni (a division of the negroid Bantu peoples) centred on the eastern coastal belt of southern Africa, with tribal territories extending southwards from Swaziland to the Great Fish River. The Nguni comprise a variety of peoples with dark brown skins and robust physiques, speaking variants of the same language and sharing a number of cultural phenomena such as widespread polygamy and taboos against cousin marriages.

The first Bantu tribes had evidently settled in South Africa by AD300 (much earlier than was once thought) and were the vanguard of an extended process of migration from central Africa by communities which apparently engaged in mixed farming and metal-working. They arrived in a region long inhabited by earlier settlers, the San and Khoikhoi (popularly known as the Bushmen and Hottentots), related non-Negroid peoples of small stature, with light brown or olive skins and features that differed from those of the newcomers. The San were Stone Age hunter-gatherers while the Khoikhoi were pastoralists. Conflict between the Bantu groups

17

and the indigenous peoples occurred, but so too did peaceful interaction, including intermarriage. For instance, the speech of the southernmost Nguni people, the Xhosa, strongly betrays Khoisan influence in the form of many click sounds.

Just when the Nguni first arrived in Zululand is uncertain. Monica Wilson has drawn attention to the fact that in 1554 people 'very black in colour' were mentioned south of the Mthatha River, and that in 1594 the survivors of a shipwreck recorded Nguni speech in the same area, indicating that the foremost Nguni were already settled far down the coast from Zululand by the sixteenth century at the latest. More recently Laband has commented:

> After about AD1500 the evidence indicates that the Iron Age people of the Natal–Zululand region were culturally, linguistically and physically the direct ancestors of today's black population, and that their distinctive Nguni-speaking culture had developed within their own region.

Hunter-gatherer communities continued to inhabit the region, however, and were present in the days of Shaka, having withdrawn to the inaccessible fastnesses of the Drakensberg.

Shaka's subjects lived in family homesteads or kraals known as *imizi* which dotted the countryside. They were normally located on an east-facing slope and consisted of a collection of thatched, domed huts, situated in a circle around a central cattle pen, and surrounded by a stockade. Each hut contained a shrine where the spirits of dead forebears were believed to reside. Facing the entrance, at the far end of the kraal, was the hut of the most senior wife, while those of the junior members of the family or dependents were located nearer to the entrance. The family head spent his time in the huts of his wives, although if he were a man of importance he would have a hut of his own into which he could retire for privacy. When a son married (and because the Nguni practised exogamy he could only marry a woman from another clan), he forsook the homestead and established one of his own, and in time his descendants might develop into a new clan.

Daily life for men entailed tending cattle and undertaking other tasks such as building kraal fences or erecting huts. Women, in addition to household duties, spent much of their time cultivating vegetables and grain in small plots close to the homestead – work normally deemed beneath a man's dignity.

Everyday costume was basic. Men were required to wear a sheath of plaited grass and leaves over the end of the penis. This constituted decent dress, but was normally overlaid by a loin covering which consisted of a kilt of fur strips twisted together to resemble tails, although by the 1830s it comprised a bunch of tails in the front and bullock-hide over the buttocks. Unmarried females wore a small leather skirt or a fringe of brown strings low on their hips, while married women were distinguished by a large pleated skirt.

Among important members of society were medicine men, *izinyanga* (who employed a wide range of herbal remedies and poultices to cure or treat wounds) and diviners, *izangoma*, frequently women, who officiated at 'smelling out' ceremonies to detect persons believed to be possessed by evil spirits, and thus deemed to be either wizards or witches. The diviner, dressed in exotic garb and arrayed with magical charms, danced around in the midst of a chanting circle of people and eventually struck one of those present with a gnu's tail, whereupon the hapless victim was dragged off and despatched by having a sharpened stake rammed up the anus.

As king, Shaka was paramount. Final decisions of state rested with him, as did ultimate command of the army. But he was also invested by tradition with other powers. He was viewed as the mouthpiece of his nation with the spirit realm – a role of crucial importance – and played a decisive part in the annual first fruits ceremony which ushered in the new harvest.

Shaka's kingdom of course consisted of a conglomeration of many clans. As mentioned, some of these had allied themselves with the ascendant Zulu, but others had been brought under his sway by conquest, and their chiefs replaced by more acceptable nominees. His practice of regularly moving about his kingdom was doubtless due largely to his desire to keep an eye on things. Although inevitably subordinate to Shaka, clan chiefs nonetheless enjoyed a considerable degree of power over their own people and in many cases were members of the advisory royal council of 'great ones'. Not that Shaka necessarily deferred to its wishes. Indeed, he was not beyond executing councillors who disagreed with him, which no doubt discouraged others from speaking their mind.

Key figures in the Zulu state were officials known as *izinduna* (popularly referred to as indunas), who were representatives of the king. They held important administrative or military posts and indirectly served to counter-balance the influence of clan chiefs. Indunas were appointed by the king and were often of exalted birth, but Shaka had no qualms about elevating men of modest birth if he deemed them worthy of such promotion.

Shaka's army
Something has already been said about traditional Nguni warfare, and how Shaka promoted a more aggressive form of combat. But Shaka's army, or impi – the great power-house of the Zulu state – must now be described in more detail.

19

The military system was based upon the institution of age-set units called *amabutho* (sing. *ibutho*) which evidently developed from the ancient practice among the Natal Nguni of assembling male youths for circumcision shortly after they had reached puberty. By the early nineteenth century, though, in the area later dominated by the Zulu kingdom, the practice of circumcision had died out, or was in the process of doing so. Nonetheless, chiefs continued to band together young men of comparable age who would perform various services on their behalf, both economic and military, when called upon to do so. Ian Knight, in *The Anatomy of the Zulu Army*, states:

> There is considerable evidence to suggest that these guilds were already being used as battlefield tactical units during the wars which preceded Shaka's rise, and that Shaka simply went one step further, turning them into the basis of a fully-fledged national army.

Amabutho thus formed the principal units of Shaka's army, and were commanded by indunas appointed by him. The regiments were not organised on a clan basis for that could have undermined the stability of the state. Instead, in line with the old practice of bringing youths together for initiation purposes, Shaka's regiments were organised on an age basis, those in their late teens being assembled from the various clans to form a new regiment. The majority of them would have already experienced a period of cadetship in their respective localities.

A newly formed regiment would be given a name, a distinctive uniform, and be ordered to construct a regimental barracks or *ikhanda* (pl. *amakhanda*). These were located at strategic points around the country and served as centres of the king's authority, for in addition to housing regiments they also functioned as royal homesteads and were often placed in the charge of female members of the royal house. The *amakhanda* were enclosed by a stockade, and at least in some cases these consisted of two rows of stakes pointing inwards so that they crossed at the top, with thornbush filling the gaps in between. The warriors occupied shared huts arranged in a circle around a central open space that not only accommodated the regimental cattle – which belonged to Shaka – but also functioned as a parade ground. At the top of each barracks was a fenced area, the *isigodlo*, where the king or his representatives dwelt when in residence. It also housed young women reserved for royal service and when a regiment (or regiments) were present, guards were posted outside it to keep the warriors at bay.

When resident at *amakhanda*, warriors were provided with meat and drink by the king. Other sustenance, however, had to be provided by members of their families who would bring grain and other provisions;

and for warriors whose relations lived some distance away this could, and did, result in hardship, for they might receive supplies intermittently and undergo periods of hunger.

The warriors based at these military homesteads were bachelors and remained such until their regiments were given royal permission to marry, usually granted when the men were nearly forty. It is sometimes maintained that when not engaged on military or other service, unmarried warriors spent all their time in their respective barracks, but it appears that after a few months of rudimentary training, members of a newly raised regiment would be allowed to return home. Thereafter they would assemble at the *ikhanda* for a few months every year.

Single warriors were effectively subject to whatever national service the king dictated. In addition to military training, they tended the royal cattle and, in contrast to life at home, sowed and reaped his crops. They looked after their huts and participated in organised hunts and ceremonial gatherings. By prolonging the bachelor years of his warriors, Shaka was able to utilise the manpower of his state to maximum efficiency; and as the single warriors had no resources of their own, they were dependent on his bounty.

Upon being granted permission to marry, the men usually chose their brides from a specified group of younger women, for they too were formed into age-grades, though not required to live in *amakhanda*. There were no ceremonial, mass marriages. The regiment simply dispersed and the men found themselves suitable partners, often women with whom they had already formed an attachment and in many instances had engaged in love-making, at least theoretically, short of full sexual intercourse. The married men would then set up homesteads of their own; henceforth their primary allegiance was to their family and clan chief, although they nevertheless remained within the *amabutho* system and could be called up again to serve alongside their former colleagues if exceptional circumstances so required.

Apart from assembling for major military campaigns, the army gathered to observe the all-important annual harvest festival, the great *umKhosi* or first fruits ceremony, which was usually held at the end of December or in early January. Its main purpose was to secure the blessing of the ancestral spirits of the Zulu clan on the new harvest. Prior to the ceremony, messengers were despatched to order the commanders of distant regiments to converge with their men on what was normally the king's principal homestead: regiments whose barracks were closer to hand would use them as a base throughout the subsequent rituals, while the less fortunate warriors from further afield would have to erect temporary huts nearby to serve as accommodation.

The regiments mustered for the *umKhosi* were resplendent, sporting their full regalia. During the ensuing rituals, which lasted several days, the king would repeatedly be smeared with medicine by *izinyanga*, both with the aim of warding off evil spirits and making him receptive to the influence of his deceased ancestors. At the height of the ceremonies, a young regiment was ordered to kill unarmed a fierce black bull taken from the herd of an enemy, the animal not always being the only fatality on such occasions.

Regiments varied in strength, from about 600 men to 1,200 men. Organisationally, they were divided into two wings, one led by the regimental commander, the other by a subordinate induna, both of whom were chosen by the king and usually came from an experienced regiment which had been granted permission to marry. Regiments were further subdivided into *izigaba* or sections with their own commanders. Each of these divisions was made up of companies consisting of men who had spent their period of cadetship at the same *ikhanda*. The strength of both *izigaba* and their constituent companies varied within regiments and from one regiment to another. Some companies, for instance, numbered only some 50 men whereas others were about 200 strong.

The Zulu armoury included the knobkerry – a club cut from a single piece of wood with a stout straight handle and a heavy knob at the end. The standard weapon, however, was the stabbing spear or *iklwa*. This evidently had a tapering blade about 18 inches long and 1½ inches wide. In contrast to shields, which were the property of the king, warriors had to obtain their own spears.

Warriors' oval shields were made from the hides of the king's cattle – and were kept in stores in each barracks until required for a campaign. Made of cowhide reinforced at the back by a vertical piece of wood held in place by a double row of hide lacing, they could measure more than 50 inches long by 30 inches wide. The top and bottom of the stick projected beyond the hide, and while the top was ornamented with a piece of fur, the base was cut to a point so that it could be jabbed in combat at an enemy's feet and ankles. Each man would choose a shield appropriate to his height.

Every regiment had its own uniform and distinctive shield, although the variations were sometimes slight – for when Shaka established a new *ibutho* he granted it a herd of cattle comprising animals whose hides, used for the shields, were fairly uniform. On this point Ian Knight comments: 'Judging from the extensive terminology used to describe the patterns on hides used for shields, the distinctions between the different *amabutho* were, in Shaka's day at least, quite specific.' Moreover, the colour of shields indicated the standing of a regiment. Newly formed *amabutho* had shields which were predominantly black while those of senior regiments were generally white.

22

Although the identifying shield is sometimes said to have been a novel feature introduced by Shaka, Fynn tells us that at an earlier date Dingiswayo's regiments were distinguished 'by the colour of the shields carried by the men'. Furthermore, Shaka is also often credited with introducing impressive uniforms. However, again, Fynn comments that these were likewise not an innovation, for Dingiswayo had 'introduced imposing war-dress' among his *amabutho.*

In addition to a distinctive shield, each regiment had its own uniform. These consisted of furs, cows' tails and bird feathers. Originally, the raw materials were found within Zululand itself but as Shaka's army grew, the kingdom's wildlife was insufficient to meet the demand and so pelts and feathers were obtained from elsewhere, either as tribute or through trade, most notably from Tsonga groups bordering Zululand's north-eastern boundary. The ends of cows' tails were worn suspended from thongs around the elbows and the knees, and sometimes at the wrists and ankles as well. Fynn tells us that some warriors also wore 'a dress of oxtails over the shoulders and chest' (certainly at a later date, and perhaps in Shaka's time as well, cows' tails sometimes hung in bunches that reached to the waist in front and the knees behind), while other warriors sported on their chests the skins of monkeys and genets cut into strips and twisted to resemble tails. Around the waist, the warriors wore kilts of twisted monkey and genet skins extending to the knees.

The uniforms included splendid and often complex headdresses. The basis of the headdress was a padded band of animal skin, usually leopard skin in the case of junior regiments, otter skin for the senior regiments. Square or oblong earflaps, normally of samango monkey skin, but sometimes of leopard skin, were attached to the headband and hung down to the jawline. Some regiments also had flaps hanging from the back of the head and reaching down to the shoulders. In addition, each regiment wore distinctive plumes fixed to the headband. Young regiments, for instance, usually sported the long black tail feathers of the sakabuli bird, while members of married regiments displayed blue crane feathers. Individual warriors who had distinguished themselves for bravery were awarded small bunches of the scarlet feathers of the lourie bird, and/or a brass armband for the right forearm and a necklace of interlocking wooden beads.

When Shaka summoned the army for a campaign, the regiments rapidly made their way to the capital. Once assembled, they underwent various ceremonies (including ritual vomiting) aimed at binding them together and rendering them invulnerable both to enemy weapons and supernatural attempts to bring them misfortune. A key feature of the preparations was the *giya*, in which prominent warriors (or regiments) were called upon to perform an aggressive dance in front of their colleagues. James Stuart was told that the *giya* was intended 'to sharpen the heroes'. A warrior singled out for such a distinction 'would remember his praises when the battle was on, feeling he would be worthless if he did not fight fiercely'.

The army would then set off in a column, but would divide in two when nearing the enemy. Henry Fynn witnessed Shaka's army moving off against the Ndwandwe in 1826 and observed:

> Every man was ordered to roll up his shield and carry it on his back – a custom observed only when the enemy is known to be at a considerable distance. In the rear of the regiments were the baggage boys, few above the age of 12, and some not more than six. These boys were attached to the chiefs and principal men, carrying their mats, headrests, tobacco, etc., and driving cattle required for the army's consumption. Some of the chiefs, moreover, were accompanied by girls carrying beer, corn and milk; and when their supply had been exhausted these carriers returned to their homes.

Then, as was customary, the impi had to resort to foraging.

The Zulu army was extremely mobile in comparison with its European counterparts; although the figure has sometimes been wildly exaggerated, it could cover over twenty miles in a single day without undue effort, and maintain such a pace for days. This surely testifies to the stamina of its constituent warriors, bearing in mind the often rugged terrain over which they moved.

The impi on the march was screened by scouts well to the fore, charged with the task of reporting enemy movements. Between the scouts and the main body of the army was an advance guard, consisting of warriors from each regiment sent forward with the aim of fooling the enemy into the belief that this represented the principal Zulu force.

When near enough to the enemy, if circumstances permitted, the army would draw into a circle where the warriors were given their orders and sprinkled, for the final time, with more medicine by the war-doctors.

Once battle had been joined – the preferred time for an attack was dawn – the senior commanders would normally watch unfolding events from high ground. Although the degree of control they could exercise after the warriors had been committed was minimal, they would issue fresh instructions by runner or through hand signals.

The Zulus' favourite attack formation was an encircling movement known as the 'beast's horns', comprising a centre, flanking units and a reserve. The centre or 'chest' consisted of veteran regiments which would advance to engage the enemy, while on the flanks the 'horns', made up of younger warriors, would dash forward with the aim of surrounding their opponents. The reserve, or 'loins', stayed to the rear to enter the fray when and where required. Shaka is credited with the invention of the 'beast's horns' tactic, but this is not certain. On this point Ian Knight comments: 'The best that can be said with certainty is that the *impondo zankomo* emerged early in the kingdom's history, and quite possibly under Shaka' and 'was undoubtedly in vogue in the 1830s' during the reign of his successor.

If, as so often proved the case, the battle ended in victory, the Zulus disembowelled the bodies of slain opponents, for it was believed that the spirit of the deceased was in his stomach: if not released, it would wreak havoc on the warrior responsible, sooner or later driving him to insanity.

At the end of a campaign, the army returned to the principal royal homestead. Here warriors who had distinguished themselves were singled out for commendation and rewards. But others, accused of cowardice, were executed. For example, a man who had lost his spear or had been wounded in the back could expect such a fate. Mtshapi kaNoradu (the son of one of Shaka's warriors and one of James Stuart's sources), relates the general opinion of a coward's fate:

> Shaka used to order that a person should be seized, and his arm lifted up; he would then say, 'Give him a taste of the assegai, the thing that he fears so much.' He would then be stabbed as if he were a goat, and killed.

By the mid 1820s, when Shaka's power was at its height and men more numerous and expendable, warriors are said sometimes to have been despatched in such a manner quite at random, having been selected from among their fellows simply to remind the army that it was always expected to fight courageously.

The strength of the Zulu army in Shaka's day is uncertain. Its strength has sometimes been put at about 50,000 men. Even higher figures have been suggested, but none are credible. Shaka's army was undoubtedly much smaller, and modern estimates, based on probable population levels, place its strength in 1824 at approximately 15,000 men.

Contact with Europeans

By 1824, as mentioned by Henry Fynn, much of Natal was virtually depopulated. Early in that year Fynn was a resident of Cape Town, a settlement situated on a peninsula at the south-west tip of Africa. Originally a revictualling station founded by the Dutch East India Company in 1652, it had been taken over by the British in 1806. Here he heard rumours that a powerful and very wealthy black kingdom existed far to the north. The reports stemmed from black refugees fleeing the *mfecane*, and also from certain whites. One of the latter was a merchant named John Robert Thompson who arrived at Cape Town in 1822 after returning from a

venture to the long-established but nondescript Portuguese trading settlement at Delagoa Bay. Thompson talked of 'a formidable tribe' which had
recently risen from obscurity to a position of supremacy under its chief,
'Chaka', who had 'established a barbaric kingdom of large extent'
governed through 'military despotism'.

Although some dismissed such tales as of no great consequence, Fynn
was not one of them. Neither was an ex-Royal Navy lieutenant named
Francis George Farewell. Excited and intrigued by what he heard, Farewell
decided that money could be made by opening up contact with Shaka. In
1823, therefore, he chartered two vessels and sailed up the coast, with that
purpose in view. As it happened, no such contact was made, but Farewell
did come across a suitable location for a rival port to Delagoa – the site of
present-day Durban.

On his return to Cape Town, he began to plan the establishment of an
alternative port which would draw away the ivory trade from Delagoa
Bay, to which the Zulus brought their tusks of elephant and
hippopotamus. Fynn was among those who consented to participate in
the venture. It has recently been argued that Farewell and his colleagues
were motivated by a desire to engage in the slave trade, but this view is
unconvincing.

In May 1824, a small advance group – which did not include Farewell
himself – arrived off the coast of Natal. The party was led by Fynn, whose
Diary records that they entered a beautiful bay (known to the Portuguese
as Rio de Natal), largely enclosed by jaws of land and overlooked by territory which teemed with game.

Fynn came ashore with three companions and spent what proved a
stormy night encamped on sand dunes, harassed by hyenas. He soon made
contact with a native called Mahamba, whose people had been devastated
by the Zulus and who told him that Shaka lived somewhere to the north.

Fynn promptly set off up the beach in search of Shaka's residence –
which he believed to be much closer – accompanied by Mahamba and two
black servants, one of whom was an interpreter. After walking about twelve
miles, Fynn sat down and ordered coffee. It was while the kettle was
coming to the boil that Fynn, as mentioned earlier, suddenly realised they
were not alone:

> I saw on my right a dense mass of people coming fast from the direc-
> tion I had come. My view extended over several miles of the beach,
> but I could not see the rear of this immense black and continuous
> mass of natives, all armed and in their war-dresses.

As Fynn later discovered, the warriors were part of a tired Zulu army
heading home, after having conducted a raid against the Pondo kingdom

south of the Mthamvuna River. Mahamba immediately took to his heels, and was soon followed into the bush by the servants. But Fynn stood his ground and engaged in conversation as best he could with the astonished Zulu commanders.

The existence of Europeans was of course not unknown to the Zulus, partly owing to their trade with the Portuguese, and they referred to whites as 'the makers of wonders'. They also used an older expression, *abeLungu*, roughly meaning 'pale and bedraggled sea creatures', for over the years European survivors of shipwrecks had occasionally struggled ashore along the coast, being regarded as strange inhabitants of the ocean who sometimes abandoned their watery home.

The warriors duly continued on their way, and next day Fynn, with his two servants, followed in their wake, eventually reaching a kraal on the fringe of Shaka's domain. Learning, however, that the king was not yet prepared to see him, he returned to the port, where Farewell and the rest of his party had just landed.

Word then arrived that Shaka was now ready to receive Fynn and his companions. Escorted by about a hundred of Shaka's warriors, a small group, including Farewell and Fynn, therefore set off to see the king. Progress was slow, but after several days they reached a ridge from which Bulawayo could be seen.

Farewell and Fynn were the first to enter the royal homestead where, according to the latter, much of the Zulu nation, including some 12000 warriors, had assembled to meet them. They were welcomed with an impressive display of military bravado, dancing, and exhibitions of cattle assorted by colour. 'It was a most exciting scene,' states Fynn, 'surprising to us, who could not have imagined that a nation termed "savages" could be so disciplined and kept in order.' Shaka asked whether his guests had ever seen a land as well ordered as his own and boasted that 'he was the greatest king in existence, that his people were as numerous as the stars, and that his cattle were innumerable'.

Shaka had recently heard news of the outside world from an interesting individual named Jakot, who had arrived at his court in 1823. Jakot had, for example told the king about the conflict between his own people, the Xhosa, and invading Dutch settlers, a conflict waged to the south of the Pondo kingdom and thus well beyond Shaka's sphere of influence. Now, through Jakot – who had learnt some English as a result of previous contacts – Shaka questioned his guests. Among other things, he wished to know whether the British monarch, George IV, was as great a king as himself.

Farewell returned to the bay in late July, but at Shaka's request Fynn and a servant remained behind. In further conversation, Shaka remarked that he believed Zulu weaponry to be superior to firearms, for the effectiveness of guns was reduced by the time it took to reload, so enabling his warriors to reach and overwhelm potential white opponents.

Of Shaka's attitude during such private conversations, Fynn wrote:

> In the presence of his people he placed the worst construction on everything, ridiculing all our manners and customs, though in perfect good humour [but when] none of his subjects were present he would listen with the greatest attention and could not help acknowledging our superiority. He, however, took exception to our method of imprisoning criminals, regarding it as the most horrid pain man could endure. If one were guilty why not punish the deed with death?

Within days of Farewell's departure, Fynn featured in a dramatic incident – the aftermath of an attempt to kill Shaka. The assassins' identity is uncertain. They were presumed to be either dissident Qwabe, or Ndwandwe sent by Zwide, although the assassination plot perhaps emanated from within the Zulu royal house itself. They struck during a dance, with the result that a spear passed through Shaka's arm and into his side. Hysteria erupted. The king was carried to a hut in a kraal near Bulawayo where he benefited from the ministration of a Zulu medicine man and from the attention of Fynn, who had a rudimentary knowledge of medical matters. The Englishman bathed the wound with camomile tea and bandaged it with linen. Medicines already promised by Farewell then arrived and were employed by Fynn. Even so, for four days the atmosphere was tense – Shaka's life hung in the balance. His condition then began to improve and he was soon sufficiently recovered to appear in public.

In early August, Farewell reappeared, having received word of the assassination attempt. Shaka evidently believed that his recovery was due to magical powers enjoyed by Fynn, and thus, sensing that an opportune time had come to stake his claim, Farewell presented Shaka with a written petition begging for land. His hopes were rewarded. On 7 August, the king responded by making his mark on the document, thereby, as far as the whites were concerned, ceding to them the bay where they had landed and some 3500 square miles of the surrounding countryside as well.

Following Shaka's recovery, Fynn returned to the bay with his colleagues and, on 27 August, ran up the Union Flag (Union Jack) and named the new settlement Port Natal. Farewell and his companions took up residence there, assuming the manner of local chiefs, and in some cases married native wives. They gathered supporters, refugees from Shaka's wars, whom they judged according to African law, and amassed herds of cattle and stocks of ivory at their respective homesteads.

Following the attempt on his life, Shaka moved his capital, Bulawayo, from beside the White Mfolozi in the Zulu heartland south to a ridge that enjoyed a commanding view of the Mhlatuze Valley. Here an impressive new homestead was constructed, with an outer palisade nearly two miles in circumference and enclosing some 1500 huts. The new capital, sometimes referred to as Gibixhegu, was in Qwabe country and the move was no doubt partly intended by Shaka as a means of more effectively stamping out dissent among the Qwabe.

Shaka moves against Sikhunyana
In return for permission to settle at Port Natal, the Zulu king expected the whites to serve him when called upon to do so. To him they were merely subordinate chiefs subject to his will, and not, as they saw themselves, independent masters of their own destiny. In 1826 they were called upon to join the king's army for a campaign against the Ndwandwe, whose king, Sikhunyana, had recently succeeded his father, Shaka's old adversary, Zwide. Despite the events of 1819, the Ndwandwe were still a potent force, and had raided the northern regions of Shaka's domain. So he was determined to deal with Sikhunyana, encouraged by the defection to his side of a number of dissident Ndwandwe.

According to Fynn, and another member of the Port Natal community named Nathaniel Isaacs, who had arrived the previous year as a youth of seventeen, the Europeans were reluctant to comply with Shaka's summons but deemed it wise to do so when the king informed them that he could, if he so wished, destroy them with impunity.

The army which gathered was undoubtedly one of the largest Shaka ever assembled, and he led it in person. Fynn states that 'the whole body of men, boys and women, amounted as nearly as we could reckon, to 50,000', a figure that is generally and no doubt correctly believed to be something of an over-estimate.

The Zulus and their white colleagues moved north at a leisurely pace and, after crossing the Pongola, came across the enemy deployed on a slope in the wooded country of the Dololwane Hills. Fynn (who was to watch the battle from a suitable vantage point) says that the Zulus approached 'with much caution ... till within twenty yards of the enemy'. Jakot, the Xhosa interpreter, then fired three shots, whereupon 'both parties, with a tumultuous yell, clashed together, and continued stabbing each other for about three minutes' before falling back. A brief lull followed. Then, seeing that 'their losses were about equal', they closed again and a more prolonged clash occurred. Both sides then disengaged for the second time, with the Zulus having had the better of the contest. Emboldened by this, Shaka's warriors charged once more and the Ndwandwe lines began to collapse. According to a Zulu source, at one point in the carnage Zulu killed Zulu when warriors came face to face after encircling and killing Ndwandwe in their path.

Following the disintegration of Sikhunyana's army, the slaughter began in earnest. Shaka had given orders for all the Ndwandwe to be finished off and thus women and children were likewise butchered. The Ndwandwe ceased to exist as a nation. But Sikhunyana was not among the thousands who perished. He fled and was to live on for many years in obscurity.

The death of Nandi

By defeating Sikhunyana, Shaka had effectively secured his northern border, and he now turned his eyes to the south, apparently focusing on events beyond Natal. His armies had already raided the kingdom of the Pondos some 200 miles away, bordering southern Natal. Beyond that mauled kingdom lay the territory of the Xhosa, who were in turn bordered to the south by subjects of King George IV living in Cape Colony on the far side of the Great Fish River. It has been suggested that with the encouragement of the Port Natal whites, Shaka may have contemplated extending his authority southward and opening up direct contact with the British. What is certain is that in November 1826 he moved south across the Tugela River into Natal and established a new principal residence near the sea at Dukuza.

Within a year of founding Dukuza, Shaka's mother died. Hearing of her illness, Shaka apparently hastened to her homestead near Bulawayo. Fynn, who was present, relates that he was ordered to attend Nandi, but saw no hope of saving her. She had been struck down with dysentery and her life was ebbing away. Upon receiving word of her death, Shaka appeared before the hut in which her body lay, accompanied by his principal chiefs in war attire. After standing, head bowed on his shield and weeping silently for about twenty minutes, he gave a heavy sigh and let out a series of yells which, in Fynn's words, 'fearfully contrasted with the silence that had hitherto prevailed', whereupon the chiefs and people 'to the number of about 15,000, commenced the most dismal and horrid lamentations'.

Did Nandi indeed die of dysentery? James Stuart was told a different tale: Shaka had stabbed his mother in a fit of rage in the belief that she was harbouring a potential rival and, horrified by what he had done, bound up the wound. Within days, however, Nandi died after reports had been circulated that she was ill. Stuart also heard that Shaka was responsible for his mother's death from a white informant, an early Natal settler named William Bazley, who stated that Fynn himself had admitted as much to him in private. Given that Shaka's mental state was apparently becoming increasingly troubled, it would be unwise to dismiss out of hand the reports that he might have struck down his mother, although the grief he displayed upon her death could nonetheless have been genuine.

What is beyond doubt is that Nandi's death resulted in a frenzied period of mourning on the part of those present at the kraal and those thousands

30

who travelled to Bulawayo to mourn their king's bereavement. Fear of incurring Shaka's displeasure was no doubt a principal factor in these displays of public sorrow. Deaths occurred, especially when some of those present began attacking one another. Indeed, Fynn says that the kraal and its vicinity witnessed a bloodbath in which no less than 7000 people died. But his figures are frequently on the high side and this one is hard to credit. Even so, we hear from Zulu sources, such as Jantshi kaNongila, that many of the mourners perished during this emotionally charged period in which Shaka doubtless arranged for many enemies, real or imagined, to be killed.

War and diplomacy

Shaka proceeded to call a year-long period of national mourning, with certain prohibitions affecting aspects of daily life which were to be punishable by death if broken. In the event, some of the restrictions – such as one that forbade cultivation – were soon lifted. Shaka then held a purification ceremony at Dukuza to bring an end to the period of national grief.

A southern campaign against frontier tribes soon followed. It has been suggested that it was largely if not entirely instigated by unscrupulous Port Natal settlers, who wished him to launch such attacks in the hope that it would lead to retaliation by the British authorities and pave the way for a greater British say in the affairs of Natal, with themselves as beneficiaries. Shaka may have been persuaded that by subduing the blacks who lived between Zululand and Cape Colony, a treaty of friendship could be agreed with the British authorities at the Cape, which would acknowledge his right to supremacy over the region's black population. A Scottish member of the Port Natal community named Charles Maclean states that he was told by Shaka that he wished only for two great kings in the world, himself to rule the blacks and George IV to rule the Europeans; and Fynn writes that the impi was ordered not to progress further south than the territory of the Xhosa chief, Hintza, for Shaka wished to be on good terms with Cape Colony.

Indeed, just before the army departed, Shaka sent a diplomatic mission to the Cape. It was led by one of his most trusted indunas, Sothobe kaMpangalala, and included two Port Natal settlers, James King and Nathaniel Isaacs. But the mission did not solely have a political dimension. We are told by both Fynn and Isaacs that Shaka was interested in obtaining a cosmetic hair ointment, Macassar oil, which Fynn had mentioned to him and which Shaka evidently believed had the power to restore lost youth.

The envoys sailed from Port Natal in late April on board a crude schooner constructed by the settlers as a replacement for a brig that had been wrecked at the entrance to Port Natal's harbour in 1825. It is sometimes said that the mission left shortly after the impi had set off on its campaign, but in fact Sothobe and his companions sailed before the warriors moved south.

On 4 May the embassy arrived at the settlement of Port Elizabeth in Cape Colony and King sent word of his arrival to Cape Town. But things did not go smoothly. Instead of being allowed to proceed, the party was kept waiting at Port Elizabeth for three months during which a certain Major Josias Cloete, representing the governor of the colony, subjected the Zulus to questioning, believing them to be spies. Furthermore, he told Sothobe that King enjoyed no status with George IV or any other British authority. Finally, on 2 August, HMS *Helicon* arrived at Port Elizabeth from Cape Town carrying gifts for Shaka and official word that the authorities did not wish to receive the mission. King and his frustrated colleagues therefore departed for Port Natal.

Meanwhile, Shaka's warriors had struck. Shaka accompanied the impi in person as far as the Mzimkhulu River where he halted with a bodyguard and spent some time in the company of Fynn, who had property in the neighbourhood. At the Mzimkhulu, Shaka divided the impi, despatching part of it to attack the Pondos, while the remainder were sent against the Thembus, a tribe living further inland. The Pondos avoided conflict by sheltering in strongholds in rugged country, leaving the Zulus to destroy abandoned kraals; but as they emerged from their refuges, they were struck by the Zulus who had re-entered their territory. After rounding up cattle, the warriors began to retrace their steps on the long journey home. The other arm of the impi, having devastated the Thembus, likewise headed back with thousands of head of cattle.

Upon receiving word of the Zulu invasion into what the British deemed their sphere of influence, a small force under Major Dundas was sent across the frontier and drew blood on 20 July. In a heated encounter Dundas routed what he believed to be part of the with-drawing Zulu army. It was not. The Zulus had already retired. The trounced natives were Ngwane, followers of a chief named Matiwane who had been ejected with his clan from the eastern foothills of the Drakensberg Mountains some years earlier by Shaka and had lived in the interior before moving south-east into the frontier region. A month later, on 26 August, a larger British force again encountered Matiwane and his followers and overwhelmed them, again believing that they were Zulus.

It was in late August that Shaka heard that the diplomatic mission had been a failure and examined the paltry gifts sent to him. To make things worse, Isaacs had forgotten to obtain the Macassar oil. Shaka reacted angrily. Isaacs states that he feared for his own life: 'I began to perceive that I stood on the brink of eternity.... I was incessantly abused, and often threatened with immediate execution.'

Meanwhile, instead of being allowed the customary rest period after the campaign, the army had been despatched to the north, primarily against Shoshangane, Zwide's former general who had departed with a band of followers in the aftermath of Shaka's destruction of Zwide's kingdom south of the Pongola, and had carved out a kingdom of his own north of Delagoa Bay. The tired warriors set off with little enthusiasm. Indeed, there was probably widespread dissatisfaction with Shaka. The lives of his subjects had always meant little to him. It was not unknown for him to have someone – or entire groups of people – executed for little or no reason and such deaths had become increasingly common. Shaka was greatly feared, and there can be no doubt that many of the warriors regarded their king as an extremely harsh and dangerous tyrant – a millstone around his people's neck. The millstone was soon to be shattered: a conspiracy to kill Shaka was afoot.

At its heart were two of his younger half-brothers, Dingane and Mhlangana, both of whom enjoyed the support of his powerful aunt, Mnkabayi, who is said to have encouraged them in order to avenge Nandi's death. Another conspirator was Shaka's body-servant, Mbhopa kaSithayi. As Shaka developed into an increasingly mistrustful and capricious killer, the brothers may well have feared for their own safety and concluded that it was best to strike before they themselves were liquidated. Zulu tradition has it that Dingane was motivated by a genuine desire to free the Zulu people from Shaka's bloody rule.

Shaka had ordered Dingane and Mhlangana to take part in the northern campaign. But shortly after setting off, they feigned illness and returned to their own kraals near Dukuza. Then, with Mbhopa, they finalised plans to eliminate the king. On 24 September 1828, Shaka was assassinated by the conspirators at a small homestead in the vicinity of Dukuza. He tried to make his escape when the assassins struck, but failed, and was finished off near the kraal gate. It is said that as he lay dying in a pool of blood he exclaimed words to the effect: 'You will not rule when I am gone, for the land will see white people and locusts come.'

Shaka's life ended abruptly when he was only about 41 years of age. His career had been remarkable. He had risen from obscurity as the chief of a minor clan to become the most powerful black ruler in southern Africa, and had initiated the process of forging a Zulu national identity among the many Nguni-speaking clans that he had brought under his sway.

He has often been described as 'the Napoleon of Africa'. This analogy is over-strained. Napoleon Bonaparte had an exceptional military mind: he operated on a far larger stage, commanding armies that sometimes numbered hundreds of thousands of men, and faced formidable coalitions of enemies determined to destroy him. Moreover, his intellectual abilities extended well beyond the military sphere. It is doubtful that Shaka was in the same class. He is often said to have invented the 'beast's horn's' forma-tion, but as has been seen, even this is uncertain. Nor was he the first to use *amabutho* as regiments furnished with elaborate uniforms, for, as noted, Fynn tells us that upon becoming chief of the Mthethwa, Shaka's patron Dingiswayo had formed his *amabutho* into regiments subdivided into companies and had provided them with distinctive shields and elab-orate uniforms. Moreover, as mentioned, Shaka's famous stabbing spear, the *iklwa*, may have been a refinement of a weapon already in use among the northern Nguni rather than a totally original innovation.

Nevertheless, it would be wrong to be wholly dismissive. Shaka did not achieve the power and the status he enjoyed by accident. He had a good grasp of tactics and strategy, and may well have introduced a much greater degree of professionalism into northern Nguni warfare. Of him, Ian Knight comments:

> Shaka certainly developed fighting techniques to an unprecedented degree, and there is a wealth of stories concerning his prowess as a warrior: he may, indeed, have been one of the great military geniuses of his age.... Shaka taught his warriors to advance rapidly in tight formations and engage hand-to-hand, battering the enemy with large war-shields, then skewering their foes with the new spear as they were thrown off balance.

And what of Shaka's character? This is the subject of great controversy. A number of scholars argue that his demonic reputation is undeserved, that his name has been deliberately blackened by Europeans to mask their alleged involvement in the slave trade and their occupation of land. There is undoubtedly an element of truth in this. For instance, some of what Nathaniel Isaacs has to say about the king has to be taken with a pinch of salt, for he recommended portraying Shaka in a bloodthirsty manner in order to captivate as many readers as possible, and doubtless did so himself. But as Carolyn Hamilton has recently commented:

> Examination of the image of Shaka promoted by the Port Natal traders in the 1820s reveals that, with two highly specific exceptions which were not influential at the time, the traders' presentation of Shaka was that of a benign patron. It was only in 1829, after the Zulu king's death, that European representations began to include a range of 'atrocity' stories regarding Shaka.

Yet rather than being mere invention by whites, Hamilton concludes, the stories 'drew on images of Shaka already in place amongst the African communities of southern Africa'.

In short, although Shaka was evidently capable of feelings of tenderness and affection, it is reasonable to conclude that he was essentially a harsh, brutal figure, to whom human life in general meant little. Baleka kaMpitikazi stated that people would be executed even though they had done nothing to warrant their fate, having 'neither practised witchcraft, committed adultery, nor stolen'. True, Baleka was a Qwabe, a people with little love for Shaka. Nonetheless, comparable points are made by others. Jantshi kaNongila, for instance, declares:

> Very frequently did Shaka cause people to be put to death.... Amongst Shaka's extraordinary acts was his causing a pregnant woman to be cut open in order to see what position the child took up in its mother's womb. He did this more than once.

Others concur. Maziyana kaMahlabeni told Stuart of just such an atrocity, committed just before Shaka was assassinated:

> Shaka cut open a number of women when their husbands were away on campaign in order to see how the child lay in the womb. That was one of the reasons why Dingane put Shaka to death. These women had done no wrong.

It is sometimes said that Shaka deliberately used terror as a policy, a means of inspiring awe in his subjects and maintaining an iron grip on his people. Yet over the years the killings seem to have become more whimsical; and as Leonard Thompson aptly comments: 'As with other military despots, success eventually went to his head and undermined his sense of reality.' In truth, he deserved his end.

CHAPTER 2
'KILL THE WIZARDS!' –
THE REIGN OF DINGANE

'Certain it is, as far as human foresight can judge, that we shall speedily hear either of the massacre of the whole company of Boers, or of – what is scarcely less terrible – wars and bloodshed, of which there will be no end till either the Boers or the Zulu nation cease to be.' Francis Owen

As he watched Shaka dying in a pool of blood from wounds partly inflicted by himself, Mhlangana may well have believed that he would be the next Zulu king and that a glorious future lay ahead. If so, he was mistaken. Within weeks he followed his brother to the grave, struck down by Dingane, aided and abetted by others, most notably Mnkabayi, who wished to have Mhlangana out of the way so that Dingane could become king.

Shortly after this, as 1828 drew to a close, the army Shaka had sent north began to return in dribs and drabs to find him dead. It was just as well. The campaign had been a disaster and the warriors expected a far from tranquil homecoming. After entering what is now Mozambique, they had experienced disease and hunger. Moreover, their suffering had subsequently been compounded when Shoshangane gave them a bloody reception north-east of Delagoa Bay after launching a surprise night attack. Although their commander, Mdlaka kaNcidi, had managed to rally them and regroup, Shoshangane avoided further conflict and the dispirited Zulus had headed for home. Unexpectedly, they found Dingane in a generous mood, anxious to gain their acceptance. Fynn notes that the warriors were treated with 'liberality and kindness'.

Fortunately for Dingane, the great men of the nation willingly accepted him as their new ruler, and to secure his position he inaugurated his reign by behaving magnanimously. He allowed the regiments to freely consort with women and granted a number of the older *amabutho* permission to marry.

Dingane was about 30 years old at the time of his accession and had kept a low profile during Shaka's reign. He had participated in a number of campaigns (having received a chest wound while fighting against the Ngwane), but had a less warlike nature than his predecessor. He was powerfully built, though apparently not as tall as Shaka. It is said that he rarely laughed or smiled, because he was self-conscious about the small size of his teeth. He is reputed to have had a sensuous disposition, with an eye for fat young women with pretty faces: 'women, luxury, and ease' were uppermost in his mind, states Isaacs. Dingane was more artistic by disposition than

Shaka, and had an inordinate fondness for material goods. His reign was characterised by great pageantry. Although, according to Fynn, rituals and ceremonies displayed 'sedateness and formal regularity', they were of unprecedented splendour, and Dingane cut a dashing figure, though somewhat vitiated by increasing corpulence.

Dingane faced his first major test as king in early 1829 when Nqetho, the chief of the Qwabe, one of the most powerful clans in the kingdom, decided to go his own way. He sent messengers throughout Zululand calling upon members of his clan to revolt. Many warriors responded and began making their way to the clan homeland in south-eastern Zululand, in some instances stealing cattle en route. Nqetho and his followers crossed the Tugela into Natal and plundered the territory of the Cele before pressing on further down the coast.

When about 40 miles north-west of Port Natal, Nqetho was caught by a Zulu force despatched by Dingane and both sides began preparing for battle. Fynn states, however, that neither side 'felt disposed to attack the other'. Instead, Dingane's warriors merely rounded up some of the stolen cattle before setting off home, while Nqetho continued down the coast and invaded the Pondo kingdom. Here he created havoc and, in September 1829, murdered Lieutenant Farewell and two white companions who were heading back to Port Natal from the eastern Cape with a wagonload of goods.

Dingane reacted to the defection of Nqetho and his Qwabe supporters by executing a number of clan chiefs located across the Tugela. The most notable to die was Magaye of the Cele, a favourite of Shaka, who had been entrusted by the late king with control of the country south of the Tugela and whom Dingane believed should have done more to prevent Nqetho's escape.

The defection and its consequences did much to weaken the Zulu state, leading to the alienation of the clans of the trans-Tugela region, territory that comprised well over one-third of the Zulu kingdom. To retain his hold over the area, Dingane appointed Sothobe – Shaka's former ambassador to the Cape – viceroy over the country south of the Tugela and in 1831 Sothobe virtually eliminated the Cele on Dingane's behalf.

By now Dingane had established a new capital, uMgungundlovu, to replace Dukuza. It was built in 1829 in the Zulu heartland of the emaKhosini Valley, approximately half-way between the Mhlatuze and White Mfolozi Rivers, on a gently sloping hillside with streams on either side flowing towards the White Mfolozi. It was more than a mile in circumference and contained some 1400 to 1700 huts, likely capable of accommodating up to 7000 people.

It was at uMgungundlovu that Dingane soon killed several of his brothers. According to Jantshi kaNongila, he denounced them early one

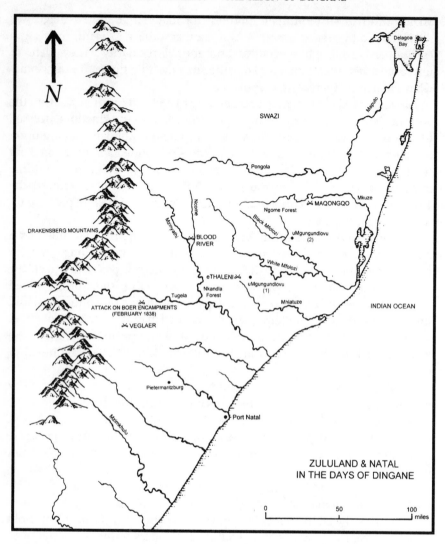

ZULULAND & NATAL
IN THE DAYS OF DINGANE

morning and had them clubbed to death with thick sticks. Jantshi also states that one of the brothers, Mpande, was about to be killed when Ndlela kaSompisi, Dingane's chief councillor and commander-in-chief, interceded on his behalf, exclaiming: 'Surely you are not going to kill Mpande, one who is just a simpleton.' Mpande undoubtedly survived the purge and Ndlela, as Jantshi avers, evidently played a part in saving his life.

Strained relations
Dingane wished to establish friendly relations with the British authorities in the Cape and thus in 1830 he appointed a white trader, John Cane, a rough, injudicious member of the Port Natal community, to act as his emis-

sary and assigned several Zulus to accompany him, while an unwilling Jakot was charged with acting as the interpreter. On 21 November, the delegation arrived at Grahamstown, headquarters of the eastern frontier garrison, but the mission was to prove a failure. Dingane had sent a gift of four elephant tusks for the governor but this was declined, whereupon Cane sold them and bought beads, cloths and blankets for Dingane before setting off for Port Natal without having received a reply to the king's message. He arrived at the port on 10 March. But instead of pressing on to uMgungundlovu to report and deliver the presents (a task he entrusted to native carriers), he decided instead to go hunting.

Isaacs describes Jakot as a 'perfidious and designing villain' who now misrepresented Cane, with whom he was on bad terms. He alleged that the British authorities in Cape Colony, on the advice of Cane, intended to attack the Zulus. Isaacs's account is corroborated by Fynn, who describes Jakot as 'an atrocious character' and 'a dissimulating wretch'.

Dingane reacted angrily and sent a punitive force to punish Cane, who fled upon receiving word of its approach. On or about 18 April 1831, the Zulus destroyed Cane's homestead and seized his cattle. Meanwhile, Isaacs and Fynn's brother, William, had made their way to see Dingane. They arrived on 17 April and were told of his orders to deal with Cane. Isaacs denounced Jakot as a trouble-maker and promised Dingane that there was no prospect of a British invasion – an assurance that the king appeared to accept.

Isaacs and his companion then set off for Port Natal. They arrived on 24 April, and were joined later that day by Henry Fynn (who had feared for their lives) and had temporarily abandoned the port with his followers after hearing rumours that hostile Zulu forces were approaching.

On 5 May the settlers received word from Dingane that he felt regret at having alarmed the community as a whole. Isaacs reports that they rapidly 'recovered confidence ... and began to believe [Dingane's] expressions of sorrow'. On the 14th, therefore, Henry Fynn set off for uMgungundlovu with his brother, accompanied by porters carrying muskets and other presents for Dingane. In exchange, the king gave the traders ivory, but was angered by Fynn's evident displeasure at the amount offered. Moreover, although Fynn attempted to expose Jakot, the king's advisers 'were prejudiced from the effect of [Jakot's] report, and implicitly believed all he had asserted'.

Fear thus returned to the settler community, so much so that a decision was taken to abandon Natal. Isaacs sailed to Delagoa Bay, while Henry Fynn's party, which included his five Zulu wives and his many children, began moving south by land. They were attacked one morning before daybreak in a half-hearted manner by a Zulu impi while encamped near a river mouth in southern Natal. Fynn relates that they were awoken by a sudden 'violent noise and commotion, which proved to be the Zulus stabbing our people while we were all still asleep'. In the confusion, Fynn and other fortunate members of the party escaped into the surrounding bush where they rallied. Fynn, and eight of his colleagues, had guns, though these were in poor condition for the best weapons had been given to Dingane.

After its initial assault, the impi divided into three groups. One remained on the spot, letting out shouts of 'There he is! There he is! Stab him!', while the others moved off in Fynn's direction, one by an inland route and the other along the beach. The former found its way barred by a steep precipice while the warriors on the seashore were checked by the defenders' gunfire. The Zulus then withdrew, having lost thirteen of their number. Fynn's losses were higher – five men, twenty women and fifteen children. Moreover, 150 head of cattle and two horses had been taken, together with cloth, beads and medicine. The 70 or so survivors eventually reached a mission station in the heart of Pondoland in early July where they received sanctuary.

Cane had remained in Natal, albeit in hiding, and duly made contact with Fynn, telling him that Dingane wished him and the other traders to return. In September, therefore, Fynn was back on the scene, having returned with a party of settlers from Grahamstown. Several months later, in late January 1832, Jakot was shot by one of the traders named John Ogle, acting on Cane's behalf after Dingane had granted the latter permission to execute the wayward Xhosa, who had to some extent sealed his own fate by stealing royal cattle.

Dingane flexes his muscles

In 1833 Dingane sent an impi southward against the Pondos and the Bhaca clan whose territory bordered Pondoland. A previous expedition in 1830 had proved a failure and history now repeated itself. The army was ordered to take an unfamiliar route to fall upon their opponents from an unexpected quarter, but wandered so far into the interior that, according to Fynn, 'they became bewildered' and were near to starving in depopulated country. 'Famine began to be felt to such a degree that their shields were consumed for food, and thousands of them perished in the trackless wilderness in which they found themselves entangled.'

In June the demoralised impi neared Port Natal, homeward bound, 'in the most wretched, dispirited and disorganised state' (commented Ogle in the 10 October 1833 issue of the *Grahamstown Journal*), only to be attacked by a force under Cane. A rumour had reached the port that the Zulus had killed absent white members of the community, whereas they had in fact attacked a party of Khoikhoi hunters. The majority of Cane's force was black, consisting of natives associated with the settlers. According to Ogle, the Zulus did not resist and 'a dreadful slaughter took place. I should think that 200 must have been killed. Many more shields and assegais than this number were brought in, but some, in all probability, were thrown away to facilitate escape.'

Fearing retribution, the settlers hurriedly abandoned Port Natal once again and fled to Pondoland, until assured later in the year by Dingane that it was safe to return, for he was aware that the attack had been due to a misunderstanding.

Dingane was not only involved with the whites in Natal. The Portuguese of Delagoa Bay also engaged his attention. In 1830 he sent a message to its newly appointed governor, Dionisio Antonio Ribeiro, who commanded a garrison of half a dozen Portuguese soldiers and some 100 or so native levies, demanding that he pay tribute just like subject black chiefs: failure to do so would result in a Zulu army descending on the settlement and installing a trader named Anselmo Nascimento in Ribeiro's place. The governor was not overawed. He showed the envoys two cannonballs and declared that they were the best beads he had to offer. Dingane decided not to take up the challenge and instead sent some cattle as a peace offering.

Harmonious relations prevailed during the next couple of years but then turned sour when Ribeiro apparently made the mistake of capturing Zulus for the slave trade. Hence in July 1833 Dingane despatched an impi against Delagoa Bay. Several villages in its vicinity were burned and the warriors then withdrew after receiving a gift for Dingane from the governor. Within weeks, though, the impi was back and on 17 September it entered the settlement unopposed and sacked the fort. Neither the soldiers nor the traders were harmed. Ribeiro, however, had withdrawn to an island in the bay and, since he was their quarry, the Zulus settled down on the shore opposite his sanctuary. Three weeks later, the governor, intent on escape, boarded a boat but was blown ashore, taken captive back to Delagoa, and paraded before the assembled community. According to one Portuguese trader, the Zulu commander then made a speech denouncing Ribeiro for treachery and tyranny, for having usurped the land of Dingane and of a Zulu tributary named Makasana, and for seizing Zulus for slavery. Ribeiro was then killed, perhaps by having his neck broken with a wrench to the head, a common method employed by Zulu executioners, whereupon a more cooperative governor was installed. The raid strengthened Dingane's control over southern Mozambique and raised Zulu influence in the region to an unprecedented height.

The arrival of Allen Gardiner

On 10 February 1835, an English missionary named Allen Gardiner arrived at uMgungundlovu, intent on preaching the word of God to Dingane and his people. En route to Zululand he had met Fynn at Grahamstown – where

41

the latter was now working as a colonial official, having left Port Natal the previous September – and from whom he received first-hand information about Dingane.

Gardiner told the king that he had come to instruct the Zulus about the Bible, whereupon Dingane questioned him on such matters as God's whereabouts and the Last Judgement. When Gardiner requested permission to build a mission station at the royal kraal, Dingane, who had heard unfavourable reports of the activities of missionaries further south from Jakot, replied that he would consult with his principal indunas, Ndlela and Nzobo kaSobadli, better known as Dambuza. Both were men to whom the increasingly slothful king (who spent much of his time relaxing on a reed mat) had delegated more and more responsibility.

For four weeks, much of which was spent in the capital, Gardiner awaited a reply. His mood was far from ebullient. A tense atmosphere prevailed. uMgungundlovu was a 'place of death,' states Lunguza kaMpukane, one of James Stuart's informants. 'One always lived in a state of dread and trembling at uMgungundlovu, and was only relieved when one went home.' Like Shaka, Dingane had people killed for little or no reason. But whereas in Shaka's day only the king could order an execution, Dingane now gave such authority to his two indunas. Although Ndlela was not a cruel man, magnanimity was not one of Nzobo's dominant attributes. It is reported that many hapless Zulus became all too well aware of this fact, especially if he had set his eye on their property, cattle or women. Gardiner wrote of him that his 'scowling profile' reflected 'too exactly ... a character for tyranny and insolence', and more than once during these weeks Nzobo's attitude was so openly hostile that the missionary feared for his life.

On 7 March, Gardiner was finally summoned by Dingane to discuss the matter of the mission station after the court had moved to another kraal, emBelebeleni. During the proceedings Nzobo stated that the Zulus were not interested in hearing about the Bible. The only instruction they wished to receive was how to use muskets brought by traders. Ndlela agreed, and Gardiner was dismayed when the king stated in conclusion that he felt likewise. Gardiner promptly set off for Port Natal, where in late March he established a mission station on a hill overlooking the bay.

The following month the traders chose him to act as their intermediary with Dingane, for a simmering crisis now threatened to come to the boil. Port Natal's male white community had grown to some 30 or so traders and hunters, but the bulk of the population consisted, according to Gardiner, of about 2500 black dependents and refugees. Some were survivors of Shaka's raids, while others were fugitives from Zululand. In late 1834, for example, a regiment stationed on the Tugela to prevent flight into Natal had itself deserted to the port. Such losses could not be ignored. Port Natal, with its relaxed lifestyle, was increasingly proving a magnet for discontented Zulus, thereby sapping the nation's strength and helping to undermine the stability of the Zulu state.

Nzobo favoured a bloody response – sending an impi against Port Natal to wipe out both the Europeans and associated blacks. Others agreed. Dingane's annoyance, however, was tempered by his fondness for the objects that he received from the Europeans – ever more splendid as the whites tried to mollify him, aware that it was vital to retain his goodwill.

In April, therefore, Gardiner set off to see Dingane with a promise that henceforth all fugitives from Zululand would be returned if he would guarantee the safety of Natal's European and native residents. Gardiner was also armed with a variety of gifts, including a telescope and a portrait of William IV. Early in May, having crossed the Tugela, he was conducted to a military homestead where Dingane was then resident and met with a positive response. The king was delighted with the proposed treaty, while Nzobo declared that he, too, was glad and that Gardiner was a good man who could be trusted.

Much to his joy, moreover, Gardiner was now granted permission to establish a mission in Zululand. Later in the month, after returning to Port Natal, he was put to the test, charged with the unpleasant task of returning to Zululand several fugitives, including a woman of high rank alleged to have committed adultery, where they were to be put to death. As a result, he gained Dingane's confidence and was told by the king, 'Now we see you belong to the Zulus.'

Some of the traders, however, soon broke the treaty by helping Zulus to desert to Natal: a number of women, for example, were smuggled out in wagons. Dingane responded by halting all trade with Port Natal. At a further meeting with Gardiner in July, the king granted the missionary full authority in Natal; 'You must be the chief over all the people there.' Henceforth anyone who wished to trade with the Zulus was obliged to obtain Gardiner's clearance.

By this time the Port Natal community had decided to rename their burgeoning settlement Durban, in honour of the Governor of Cape Colony, Sir Benjamin D'Urban. Gardiner accepted Dingane's offer, subject to the approval of D'Urban, whom he met in December. The governor responded by sending a letter and gifts to Dingane in the care of a Jewish merchant bound for Durban and Zululand. Among other things, the letter stated that on behalf of the King of England, D'Urban was going to send an officer to administer the port and to 'communicate with [Dingane] upon all matters concerning the people of Natal' in Gardiner's stead.

Gardiner himself set sail for England, taking a despatch from the governor urging the British government to occupy Durban. On his arrival in February 1836, he duly presented the document and begged the Church Missionary Society to provide him with assistance in preaching to the

Zulus. He stayed for some time in England and did not return to Natal – where he was to devote his time to missionary work – until May 1837.

By this date Dingane was anxious to procure firearms, whose value as weapons of war he had long realised. Indeed, he had already acquired some guns from traders at the port, and others were supplied via Delagoa Bay. But more recently he had decreed that henceforth firearms would be demanded from whites in return for the privilege of hunting and trading in Zululand. The value of the weapons, however, was restricted by the Zulus' lack of training and because many of the guns were unusable. An article in the *South African Commercial Advertiser* of 21 January 1837 quotes one white trader as commenting that 'the traders trading with Dingane in guns and powder were becoming rich' and that they had 'hit on a happy expedient of cheating the chief' by removing, prior to delivery, 'either the mainspring out of the lock, or some screw', thereby rendering the guns useless. Dingane, however, had 'at last discovered the roguery'.

The Great Trek
Events were soon to take a dramatic new turn. Migrants from Cape Colony known as Afrikaners or Boers, who were mostly of Dutch, German and French origin, would shortly appear on the scene, intent on settling in Natal.

In 1652, as mentioned, a revictualling station had been established at the Cape by the Dutch East India Company. The settlement of Cape Town had thus come into being beneath majestic Table Mountain, and in due course it was followed by others, such as Stellenbosch and Paarl, as whites began moving further afield at the expense of the Cape Peninsula's aboriginal population of San and Khoikhoi. Some of the Europeans journeyed eastward into what is known as the Eastern Cape, and during the course of the eighteenth century came into contact with the southernmost of the Nguni, the Xhosa, whose vanguard lived on fertile plains between the Great Fish and Sunday Rivers, and with whom in 1779 they were to fight the first of a long series of wars known as the Frontier or Kaffir Wars.

In 1795 – after the Netherlands had been invaded by France during the Revolutionary Wars – the Cape was temporarily occupied by Britain with the aim of securing the route to India. It was restored in 1802, only to be taken over by the British again in 1806. Boer resentment at finding themselves under permanent alien rule intensified after 1 December 1834 when slaves in Britain's colonies, including some 39,000 in the Cape, were emancipated. This was a financial blow to the Boers who were angered by the inadequate compensation offered and by the fact that it was only payable in London.

To make things worse, later in the same month trouble erupted on the eastern frontier. This had been extended more than once by the British, entailing the expulsion of many Xhosa, and now rested on the Keiskamma River east of the Great Fish. About 12,000 Xhosa, angered by white encroachment and the killing of one of their chiefs, invaded the colony. Farms and stores were set alight, cattle plundered and, most seriously, white settlers slain. Reinforcements were sent to the area and the Xhosa fell back into the Amatola Mountains where they waged a skilful guerrilla campaign.

The combination of the abolition of slavery and the Sixth Frontier War of 1834–5 heightened disenchantment among many of the Boers living in the Eastern Cape. For many, the prospect of escape to fresh pastures was becoming increasingly attractive, and thus a report they received about conditions in Natal was music to their ears. As December 1834 drew to a close, a party of 22 Boers, led by an Uitenhage farmer named Piet Uys, returned from an extended reconnaissance mission up the eastern coastal belt designed to test the truth of reports that had been received from various quarters about Natal's suitability for settlement. Uys's findings corroborated what had already been heard – Natal was well-watered, grass grew taller than the height of a man, and sheep could grow as fat as cattle – a veritable paradise.

The glowing reports helped to encourage a number of frontier Boer families, many of whose menfolk were fine horsemen and good shots, to move north and establish a new life for themselves free of British rule, and with a strong religious conviction that God would ensure their ultimate success: they were thus to spearhead a movement known to history as the Great Trek.

The Great Trek began on a small-scale in 1835 when a trickle of Boers bought large supplies of gunpowder, gathered up their livestock, loaded other property on to their ox-wagons, and forsook their farms, accompanied by their non-white dependents. They left Cape Colony by fording the mighty Orange River, and a number of them then gathered in the vicinity of a mission station named Thaba Nchu, east of the present-day city of Bloemfontein. They were followed by more and more Afrikaners from along the frontier, and in early 1837 most of them pressed on from Thabu Nchu and began settling in country to the north, most notably at what was soon to become the town of Winburg.

By mid-1837 approximately 5,000 Voortrekkers, as they later came to be known (from *voor*, meaning 'the one who goes in front'), had crossed the Orange, intent on founding a new homeland where they could be independent, hopefully enjoy access to ports beyond the British sphere of control and, if possible, live on peaceful terms with the blacks they encountered.

One of the trekkers was Piet Retief, who although born near Cape Town in 1780, had become a respected eastern frontier farmer. He was a tall bearded man with a commanding presence, who had distinguished himself in the recent Kaffir War. Retief arrived at Winburg at the head of a trek party in April 1837 and was soon elected governor and chief commandant. Other migrants subsequently appeared at Winburg, including Piet Uys, who had left Uitenhage in April.

By this time the trekker community was weakened by doubts and arguments, principally over the best course of action to take. Should they head north to the open grasslands of the highveld beyond the Vaal River into today's province of the Transvaal, where they could settle and open up a trade route with Delagoa Bay? Or was it better to make for lush Natal? Retief favoured the latter option and set off to the south-east, followed by the other trekkers, although some of them, such as Hendrik Potgieter, leader of one of the parties, were in rebellious mood. Things came to a head in mid-September when Potgieter and like-minded Voortrekkers finally decided to part company with their fellows, their hearts set on the Transvaal.

Retief arrived at Durban (at this date still generally referred to as Port Natal) on 19 October with a small party of men after crossing the Drakensberg. The majority of his followers were left west of the mountain range with orders not to cross until instructed otherwise. Retief spoke English fluently and received a generally friendly welcome from a British community that was anxious about its security and eager to see Voortrekkers settle in Natal, for relations with Dingane had worsened once again after further asylum had been offered to refugees. Defensive measures had thus been taken in the preceding months, including the building of fortifications and the establishment of a militia.

Recognising that it would be important to live on peaceful terms with Dingane, Retief soon headed for uMgungundlovu, accompanied by some of his men and a young member of the Durban community named Thomas Halstead who spoke Zulu and was to act as interpreter. They arrived on 5 November and Dingane proceeded to entertain them, partly with martial displays by thousands of his warriors. Retief recalled later in the month that Dingane did not give him an audience on the subject of his mission until the third day after his arrival. On 8 November Dingane announced that he was 'almost inclined' to grant Retief land in Natal, but that Retief had first to demonstrate his goodwill by recovering Zulu cattle that had been stolen by raiders.

Retief agreed to do so, and rejoined his followers on 27 November, after first returning to Durban. He met them east of the Drakensberg for in the meantime they had crossed the mountains and encamped around the headwaters of the Tugela and its tributaries. Then, in late December, he recrossed the Drakensberg with a commando and in early January 1838 seized the man he knew was responsible for stealing the livestock, Sikonyela, chief of the Mokotleng Tlokwa, holding him until the cattle had been surrendered. He also compelled the Tlokwa to hand over their horses and guns.

Back at the Boer encampments, Retief rejected warnings from fellow trekkers against revisiting Dingane. He was thus advised to take only a couple of men, to minimise losses if Dingane acted treacherously. One of those who advocated such a course was a leading figure named Gert Maritz who, though pessimistic, boldly declared that he was prepared to take Retief's place. But Retief remained adamant: he would go himself. He asked for volunteers to accompany him. Just how many did so is uncertain. Some put the figure at 65 Boers and five coloureds, while others state that 66 Boers and 30 non-whites volunteered. Retief then set off to see Dingane from whom he expected to receive his reward, to use Leonard Thompson's phrase, 'the foundation deed for the Promised Land'.

Retief and his companions arrived at uMgungundlovu on Saturday 3 February. With Dingane's permission, the Boers put on a display in the arena at the centre of the kraal, conducting mock charges against one another and making 'the air resound with their guns'. Dingane then asked Retief to hand over the guns and horses seized from the Tlokwa in the previous month's raid on his behalf, but Retief declined. According to Francis Owen, a missionary who had recently settled just outside uMgungundlovu, Dingane wished to establish a mounted force of gunmen comparable to a Boer commando.

Dingane entertained his guests with massed singing and dancing, and among the participants were many warriors he had assembled at his capital. Then, on 4 February, he put his mark to a document drawn up by Retief which is claimed to have granted the Voortrekker and his countrymen 'the place called Port Natal, together with all the land annexed, that is to say from [the Tugela] to the [Mzimvubu River] westward and from the Sea to the North, as far as the Land may be useful [and] in my possession'. Further dancing and displays followed on the next day.

On the morning of Tuesday 6 February, as Retief and his party were about to set off from their temporary encampment outside uMgungundlovu, Dingane invited them for a farewell drink. The Voortrekkers and the majority of their coloured dependents complied. They entered the royal homestead and, after being greeted by the king, sat down on mats and were served with milk and beer. As they drank, warriors encircled them, performing a war-dance with a slow forward and backward movement. The dancing became increasingly frenzied, with the warriors moving closer and closer to Retief and his companions. Suddenly, Dingane shouted 'Seize them!', whereupon Retief and his terrified party were set upon. Dingane then cried *Babulaleni abathakathi!* ('Kill the wizards!') Some of the trekkers attempted to defend themselves with knives they had been allowed to bring with them (they had not been allowed to bring their guns), but it was futile. The hapless Retief and his colleagues were overpowered, unceremoniously hauled out of the kraal by groups of warriors and their hands bound with thongs. They were then dragged down towards the Mkhumbane stream and up to a place of execution, kwaMatiwane (where the remains of previous victims lay scattered among the rocks and bushes), and where executioners now set to work once again. How Retief and his men died is uncertain. Oral tradition maintains that their necks were broken. But William Wood, a thirteen-year-old who witnessed the scene with Francis Owen, tells us that they were clubbed, with Retief being kept for last. Moreover, another source, who subsequently saw the bodies of the slain Boers, relates that some of them had been rectally impaled.

Owen, who had been promised that Dingane meant him and his companions no harm, states that once the last of the seized men had been put to death, 'the whole multitude' of Zulus on the hill began returning to Dingane, who had stayed at uMgungundlovu, and that as they neared him 'they set up a shout ... which continued for some time'. Shields and spears were issued and the warriors began dancing jubilantly, praising their king and working themselves into an increasingly aggressive mood. At about midday they streamed out of uMgungundlovu, heading south-west and intent on further bloodshed. Their mission? To kill the other Voortrekkers who had crossed into Natal.

Conflict between Zulu and Boer

Sections of the impi struck isolated Boer encampments before midnight on 16 February. The surprised and terrified trekkers stood little chance. The Zulus were soon among their wagons. A few of the whites had time to fire one or two shots, or managed to escape, but for most there was only death. The easternmost Voortrekker encampments largely ceased to exist.

Further west, as well as to the south on the upper reaches of tributaries flowing north to the Tugela, groups of Boers were alerted by the sound of gunfire or were stirred to action when a breathless rider or two appeared, shouting warnings. The men grabbed their muskets and prepared to make a stand: if sufficiently charged with powder, the muskets had a range of over 200 yards (though they were only really accurate at up to about 80 yards) and the average rate of fire would probably be about two to three shots a minute. Consequently, these Zulu assaults fared less well. Among the Boers attacked was the party of Gert Maritz, laagered beside the upper reaches of the Bushman's River. Retief had left Maritz in command during his absence, and in previous days he had ridden from encampment to encampment warning the trekkers to go into laager in expectation of attack. Many had, to their cost, taken no heed, whereas Maritz's precautions had contributed to his party's survival.

Clashes occurred well into the daylight hours of 17 February. Sarel Cilliers, an Afrikaner in his late 30s, was to recall: 'I shot that day until the muzzle of my gun was so hot that I became scared that the powder would explode as I put it in.' By that evening the Zulus had suffered heavy losses during Boer counter-attacks and were in full retreat, but were driving off about 35,000 captured sheep and cattle. At first the Voortrekkers, tending to the wounded and bereaved, did not offer a pursuit, but the next day Maritz set off towards the Tugela with a commando. Although most of the warriors and the bulk of the animals had already crossed, he nonetheless fell upon Zulus he encountered on the south side of the river and put them to flight before turning for home, having rounded up only a small fraction of the lost livestock.

The Boers gathered at Retief's laager at Doornkop, which had not been attacked by the Zulus, and assessed how many of the trekkers and their servants had perished, with emphasis on the exact number of Europeans killed. The death toll was 41 white men, 56 white women and 185 white children, with over 200 of their servants. The survivors – who inevitably feared the worst concerning Retief and his party – were in sombre mood, shocked, saddened and, above all, angry. Revenge was in the hearts and on the lips of many. Susanna Smit, the redoubtable sister of Gert Maritz, declared: 'God will not leave [Dingane] unrecompensed nor will our men acquit him.'

In March they were joined by commandos under Hendrik Potgieter and Piet Uys who had crossed the Drakensberg from the highveld to help wage war against Dingane. Then, as the month drew to a close, successful overtures were made to the British at Durban (who were mourning the loss of one of their own number, Thomas Halstead, who had accompanied Retief to Dingane as interpreter) concerning the prospect of a twin-pronged invasion of Zululand.

On 6 April a force of 347 mounted Boers under the command of Uys and Potgieter – who were not even on speaking terms – set out from Doornkop and soon divided into two sections. They crossed the Tugela and pressed on, heading towards uMgungundlovu. On 11 April, in the vicinity of eThaleni Hill, they caught sight of a huge herd of cattle being driven between two hills down into a rocky basin containing deep dongas. They rode forward to round up the cattle. But the herd was part of an ambush laid by Nzobo, for on either hill was a Zulu force, while a third was stationed to cut off the Boers' line of retreat. In all, there were several thousand warriors. Seeing the enemy, Uys engaged those on the northernmost hill who drew him towards the difficult ground of the basin.

Potgieter initially led his men against the Zulus on the southern hill but, given the rough nature of the terrain, soon deemed it sensible to withdraw, whereupon the warriors charged down towards him and put his force to flight. The third Zulu division attempted to intercept his force but failed.

Meanwhile, Uys and his men soon found themselves being encircled and desperately began trying to fight their way clear. Eventually most of them managed to make good their escape but Uys was not among them. Neither was his fourteen-year-old son Dirk who, seeing his father in trouble, turned back to die beside him.

Later in the month, Robert Biggar, Cane and John Stubbs led a force, mostly consisting of black levies, into Zululand from Durban in support of the trekkers. Cane had led a successful raid in March into Zulu territory but history did not repeat itself – events unfolded according to a different script. On 17 April, after burning the large homestead of Ndondakusuka on the Zulu side of the Tugela and killing many of its inhabitants, the invading force was ambushed and virtually annihilated in a desperate struggle by a Zulu impi nominally led by Mpande, Dingane's half-brother. Biggar and Cane were among the dead.

The survivors fell back on Durban where, as William Wood states, the European population decided 'to make for themselves the best shift they could'. They did so by taking sanctuary on a brig called the *Comet* which happened to be moored in the bay. Among them were American missionaries who had recently arrived in Dingane's kingdom, and Francis Owen, who had fled Zululand despite assurances from Dingane that their lives were not in jeopardy.

The whites evacuated Durban just in time, for on the following morning, 24 April, a Zulu impi appeared and proceeded to sack the settlement. Abandoned homes were looted and exiles who had not fled were slaughtered. When, after several days, the Zulus began heading home, a few of the more daring or foolhardy whites on the *Comet* went ashore. The majority, however, set sail for Cape Town on 11 May. As Stephen Taylor comments: 'Across the Zulu country, gun and gospel were in retreat.'

Yet not, presumably, if the Boers who had remained in Natal could prevent it. Some, under Potgieter, had decided to recross the Drakensberg with a view to settling on the highveld. The fate of Retief and his colleagues and the deaths of other trekkers were deeply etched on the minds of the surviving Afrikaners. The hearts of many were aflame with righteous indignation and burning for revenge. Nevertheless, they were beset by problems. Not only could the leaders not agree on a plan for a punitive expedition against Dingane, but, with the exception of meat, supplies were running low, and they were also having to contend with frequent heavy rain. Then disease broke out: foot-and-mouth among the cattle, fever among the trekkers.

In mid-August Dingane despatched an impi under Ndlela to root out the Voortrekkers. It came up against a Boer laager of some 290 wagons at Gatsrand near the Bushman's River. Early in the night of 12 August, after a day marked by rain and thunder, the encampment was startled by the sound of a gunshot. One of the lookouts had fired at what he thought was a spy. Nothing happened thereafter and peace resumed. Then on the morning of the 13th, native herdboys staggered into the camp, exclaiming that the Zulus were approaching. The news caused little alarm, for reports had been heard previously and had proved false. Even so, a patrol was sent out to reconnoitre. Before long it was dashing back. Dingane's warriors were at hand, having killed a Boer out tending sheep and an elderly female servant gathering firewood.

Hurried preparations were made to receive them. The laager was a strong one, wedge-shaped, with its base resting on the bank of the Bushman's and a cannon deployed at its apex. But manpower was scarce. There were only 75 Afrikaner men capable of fighting and, to make things worse, rain was in the air, so that much of the powder was not sufficiently dry. As the defenders gathered around their minister to pray, they caught sight in every direction of marching columns of Zulus. Before long, the Boers were surrounded by perhaps 10,000 warriors, some of whom were carrying guns captured from Retief's and Uys's commando.

Some of the Zulus opened fire on the trekkers, others hurled throwing spears (which had been reintroduced by Dingane), but no mass charge against the wagons was attempted, so that the defenders were able to move freely from sector to sector, reinforcing colleagues under pressure. The Boers fired and loaded in rotation, thereby maintaining a constant rate of fire. At about midday the enemy attacks died down, whereupon a mounted party sallied out of the laager and skirmished with the Zulus, forcing a with-drawal. Both sides then settled down for the night. The trekkers took no chances. Sentries were doubled and lanterns hung out on whipstocks around the laager, to deter any attack under cover of darkness and facilitate the loading of muskets. For their part, the Zulus spent much of the night feasting on captured Boer livestock.

Dawn brought renewed action when mounted Boers made a sortie before falling back, drawing the Zulus after them and into the defenders' zone of fire. The warriors attempted to storm the defences by setting the wagons alight with spears wrapped in burning straw but were repulsed.

That night again proved an anxious one for the Boers, with the Zulus still close by. On the following day, however, the impi chanted a war-song and set off for home with captured livestock, some of which were retaken by the Afrikaners when they gave chase.

Following the battle of Veglaer, (as it became known), the Boers broke camp and moved closer to Gert Maritz's laager beside the Little Tugela in the shadow of the Drakensberg. But bad weather, depleted supplies and illness continued to beset the trekkers and Maritz's death from fever in late September further undermined morale.

Good news, however, was to follow in October. A ship docked at Durban from Cape Town bearing supplies of all kinds sent by well-wishers. Moreover, word arrived that reinforcements were on the way under a dynamic, experienced commando leader named Andries Pretorius, who had spent some time with the Voortrekker groups in 1837 before returning to his home in the Graaff-Reinet district, intent on leading a trek north with his friends and relations to Natal. Pretorius had received an urgent summons from the trekkers in Natal to come post-haste, and on 22 November he duly arrived, having pressed ahead of the bulk of his party with 60 mounted men and a small ship's cannon. He was appointed commander-in-chief and, on 28 November, set off for Zululand at the head of a commando. En route he took steps to ensure that it was a disciplined force. He established a proper chain of command, posted sentries, punished insubordination and at night formed strong laagers. On the sixth day after departure, and before crossing the Tugela, the slow-moving force was joined by a contingent from Durban consisting of a few Englishmen under Alexander Biggar (the father of Robert Biggar) and some 60 Natal Zulus.

Shortly after Pretorius left the Boer camp, a message arrived there warning him to refrain from 'offensive measures against the Zulu chief'. It was sent by Major Samuel Charters, who had just landed at Durban with about 100 troops, bearing orders from the Governor of Cape Colony to keep the peace.

As was customary, on Sunday 9 December, Pretorius's commando observed the Sabbath. They did more. They vowed that if God granted them victory against the Zulus they would build a church and commemorate the event as a day of thanksgiving. Pretorius then continued his march and crossed the Mzinyathi River.

On Saturday 15 December, the commando (which was under surveillance from Zulu spies) reached the west bank of the Ncome River and formed a laager. It was the eve of one of the most momentous battles in the history of South Africa – Blood River – of which F. A. Van Jaarsveld has commented: 'No other battle in South African history has excited as much attention or such diverse interpretations.'

The Battle of Blood River
Unfortunately, sources relating to this epic engagement are not as full as could be wished and are somewhat contradictory. Indeed, one authority on the subject, F. J. du Toit Spies, has concluded that no final solution regarding the course of the battle is possible.

Nonetheless, certain facts are known. The laager was located in a strong defensive position, for the terrain was open, providing a good field of fire once an early morning mist had cleared. Its east side was protected by the river, which was of sufficient depth at this point to prevent or at least greatly impede an advance from that quarter. Additionally, a deep donga or ditch, down which a small stream flowed into the Ncome, afforded a barrier to the south. Effectively, then, the Zulus could only really attack from the north and west, thereby enabling the defenders to concentrate their fire; and fortunately for the Voortrekkers, because the day was to prove fine and sunny, they were able to keep their powder dry. Furthermore, Pretorius issued the men with small leather cartridges of buckshot which, when fired, would burst at about 40 yards. There were also three cannon, the largest of which had a range of several thousand yards.

The shape of the laager is disputed, but it was probably formed up like a capital D. There were at least 57 wagons (some put the number at 64) and they were lashed together to prevent the Zulus forcing an opening through them. Furthermore, hurdles especially brought by Pretorius were used to block the gaps between them, while lanterns were again hung from whip-stocks.

Different figures have been given for the strength of the commando. Among the most reliable are those of B. J. Liebenberg, who states that the laager's European element numbered 468 Afrikaners and three English settlers from Port Natal. There were, moreover, many non-whites, including about 120 Port Natal blacks. The laager also contained approximately 1400 horses and oxen.

Reasonable estimates place the strength of the impi, which was commanded by Ndlela, at some 8000 to 10,000 men. Among the regiments present was Dingane's favourite *ibutho*, the uDlambedlu, the first regiment he had established following his accession. About 200 of the Zulus possessed guns.

Before daylight dawned on 16 December, the Zulus moved forward from the south-east, with the left horn (consisting of young *amabutho*) well to the fore. The left horn crossed the Ncome by way of a drift downstream of the laager and circled around to the north-west of the Boer position before settling down and awaiting daylight.

At about 6.30 the early morning mists began to lift, enabling the Voortrekkers to see the Zulu left horn arrayed about 170 yards away. Suddenly the warriors rose to their feet, shouted war-cries, rattled their spears against their shields, and began surging forward before the rest of the impi was in position. One of the Boers who watched the spectacle later recalled: 'Their approach, although frightful on account of the great number, yet presented a beautiful appearance.'

Trekker marksmen responded by firing buckshot and many of the Zulus fell, as did others hit by grapeshot from one or more of the cannons. Soon the north-western side of the laager was enveloped in thick black smoke. Valiantly, nonetheless, the Zulus repeatedly endeavoured to press home their attack. Eventually, however, they realised that it was futile to try to penetrate the defenders' zone of fire and fell back, but some groups of warriors broke away to occupy the donga only a few yards from the laager. Pretorius ordered a sally and some of his men lined the lip of the donga, pouring fire into the Zulus below. The survivors retired in a southerly direction, some of them making for the drift. At about the same time, mounted trekkers moved against the rest of the left horn, which took to its heels, many of the warriors fleeing towards a hill to the south-west. At about 8 a.m. the Boer pursuit was called off.

The day's bloodshed, however, was far from over. The Zulu chest and right horn were closing in. The right horn, in the lead, attempted to cross the Ncome just to the north-east of the laager but was prevented from doing so when Pretorius deployed mounted horsemen on the river bank; their withering fire led the Zulus to veer south to ford the river at the same point as the left horn had done earlier. The chest, coming up behind, did likewise. In the meantime, cannon fire from the laager had been directed against the senior Zulu commanders who had taken up a position on a hill on the east side of the Ncome and had inflicted casualties, forcing them to scatter.

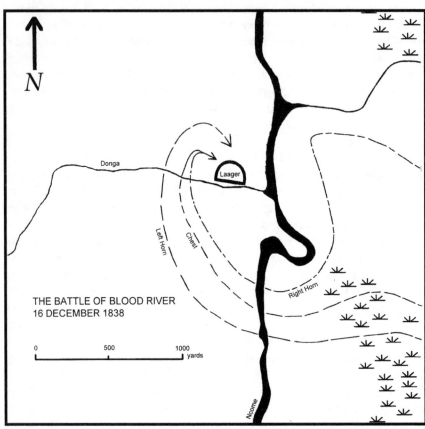

THE BATTLE OF BLOOD RIVER
16 DECEMBER 1838

54

Having crossed the river, the right horn surged forward and attacked the laager from the north-west. Repeatedly it charged, but once again enemy fire proved too hot to penetrate and the Zulu toll of dead and wounded rose rapidly. When the more senior warriors of the chest arrived on the scene, some of them jeered the younger men of the right horn (it is said that warriors actually came to blows), and tried to force a way through their ranks to close with the enemy themselves. Congestion and disorder soon prevailed, and the assault crumbled as a number of Zulu units began to retire at about 11 a.m.

Seeing this, Pretorius ordered some of his men to mount. As gaps between the wagons were opened, they galloped out against their weakened and demoralised opponents, who began fleeing in various directions, mostly towards the Ncome. Lunguza kaMpukane, our only Zulu eye-witness of events, who was with a youthful regiment deemed too young to participate in the battle other than to help finish off the trekkers, sets the scene:

> After our troops had been repulsed there was a general flight in various directions. The Boers charged; four came in our direction riding red horses, five in another direction, six in another. They fired on the Zulus with their guns. Our men hid in ant-bear holes, under ant-heaps, stuffing their heads in though otherwise exposed, whilst others hid themselves under heaps of corpses to be found in every direction. Men were shot who were already dead. I found men shot dead in front as well as behind me as we fled.

Fleeing warriors leapt into the Ncome or scurried down the donga, desperate to escape. Some made it, but many did not. From the banks, the Boers had a wealth of targets to aim at, and more and more Zulus perished. Some submerged in an attempt to save themselves. Examining the bones of many who had died, the French naturalist, Adulphe Delegorgue, who visited the battle-site the following year, noted: 'Obeying the instinct of self-preservation, they dived underwater until forced to the surface, where their heads were immediately shattered by the avenging bullets of the Boers.' Other Zulus died some distance from the laager, for the Voortrekker pursuit was conducted far across the Ncome until their mounts were exhausted.

The *Annals of Natal* vividly describes the battle as a scene of 'shouting and tumult and lamentation, and a sea of black faces, and a dense smoke that rose straight as a plumb-line upwards from the ground'. It had certainly been a hard-fought encounter, in which, so it is said, the trekkers' guns almost became too hot to handle. Nevertheless, the casualties were terribly disproportionate. None of the Europeans was killed and only three were wounded, among them Pretorius. In contrast, Zulus perished by the thousand – the Boers put the figure at 3000. The *Annals* states that bodies were piled beside the laager 'like pumpkins on a rich soil'. Indeed, so many Zulus were killed in the Ncome that its waters literally turned red, leading the Boers to give it the name 'Blood River.' Of the engagement, F. Lion Catchet was to declare years later: 'It was not a battle; it was an execution.'

Within days of the battle, Pretorius wrote:

> The venture was great and our army puny ... hence we could do nothing but trust in the justice of our cause and the God of our fathers.... However, it pleased the Almighty ... to grant us victory with no loss of life.

It was an opinion shared by other members of the victorious commando who likewise attributed the battle's outcome to divine intervention, and it is a view still held by many Afrikaners today.

After Blood River, Pretorius hurriedly pressed on, unopposed, towards uMgungundlovu. On 20 December he found the royal kraal abandoned and in flames. It was less than a year since the 'wizards' had been butchered – how the wheel of fortune had spun.

Dingane was fleeing north, having given orders to regiments to decoy and harass the enemy. On 27 December, a clash occurred in the valley of the White Mfolozi when a 300-strong Boer commando under Carel Landman, accompanied by some 70 dismounted Port Natal blacks under Biggar, descended into the valley to round up a large herd of cattle that turned out to be a mass of Zulu warriors with shields on their backs, creeping about on all-fours. Soon Landman found himself under attack, with hitherto concealed *amabutho* moving in from all sides. The trekkers managed to fight their way clear – although four of them perished – but most of the Port Natal blacks were cut off and slaughtered, and Biggar died with them rather than abandon them to their fate. The Boers claimed that they had killed about 1000 Zulus, though this no doubt has to be taken with a pinch of salt. So, too, must Zulu claims that when Pretorius and his colleagues withdrew to Natal in early January (incidentally taking with them fewer livestock than they wished), they did so with unseemly haste.

The last days of Dingane
Meanwhile, what of Dingane? The badly mauled king founded a smaller capital, again called uMgungundlovu, just beyond the Black Mfolozi and about nine miles from present-day Nongoma, and began to consolidate his position. His hopes were revived by news that the British objected to what had occurred and had warned the Boers – whom they maintained were still subjects of the crown – that any future aggression would be 'followed by the strongest marked displeasure'.

The Voortrekkers, however, were dismissive and proceeded to establish their own republic governed by the Volksraad, an elected assembly consisting of 24 members. The capital was a fledgling town (founded in 1838) on high ground about 50 miles north-west of Durban and named Pietermaritzburg in honour of Piet Retief and Gert Maritz.

Relations between the Boers and the British soldiers at Durban were nevertheless amicable, and the latter's new commander, Captain Henry Jarvis, worked towards bringing about harmony between Afrikaners and Zulus. Consequently, on 25 March 1839, peace was concluded. Dingane agreed to leave the Boers unmolested south of the Tugela and to return captured Voortrekker arms, horses, cattle and sheep, while Pretorius promised to punish Afrikaners who strayed beyond the Tugela and to assist the Zulus if they were unjustly attacked by a third party.

Dingane failed to comply fully with the treaty. True, by August the bulk of the firearms which had belonged to Retief's party had been handed over, but hardly any of the 40,000 cattle that the Boers claimed had been stolen from them were returned. Instead of trying to ensure that the terms of the treaty were fulfilled, Dingane concentrated on establishing a base for himself beyond the Pongola, intent on shifting the nucleus of his kingdom away from his troubled southern flank into Swazi territory. In 1839, an impi was despatched to begin the process of conquest; but it encountered stiff resistance and despite being reinforced by fresh *amabutho*, the campaign ended in failure. Dingane's hopes were dashed. So, too, was the morale of his people, many of whom now began deserting their weakened king.

Foremost among them was his half-brother Mpande, who had failed to provide effective military assistance for the Swazi campaign. In September he fled across the Tugela into Natal, accompanied by about 17,000 followers drawn from southern Zululand, after hearing that he was to be executed by his indignant brother.

In Natal, contact was made with the Boers and, on 27 October, the two parties agreed upon a combined attack on Dingane, whom the Boers wished to be replaced by Mpande. Hence in January 1840, shortly after the British garrison at Durban had been recalled by the Governor of Cape Colony (the troops had sailed on 24 December), Zululand was invaded again. Dingane had attempted to ward off an incursion by sending Nzobo and another induna to Natal with presents, but both had been seized by the Boers who charged them with complicity in the murder of Retief's party and the subsequent assault on the trekker encampments.

The invasion force consisted of two separate columns. Mpande (who was threatened with death if his men deserted to Dingane) crossed the Tugela with Pretorius and a commando of 308 armed men plus ancillaries. Several thousand Zulus, under Nongalaza kaNondela, followed suit further to the east.

On 29 January, after Dingane had abandoned his second capital, Nongalaza clashed with Dingane's forces under the leadership of Ndlela among the Maqongqo Hills in the far north of Zululand. It is sometimes said that the battle was watched by the Boers, who remained aloof, allowing Zulu to kill Zulu, but in fact they were miles from the scene. Details of the engagement are scarce but it was evidently a bitter encounter that turned in Nongalaza's favour when some of Dingane's warriors deserted to his side. Eventually, Dingane's impi was forced to withdraw.

On the evening of the 30th, when just south of the White Mfolozi, the Boers received word that Dingane's forces had been defeated and that the king was in flight. The following day they arraigned Nzobo and his fellow envoy before a military court in which Mpande testified against them, declaring that they had been largely responsible for the murder of Retief's party. Nzobo boldly admitted to the allegations, but asked that his companion be spared as he was innocent. Both men, however, were sentenced to death by firing squad. The execution was witnessed by Dele-gorgue. The first volley killed Nzobo's companion but only wounded the former, who, 'as calmly as ever, and in spite of his suffering ... arose and stood steadfastly facing the guns, until the second round of shots rang out'.

On 10 February, after Pretorius's men had assisted Nongalaza's warriors in an attempt to hunt down Dingane and his remaining followers, the Boer leader proclaimed Mpande king of the Zulus. Within days, however, Mpande was told that he was to rule over a substantially diminished domain, for all the land below the Black Mfolozi was no longer to be part of the Zulu kingdom. The Boers then withdrew south of the Tugela, driving an enormous herd of cattle (though less than the 40,000 they had demanded from Dingane). But although the Volksraad went on to register claims to farms north of the river in the area of Zululand annexed by the Boers, Mpande was to act as *de facto* ruler of the territory.

As for Dingane, he had fled across the Pongola and had established a homestead in the territory of the Nyawo people in the Lubombo Mountains. Ndlela was not with him for Dingane had executed his commander-in-chief, blaming him for his downfall. After all, had it not been Ndlela who had interceded when Dingane was about to execute Mpande years before? Ndlela had thus been strangled after the embittered king declared: 'You were harbouring a snake for me.'

In March, Nyawo and Swazi warriors combined against Dingane, and one night a group of them managed to infiltrate his homestead. Alarmed by the barking of his dog, Dingane emerged from his hut spear in hand, only to be fatally stabbed.

Of Dingane, F. A. van Jaarsveld has commented: 'Few historical figures have been depicted in such derogatory terms as Dingane.' Felix Okoye (who believes that the king has been treated harshly) states: 'Almost every commentator on this period of Zulu history has portrayed him as a man with hardly a redeeming quality: bloodthirsty, capricious, treacherous, self-indulgent, an absolute despot, an ingrate and an inveterate liar.'

More than anything else, Dingane's execution of Piet Retief and his colleagues at uMgungundlovu on 6 February 1838 has blackened his name and consigned his reputation to the realms of iniquity.

It is sometimes said that Retief acted foolishly and was thus partly responsible for what occurred. For example, in November 1837, upon returning to Port Natal following his first visit to uMgungundlovu, he wrote a letter to Dingane in which he referred to a powerful black potentate named Mzilikazi. On a previous occasion he had alluded to the fact that Boers had recently got the better of Mzilikazi's warriors on the highveld and he now bluntly informed Dingane: 'The great Book of God teaches us that kings who conduct themselves as Mzilikazi does are severely punished, and that it is not granted them to live and reign long.'

Dingane had every right to conclude from this letter that Retief was trying to intimidate him. Nevertheless, there is reason to believe that even before it was penned he had decided to murder Retief, for a chief named Silwebana (who fled to Port Natal to escape Dingane's wrath) maintained that Dingane had instructed him to murder Retief and his companions when they were en route to the port after leaving uMgungundlovu.

In short, it seems reasonable to conclude that under strong pressure from his advisers and *amabutho*, Dingane determined on a pre-emptive strike, entailing the elimination of Retief and his followers, fearing that sooner or later they would seek to destroy him and his kingdom. This plan backfired, for, as has been noted, after wiping out Retief and his companions at uMgungundlovu, Dingane's warriors failed to eliminate all the trekker parties in the foothills of the Drakensberg. Once reinforced, the Boers exacted bitter revenge, inflicting upon the Zulu people the most bitter defeat they had ever known, thereby undermining Dingane's position and ultimately sending him to his grave.

CHAPTER 3

CONSOLIDATION AND CIVIL WAR

'The whole air was tainted with dead bodies for the last twelve miles, which I walked against a head wind. They were lying in every possible attitude along the road, men, women, and children of all possible sizes and ages; the warriors untouched, with their war-dresses on, but all in a dreadful state of decomposition.... I saw many instances of mothers with babies on their backs, with assegais through both.' *W. C. Baldwin*

Mpande was born in the latter half of the 1790s and has often been described as the Zulu Claudius. For much of his life, before ascending to the throne, he was viewed as an insignificant weakling, an indolent and feeble-minded character who posed little or no threat. He was undoubtedly lazy – something that contributed to his enormous bulk – but his mind was far from that of an imbecile for, as John Laband comments, he possessed 'the real abilities of a shrewd and determined survivor'. Nor was he bloodthirsty – Delegorgue for instance relates that a missionary described Mpande as 'a Caffir gentleman'.

As king, Mpande set about reconciling his own supporters with those who had lately stood by Dingane, ordering his followers to refrain from ridiculing and ostracising warriors who had recently fought on his half-brother's behalf.

As Charles Ballard comments:

Mpande had become king because he had won the support of the leading chiefs of the kingdom, who sought an alternative to the murderous absolutism of Dingane. These chiefs had no intention of allowing the new king to impose the same degree of centralised control over them or their followings.

It would be wrong, nonetheless, to regard Mpande as a mere puppet of powerful subordinates. Furthermore, it is erroneous to state, as is sometimes done, that the days of arbitrary killings were over, for Mpande's prime minister, Masiphula kaMamba (who had come to power by the 1850s) had a fearsome reputation and was quick to execute people guilty of even trivial misdemeanours.

For obvious reasons, Mpande was anxious to live harmoniously with his white neighbours and in this respect the tension between Boer and Briton proved beneficial. In 1840, the growing Boer community in Natal sought British recognition of its independence and for a while there was a strong

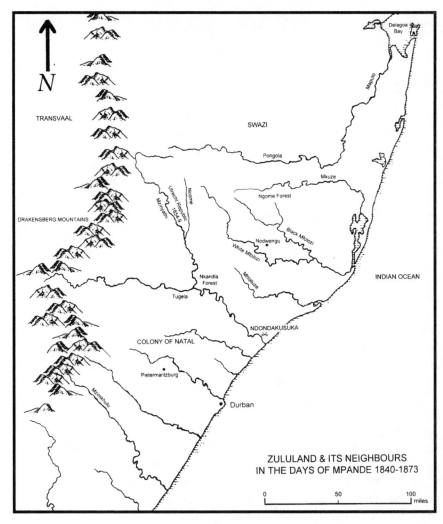

N

TRANSVAAL

SWAZI

DRAKENSBERG MOUNTAINS

Delagoa Bay

Maputo

Pongola

Mkuze

Utrecht Republic 1854-9

Ncome

Mzinyathi

Ngome Forest

Black Mfolozi

Nodwengu

White Mfolozi

Mhlatuze

Nkandla Forest

Tugela

INDIAN OCEAN

NDONDAKUSUKA

COLONY OF NATAL

Pietermaritzburg

Mzimkhulu

Durban

ZULULAND & ITS NEIGHBOURS
IN THE DAYS OF MPANDE 1840-1873

0   50   100
                            miles

possibility that this would occur, but subsequent actions by the republic prevented this. One such was a decision in August 1841 to move 'surplus' natives from Natal southward to between the Mthamvuna and Mzimvubu Rivers (territory claimed by the Pondo chief, Faku) with the aim of reducing Natal's vast and numerically dominant black population. Consequently, the Governor of the Cape, Sir George Napier, ordered the reoccupation of Durban; and early in May 1842, Captain Thomas Smith and 237 men marched into the port after making their way up from Pondoland.

Conflict erupted with the Boers, whose population in Natal numbered 6000, although the Afrikaners did not rise as one against the British presence. Pretorius was in command of the Boer forces and proceeded to besiege Durban. The garrison found itself in dire straits until reinforcements under

Colonel Josias Cloete arrived by sea in June, 34 days after the investment began. Pretorius's force then suffered from desertion and he withdrew and subsequently asked for terms.

On the day that Pretorius's flag of truce arrived at the British camp, messengers from Zululand appeared with a dramatic report. Mpande had decided to assemble an impi with the aim of descending on Natal and marching against Pietermaritzburg, having transferred his allegiance from the republic to the ascendant British. But Cloete promptly instructed him not to do so and the king complied.

The question of whether Britain should annex Natal was now in the air, and by the close of the year the Colonial Secretary, Lord Stanley, had decided in favour of doing so. A special commissioner, Henry Cloete (Josias's brother), was thus sent to Natal in 1843 to negotiate with the Boers. While some of the Afrikaners wished to oppose British authority, others were prepared to deal with the commissioner, and in 1844 – events moved slowly – the Boer republic ceased to exist and Natal became a detached district of the Cape Colony: the first lieutenant-governor duly assumed duty in December 1845.

By this time the number of Boers had dwindled to about 3000, for the remainder had set off for the highveld, a process which was to continue. By the end of 1848, the overwhelming majority of Boers had left, though the arrival of British settlers from 1849 onward reversed the decline of Natal's white population, which was to become some 18,000 strong by 1870.

Commissioner Cloete did not only deal with the Afrikaners. He also came to terms with Mpande, whom he recognised in October 1843 as the independent ruler of the Zulu kingdom, the southern boundaries of which were accepted as resting on the Tugela as far inland as its junction with the Mzinyathi, and then north up that river as far as the foot of the Drakensberg. St Lucia Bay, however, at the mouth of the Mfolozi, was annexed by Cloete in case it had potential as a port. For his part, Mpande agreed to withdraw those of his subjects living in Natal into Zululand.

Bloodshed, missionaries and Boers

When Cloete visited Mpande in 1843, the king was resident at an *ikhanda* in the emaKhosini Valley, but shortly thereafter he built a homestead called Nodwengu, north of the White Mfolozi on the Mahlabathini plain, that was to serve as his principal place of residence.

Prior to this meeting, in 1842, Mpande had killed the small number of Zulus in his kingdom who had converted to Christianity, deeming that they had compromised their allegiance to him, and had put an end to all missionary activity. Moreover, some months before Cloete's arrival, Mpande's policy of consolidating his position led him to get rid of his closest rival for the throne, for a dissident party seems to have been forming around the person of his only surviving brother, Gqugqu. In mid-1843, therefore, Mpande sent a force to wipe out him and his household. The deaths were followed by the flight to Natal of one of Mpande's aunts named Mawa, and of several thousand followers who feared that they too would be struck down. The haemorrhage continued, with a significant but indeterminate number of other Zulus subsequently making their way into Natal. Some were fugitives, but many headed for Natal in quest of a life that they felt would offer more freedom: they migrated to find work and to marry when they chose.

Although the establishment of British rule in Natal and the presence of Boers on the highveld precluded those areas being used as raiding grounds by Mpande's army, his *amabutho* nonetheless campaigned elsewhere. In 1842, for instance, Mpande began raiding a number of tributary kingdoms to the north-west of his domain, while in 1847 he sent his warriors into Swaziland (which was split by a dynastic dispute) and where he hoped to set up a client chiefdom in the south of the country. Much of southern Swaziland was soon brought under Zulu control, but later in the year Mpande's warriors pulled out after being subjected to hit-and-run raids by the Swazi, who enjoyed the support of Boer allies from the eastern Transvaal.

The following year, Zulu warriors once again invaded Swaziland, which was still rent by factionalism, and forced its king, Mswati, to submit. In 1852, however, Mswati attempted to break free of Zulu overlordship and Mpande responded by launching a full-scale invasion that cowed the Swazi and compelled many of them to flee. Mswati implored the British authorities in Natal to grant asylum to himself and his starving and displaced subjects, and they responded by bringing pressure upon Mpande to recall his army, which contributed to the king's decision to withdraw his forces.

Mpande also used the army to retain Zulu supremacy over the Tsonga chiefdoms and the prized networks of trade and tribute in the Delagoa region. In the early 1850s, for example, he intervened in a succession dispute in Maputoland and thereafter enjoyed the homage of the man whom he helped install. Laband comments: 'By the early 1850s, Mpande was firmly in the saddle, assured in his relations with his new white neighbours, unchallenged at home, and militarily dominant over the black polities along his northern marches.'

In 1850 he had felt sufficiently secure to allow missionaries to set to work once again in his kingdom. The most notable missionary active in Zululand during Mpande's reign was Hans Schreuder of the Norwegian Missionary Society, who, following his arrival in 1850, proceeded to establish seven mission stations during the next two decades. Moreover, he tended Mpande medically and acted as his principal conduit with the colonial world. From the mid-1850s on, Mpande also permitted other missionary bodies to operate in Zululand. It must not be supposed, however, that he was anxious to see his people converted to Christianity. Rather, he wished to create a favourable impression with the authorities in Natal and used the missionaries as advisers and intermediaries with colonial officials, while actively discouraging conversions.

The 1850s also witnessed the increasing presence of white traders in Zululand. Furthermore, from 1852 onward, Mpande also permitted Boers, on sufferance, to settle on the relatively empty land between the Mzinyathi and Ncome Rivers in the north-western part of his domain. Indeed, in 1854 (by which time the Afrikaners numbered nearly 200 families), he ceded the territory to them and they proclaimed the territory the Republic of Utrecht.

The return of civil war

The essential tranquillity of Mpande's reign was marred in the mid-1850s by a short but bloody civil war fought between the supporters of two of his own numerous children – Cetshwayo, (Mpande's eldest son by his first wife) and Cetshwayo's half-brother, Mbuyazi. The former, born in about 1832, was a handsome and imposing figure over six feet tall whom Mpande had proclaimed as his successor in Natal in 1839. But in the early 1850s Mpande began to favour Mbuyazi, who we are told was even more prepossessing than his half-brother, and a man whom Mpande viewed with deep affection. He had inducted both princes into the newly formed uThulwana regiment in 1850 or 1851.

Cetshwayo became increasingly sidelined. Indeed, when Mpande was challenged by an induna that he appeared to be renouncing his eldest son, the king responded by stating that when he was a commoner he had intended Cetshwayo to be his heir but had decided, now that he was king, that Mbuyazi was to be his successor. Many in the kingdom felt otherwise. Factions began forming around the princes, with Cetshwayo enjoying the greater degree of support, and by the mid-1850s this included many of the kingdom's most senior figures such as Masiphula kaMamba and Mnyamana kaNgqengelele of the Buthelezi, commander of the uThulwana *ibutho*. Cetshwayo's faction was known as the uSuthu, while Mbuyazi's was called the iziGqoza.

Civil war erupted in late 1856 after Mpande granted Mbuyazi a tract of land in the south-east bordering Natal, the region where the king's own influence had been at its greatest before the downfall of Dingane. Mpande hoped that Mbuyazi would be able to widen his own power-base at Cetshwayo's expense, and would also manage to obtain support from Natal, which could serve, if need be, as a safe haven.

In November, Mbuyazi and his followers settled in the region. Cetshwayo's homestead was nearby and he reacted angrily. Messengers were sent out to raise the uSuthu, and men from all the king's regiments rallied to Cetshwayo, who was soon at the head of a potent force, which grew as he marched through southern Zululand.

Outnumbered, Mbuyazi retreated towards the Tugela, and in a desperate attempt to increase his support, crossed the river with two of his brothers and asked for British assistance. An official named Joshua Walmsley responded by allowing his young, fluent Zulu-speaking administrative assistant, John Dunn, to cross into Zululand with a small force that included 35 frontier policemen. Dunn crossed the Tugela on 28 November and proceeded to join Mbuyazi's host encamped on high ground above a tributary of the river. Mbuyazi had approximately 7000 warriors and about twice as many dependents.

Early on 2 December, by which time heavy rains had transformed the Tugela into a raging torrent, Cetshwayo and between 15,000 and 20,000 warriors moved against Mbuyazi from an encampment to the north-west. Mbuyazi deployed to meet the threat and battle was joined near the Nwaku stream, a short distance to the west of Mbuyazi's camp. Cetshwayo's right horn endeavoured to outflank their opponents, but despite their numerical superiority they were repulsed by Mbuyazi's left horn, which enjoyed the support of Dunn and his gunmen. In contrast, the uSuthu left proceeded to push back Mbuyazi's right horn, thus undermining the morale of the prince's left horn which likewise began to give ground. Seeing this, the iziGqoza centre also beat a retreat in a south-easterly direction towards the Tugela, only to find it impassable.

The uSuthu gave chase and terrible slaughter ensued. Many of the fugitives were cut down beside the Tugela while others plunged into the raging river and were either drowned or swept out to sea. Dunn managed to save himself by clambering on to a ferryboat in mid-stream and thus lived to tell the tale. Few of the iziGqoza did so, and among the dead were thousands of women and children, for Dunn tells us that Cetshwayo's warriors had acted 'with terrible earnestness, hard at work with the deadly assegai, in some cases pinning babies to their mother's quivering forms', a point corroborated by W. C. Baldwin in the statement quoted at the head of this chapter.

Mpande's later years

After the battle of Ndondakusuka (so named after the most prominent hill in the vicinity), Cetshwayo headed triumphantly towards the capital, driving with him captured cattle. He intended to present the livestock to his father, whose position had inevitably been weakened. Mpande, however, was grief-stricken by the news of Mbuyazi's death, and those of five of his other sons in the encounter, and refused to receive the tribute, whereupon Cetshwayo set off for his own homestead.

Although Mbuyazi was now out of the picture, Cetshwayo was not without potential rivals. One such was a full brother of Mbuyazi, the thirteen-year-old Mkhungo. Mpande placed him for safekeeping among the uMcijo *ibutho*, but in mid-1857, when Cetshwayo moved towards their

65

ikhanda with a strong force, they abandoned the youngster. The prince managed to elude Cetshwayo by escaping to Natal where he was taken under the wing of Theophilus Shepstone, the Natal Secretary for Native Affairs, who enrolled him in an Anglican mission school near Pietermaritzburg with the ultimate aim of seeing him become a compliant king of the Zulus.

In November 1857, Mpande and Cetshwayo reached a formal reconciliation, though relations were to continue strained. Mpande pledged to allow the young Cetshwayo to play a prominent part in ruling the nation on condition that he maintained the peace and that Mpande remained the ultimate authority.

It was in 1857 that Cetshwayo engaged the services of Dunn, who set up a kraal near Gingindlovu (a homestead Cetshwayo had recently established in south-east Zululand) after being offered land by Cetshwayo in return for his services as a diplomat. Furthermore, Dunn, who was to go native and among other things acquire a bevy of Zulu wives, was to prove adept at supplying the prince with much-prized firearms.

In due course Mpande began to favour another of his sons, a lad named Mthonga, whose mother was one of the king's youngest wives, a good-looking woman with whom Mpande was besotted. Once again, Cetshwayo responded. In March 1861, warriors loyal to him were sent to kill the fourteen-year-old. But their quarry escaped, although the boy's mother was killed and Mpande himself gravely insulted. Mthonga and a younger brother fled to Utrecht which, since 1859, had been a district of the South African Republic. (The republic, also known as the Transvaal, had been established by Voortrekkers who had crossed the Vaal River years before and whose independence had been acknowledged by Britain in 1852.)

The Boers saw Mthonga as a bargaining tool. In recent years they had been encroaching on to land east of the Ncome River, and hard on the heels of the princes' arrival, they opened negotiations with Cetshwayo who had marched towards the Utrecht district at the head of a large force. Cetshwayo was told that the Afrikaners were prepared to hand over Mthonga and his brother if the safety of the two princes was assured and if Cetshwayo would recognise Boer land claims east of the Ncome. Satisfied that their conditions had been met – although Cetshwayo subsequently strongly denied conceding land – Mthonga and his brother were handed over to Cetshwayo, whom the Boers had publicly recognised as Mpande's heir during the negotiations.

May 1861 witnessed the arrival at Nodwengu of Shepstone, who had travelled from Natal to see Mpande, accompanied by a small escort. The visit was no mere courtesy call. Shepstone had been alarmed by Cetshwayo's recent alliance with the Boers and feared that it was prejudicial to British interests. 'He hoped that he would be able to shore up Mpande's authority,' states Laband, 'and thereby reassert British influence at the expense of that of

Cetshwayo and the Boers.' Upon arrival, Shepstone immediately declared that Mpande enjoyed his full support. Cetshwayo was not among the Zulu notables present – he had disobeyed his father's instruction to attend – but he soon made his way to Nodwengu, escorted by the uThulwana regiment, after Shepstone threatened that the Natal authorities would recognise Mkhungo as Mpande's heir.

Cetshwayo's meeting with Shepstone proved far from tranquil. For one thing, Cetshwayo demanded that Natal should surrender Mkhungo, which was refused. The atmosphere then became even more tense as members of the regiments, listening to the discussions, began to adopt a menacing attitude towards Shepstone, compelling Mpande and other senior figures, such as Masiphula kaMamba, to intervene in order to quieten them. Shepstone rose to the occasion with a cool dignity that won him the begrudging respect of many onlookers, Cetshwayo included. Calm was restored and, at Shepstone's bidding, Mpande formally recognised Cetshwayo as his heir.

With the passage of the 1860s, Mpande, with his increasing bulk, became ever more sedentary, seldom stirring, except occasionally to be transported around Nodwengu on a cart made as a gift for him by a white trader. Increasingly he left affairs in the hands of others, although he continued to officiate annually at the first-fruits festival. His permission was still required for new regiments to be formed or for others to disband and marry. Mpande allowed Cetshwayo's own regiment, the uThulwana, to marry in 1867; and Cetshwayo became a father the following year.

Mpande died at Nodwengu in September or October 1872. He left his successor a land that had enjoyed peace for most of his reign and whose population had grown, despite the exodus of some to Natal and the bloodshed caused by the civil war. Mpande has to share much of the blame for the conflict that erupted in late 1856 and paid a bitter price, both emotionally and politically, for his prestige suffered greatly and his hold on his kingdom was never the same again. Henceforth, senior members of Cetshwayo's uSuthu faction enjoyed greater autonomy than ever before, apparently paying only nominal allegiance to the king, while other great chiefs similarly exercised a greater measure of power and independence than in the past. Mpande's achievements, nevertheless, should not be ignored. His very survival was partly due to his diplomacy and shrewdness. Moreover, he successfully maintained Zulu sovereignty and independence by wisely avoiding or defusing confrontations with his white neighbours. He deserves to be remembered with a measure of respect.

CHAPTER 4

TWILIGHT OF AN ERA

'To emulate Chaka in shedding blood is as far as I have heard his highest inspiration.' *Sir Bartle Frere*

Cetshwayo was to prove a more dynamic and intelligent ruler than his father. A proud, straightforward man, he revitalised the army, which had become somewhat lax during Mpande's reign, and was determined to defend Zulu independence and the right to rule his people without foreign dictation. He was reserved, but self-possessed, a man to be reckoned with.

Like his father, Cetshwayo based his foreign policy on a close relationship with Natal – partly in the hope of countering the threat posed by the Transvaal – and one of his first actions was to invite Theophilus Shepstone, Natal Secretary for Native Affairs, to come to Zululand and acknowledge him as king before his people by 'crowning' him. Rumours had been circulating for years that Cetshwayo's former rival, Mbuyazi, had somehow survived Ndondakusuka and was living in Natal. Cetshwayo's half-brother, Mkhungo, was certainly in Natal, as were four other sons of Mpande, including Mthonga, who had settled there in 1865. By acceding to Cetshwayo's wish, Shepstone would demonstrate that he was not planning to supplant him with one or other of his half-brothers. Moreover, Cetshwayo hoped to secure a British commitment to Zulu interests.

By officially installing Cetshwayo, Shepstone believed, too, that he would gain ascendancy over him and further the interests both of Natal and Britain. He and his entourage, which included a number of prominent colonials, therefore arrived in Zululand in August 1873 with an armed escort of 110 officers and men of the Natal Volunteer Corps and about 300 Natal blacks.

Before the official meeting took place, at the urging of senior advisers such as Masiphula kaMamba, Cetshwayo went through the coronation ritual at a vast meeting of Zulus in the emaKhosini Valley near the White Mfolozi at a spot overlooked by the Mthonjaneni Heights. He had been anxious to discover whether certain prominent chiefs with their power bases in the north were prepared to accept him as Mpande's successor, and had consequently armed a substantial number of his followers with firearms supplied by Dunn.

The installation of Cetshwayo by his own people surprised and angered Shepstone to the extent that he contemplated heading home. However, Cetshwayo sent Dunn to mollify him by stating that only part of the coronation ceremony had been performed. Hence Shepstone proceeded to 'enthrone' Cetshwayo on 1 September at a royal homestead on the Mahla-bathini plain. A nondescript crown of ostrich feathers and tinsel, which Shepstone had brought for the occasion, was placed on Cetshwayo's head and the Secretary for Native Affairs then announced: 'Here is your king. You have recognised him, and I now also do so in the name of the Queen of England.' Shepstone also proclaimed a number of 'coronation laws' agreed upon with Cetshwayo. One such to the effect that no executions should take place without royal assent was hardly music to the ears of great chiefs, for they had begun to exercise the right of life and death over their dependents during Mpande's reign.

A topic touched on during the visit was the question of missionaries. Shepstone wished to know when Cetshwayo would allow more of them to operate in Zululand, but failed to obtain such a concession from the king. Cetshwayo, for his part, was concerned to know what Shepstone would do about Boer encroachment in north-western Zululand east of the Ncome, and received a vague assurance of support for Zulu claims in the area. Shepstone subsequently described the king as a man of 'great ability and frankness' ranking 'in every respect far above any native chief I have had to do with'.

In accordance with Zulu royal tradition, Cetshwayo built a new capital following Shepstone's visit (the site had already been chosen and prelimi-nary work undertaken beforehand) and the homestead was called oNdini. It was located on a gentle slope in the Mahlabathini plain not far from Nodwengu and contained approximately 1400 huts, the largest of which, not surprisingly, belonged to Cetshwayo. A second royal dwelling, a brick house of European design, was also erected. It was constructed of materials supplied by a Norwegian missionary named Ommund Oftebro, and its wall-papered rooms had glazed windows and contained some European furni-ture. When resident at oNdini, Cetshwayo normally spent part of the day in the house consulting his councillors and attending to other state affairs. Furthermore, Cetshwayo occasionally wore a coat and trousers, and listened to stories of colonial Natal and the world beyond, related by Dunn.

Foreign relations

For much of the 1870s Cetshwayo viewed the Boers in the Transvaal as the principal external threat to his sovereignty and he made a number of requests to Shepstone requesting his intercession over increasing Boer encroachment in the north-west. This gave added cogency to Cetshwayo's policy of reinvigorating and strengthening the army. A central figure in this policy was John Dunn. From his residence near the Indian Ocean, Dunn operated a gun-running network that resulted in thousands of firearms arriving in Zululand via Durban and Delagoa Bay, thereby adding to the significant quantity of guns Cetshwayo had begun amassing with Dunn's assistance in the late 1860s.

In 1876, relations between Cetshwayo and the Transvaal were such that open conflict appeared imminent. In fact, it was only averted when the Boers backed down. Nevertheless, Cetshwayo was shortly to find himself involved in a bitter war, indeed a fight for the very survival of the Zulu kingdom, and not against the Boers but against the British.

A key player in the events that led to the commencement of hostilities was the British Colonial Secretary, Lord Carnarvon, a staunch imperialist who wished to unite South Africa under the crown and indeed declared in 1876 that he hoped that Britain would dominate most of the African continent. The British had long viewed the interior of southern Africa as of little significance, but the discovery of diamonds in the late 1860s not far to the south of the Vaal River had changed this. Suddenly the region was seen as a source of great wealth that could be exploited in Britain's interest. Jeff Guy states:

> By confederation, it was hoped that a strong, united, white-dominated southern Africa could be created, one that was suited to the demands of expanding capitalistic development and, at the same time, would be able to carry its own administrative and military costs, thereby reducing the direct responsibility of the British Government in the region without harming its interests.

Initially, Carnarvon hoped that the Transvaal Boers would cooperate with his confederation policy, but this view, encouraged by talks in London with the republic's president in May 1875, proved mistaken. Carnarvon therefore decided upon annexation and entrusted the task to Shepstone, who entered the Transvaal in January 1877 with a small police escort – Cetshwayo had offered the assistance of his warriors but Shepstone had declined. Visiting Pretoria, the capital of the impoverished state, he caused alarm by declaring that Cetshwayo was assembling his forces, after reaching the end of his tether over Boer encroachment, and that his own influence with the king was such that he could avert the imminent invasion. The Transvaalers were bankrupt and demoralised, weakened by factionalism and an unsuccessful war against the Pedi people living in the east of the region. So pliant was the general mood that Shepstone was able to proclaim the Transvaal a British colony on 12 April 1877. He was to be its first Administrator.

By this date a new figure had just appeared on the South African scene, a man who had had a distinguished career in India. He stepped ashore at Cape Town on 31 March, having been appointed Governor of Cape Colony, High Commissioner for South Africa and Commander-in-Chief of the British forces in the region: his name was Sir Bartle Frere. He was charged with achieving Carnarvon's federation policy. Not surprisingly, Frere was a staunch imperialist. In the words of John Laband:

He was a committed evangelical and trained to act vigorously on his own initiative ... who considered that it was Britain's high mission to spread the civilising influence of Christian government and to eradicate barbarous institutions. By extending British rule over blacks ... he envisaged putting them to 'civilised' labour for wages, so they could spend their earnings on European manufactured goods to the benefit of white colonists, and to their own advantage.

Frere thus set himself energetically to bringing about the end of Zulu power and independence. Demonising Cetshwayo was central to the task. 'The monster Chaka is his model,' he told the Colonial Office, 'to emulate Chaka in shedding blood is as far as I have heard his highest inspiration.'

Shepstone worked hand in hand with Frere. In August 1877, for instance, the majority of the missionaries working in Zululand (where most of their seed was falling on stony ground) fled to Natal on his advice, for Shepstone wished to portray Cetshwayo as the 'heathen' persecutor of Christianity.

Moreover, Shepstone sent a message to oNdini requesting a meeting to discuss the long-running border dispute between the Zulu kingdom and the Transvaal. Cetshwayo responded by sending an impressive delegation to the appointed rendezvous beside the Ncome. It was composed of the most senior men in his kingdom and headed by his principal minister, Mnyamana of the Buthelezi, who had been his prime minister since the commencement of the reign. They arrived on 18 October. To their consternation, Shepstone made it clear that the Zulus could no longer regard him as an ally. Far from backing them up over the border dispute, as he had done previously, he now sang a discordant tune, for as the Administrator of the Transvaal he was eager to gain the favour of the Transvaalers who were growing restive following their annexation. He told the Zulus that they should accept the Boer boundary claims.

In short, Shepstone was no friend of Cetshwayo. Indeed, in December he wrote to Carnarvon describing the king as:

the secret hope of every independent chief, hundreds of miles from him, who feels a desire that his colour should prevail, and it will not be until this power [the Zulu state] is destroyed that they will make up their minds to submit to the rule of civilisation. The sooner the root of the evil that I consider to be the Zulu power and military organisation is dealt with, the easier our task will be.

But Cetshwayo received a glimmer of hope when the Lieutenant-Governor of Natal, Sir Henry Bulwer, eased tension somewhat in the same month by suggesting that Cetshwayo submit the boundary issue to the arbitration of a commission. The king accepted the proposal. So, too, did Frere, who had been convinced by Shepstone that the Boer claim to the disputed territory would be vindicated.

In March 1878, the boundary commission – which consisted of Natal officials – gathered at an isolated spot called Rorke's Drift just on the Natal side of the Mzinyathi. Its chairman was an Irishman named Michael Gallwey, who was Natal's attorney-general and a man of independent mind.

The commission reported its findings to Bulwer in June. The Transvaal claim to the land between the Mzinyathi and Ncome Rivers was upheld but its claim to the lands east of the Ncome was judged invalid.

Bulwer's reaction to the report was favourable. But when Frere saw it in mid-July, he found its partial judgement in favour of Cetshwayo far from welcome. Consequently, instead of sending the report to London promptly, he delayed doing so and pondered how best to act after soliciting the advice of others in South Africa to whom he communicated the commission's findings. Uppermost in his mind was the possible effect of the report on the disgruntled Transvaal Boers and hence of the entire confederation scheme. Since April, British forces had been engaged in an unsuccessful campaign against the Pedi. To quote Laband:

> In such unsatisfactory circumstances, any award that failed to demonstrate Britain's determination to guarantee Boer security against the blacks on their borders could well lead to rebellion. Such an uprising ... might draw in the Boers elsewhere in South Africa, and encourage the Zulu and their fellow members of the 'black conspiracy' to fall upon the whites. Frere began to envisage a dreadful scenario in which the choice lay between risking a Zulu war at once, or bringing about a Zulu war a few months later, preceded by a Boer rebellion.

Furthermore, Frere exploited a number of incidents that occurred on the Natal–Zululand border to soften up Carnarvon's successor, Sir Michael Hicks Beach, who had become Colonial Secretary in early 1878 and who wished to avoid a war with Cetshwayo. In July, for instance, two wives of a Zulu chief named Sihayo kaXongo (a great favourite of Cetshwayo) absconded into Natal. But as the month drew to a close they were seized by armed parties led by Sihayo's sons, who hauled them back to Zululand where they were executed. Bulwer reacted to the incursions by requesting the extradition of the raiders for trial in Natal, but Cetshwayo was reluctant to comply. After all, the women had violated Zulu law and had not been put to death in the colony.

By November, Frere had received the Colonial Secretary's response to the boundary commission's report. It was not favourable to his stance: Hicks Beach accepted the report's findings. Frere, however, was undaunted. He had begun to mass troops near the Zulu border in anticipation of conflict (Cetshwayo responded by calling up *amabutho*) and subsequently sent word to the king that the findings of the boundary commission and 'other communications' would be delivered on 11 December at the Lower Drift of the Tugela, near where the river met the Indian Ocean. The 'other communications' would prove to be an ultimatum.

On the morning of the 11th, as the Tugela was in spate, fourteen royal indunas and their attendants were ferried across the drift on flat-bottomed punts to the Natal bank where a party headed by John Shepstone (the Acting Secretary for Native Affairs and brother of Theophilus) was awaiting them. After announcing the findings of the boundary commission, Shepstone presented the British ultimatum to the increasingly incredulous Zulu embassy. Among other things, the perpetrators of the border incidents were to be handed over and Cetshwayo was to pay a fine of 500 cattle for not having already surrendered up the wrongdoers.

Much more significant, however, were demands that would render Cetshwayo politically and militarily impotent. The Zulu army was to be permanently disbanded; all Zulus were to be free to marry upon reaching maturity; missionaries were to be allowed to return and operate without hindrance; Cetshwayo was to observe his coronation oaths regarding the shedding of innocent blood; and a British Resident was to be stationed in Zululand to enforce the conditions. The ultimatum was due to expire on 11 January 1879 and, as Stephen Taylor comments: 'It was called an ultimatum but it was more a declaration of war.'

Frere expected Cetshwayo to resist and was confident that in the event of conflict the Zulu nation would soon be overcome. His confidence was based on the superiority of British military might and the knowledge that cracks existed in the Zulu polity, for certain senior Zulus had built up their own power-bases and were known to be on strained terms with their king. Internal discord and defections were expected. In fact, one of the greatest chiefs in Zululand, Prince Hamu kaNzibe, had already let the British know that in the event of war he was prepared to desert Cetshwayo in return for protection.

Within days, word of what Frere required arrived at oNdini. Cetshwayo responded by stating that he was prepared to pay the fine and hand over Sihayo's sons, but had to discuss the weightier issues with his councillors. By late December, though, he was unwilling to hand over Sihayo's sons despite strong pressure from his inner council to do so. As for the demand for the dismantling of the Zulu military apparatus, however, Cetshwayo and his councillors were in agreement – compliance was out of the question. Hence when Cetshwayo called upon his regiments to assemble on the Mahlabathini plain for the great *umKhosi* festival (the *amabutho* had stood down by early December following their previous call-up), he ordered them

to bring their arms and ammunition so that they could be ready for immediate active service during the festival, which was due to occur in January.

On 11 January 1879, British forces began to enter Zululand. Their
commander was Lieutenant-General Frederick Augustus Thesiger, second
Baron Chelmsford, an essentially decent man with a strong sense of duty.
War had commenced.

Chelmsford's plan of campaign

Instead of concentrating his available manpower, Chelmsford had decided
to divide his forces into five columns, three of which would take part in the
invasion while the others, he hoped, would protect Natal and the Transvaal
from any Zulu counter-thrusts. Moreover, by dividing his invasion force
Chelmsford avoided the logistical problems that a single column would
have entailed, for the larger the convoy, the slower it moved and the more
pressing was the problem of obtaining suitable forage. Also, by dividing his
strike force, Chelmsford no doubt hoped to induce the Zulus into fighting
a pitched battle, for he feared that they might intend to wage a protracted
guerrilla campaign.

The Right Flank Column (No. 1) was commanded by Colonel Charles
Pearson, 3rd Buffs, and was to cross into Zululand via the Lower Drift on
the Tugela. It numbered some 4750 officers and men. No. 2 Column, under
Colonel Anthony Durnford, RE, was stationed above the Middle Drift,
roughly half-way upstream from the Lower Drift and the Tugela's junction
with the Mzinyathi, and had a total strength of 3871. The Centre Column
(No. 3) was commanded by Colonel Richard Glyn, 24th Regiment,
although Chelmsford's decision to accompany it effectively reduced Glyn
to being its nominal commander. Its strength was 4709 officers and men. It
was to cross the Mzinyathi into Zululand via Rorke's Drift about 40 miles
north-west of where the Mzinyathi meets the Tugela. The Left Flank
Column (No. 4), 2278 strong, commanded by Colonel Evelyn Wood VC,
90th Light Infantry, would do so from a point known as Bemba's Kop on
the Ncome, while the remaining column, No. 5, under Colonel H.
Rowlands VC of the 34th Regiment, comprising 1565 officers and men, was
based further north at Luneburg in the Transvaal, charged with opposing a
Zulu incursion and keeping a watchful eye on restive Boers in the Transvaal.

The three invading columns were to march on oNdini. For much of the
way they would be so far apart that they would have to act independently.
Chelmsford would only be able to exercise command over the whole invasion force as the columns converged on their goal.

Space does not permit a detailed discussion of Chelmsford's forces, but
something needs to be said about their composition and weaponry. He was
in overall command of an army of 17,929 men, of whom 5476 were British
regulars, 1193 irregular colonial horse and 9350 black levies raised in Natal:

the remainder were wagon drivers, etc. To supply his men while on campaign, Chelmsford had assembled 10,023 oxen, 398 mules, 977 wagons and 56 carts, a task that had proved difficult and expensive.

Regular infantry regiments either consisted of a single battalion or contained two battalions. The latter was true of the 24th Regiment, which played a prominent part in the Zulu War. The first battalion had been in South Africa since 1875 and had been heavily involved in a recent Frontier War with the Xhosa, while the second battalion had only arrived in 1878 and had been employed in mopping-up operations. The 2/24th, on the whole, comprised younger men than its sister battalion and had a higher proportion of Welsh origin, which is not surprising, given that the regimental depot had been established at Brecon in 1873.

Officers of an infantry regiment possessed swords and revolvers, while the rank and file were armed with a Martini-Henry rifle and bayonet. The rifle weighed 9 lbs and was just over 4 feet long. It had been introduced in the early 1870s and was a breech-loading, single-shot weapon that fired a .45 inch calibre lead bullet, of which each man carried 70 rounds. Although sighted up to 1700 yards, the British Army considered the rifle's effective battle range as between 300 and 450 yards, though it was nonetheless common for firing to commence at 800 yards. Dirt in the mechanism made the rifle liable to jam, while after ten rounds the barrel became too hot to hold, a defect that had become apparent during the recent Ninth Frontier War; consequently, soldiers had begun to fit protective bullock-hide covers over the barrel and stock. A battalion's fire was normally delivered by volley, but independent firing was sometimes allowed. The bayonet was of the socket type and had a 21.5 inch blade, the longest ever employed by British infantry.

Chelmsford had no regular regiments of cavalry at the commencement of the Zulu War (the 1st King's Dragoon Guards and 17th Lancers participated in its later stages after being sent out from England) but he did nevertheless have mounted soldiers from the outset. These included the 1st and 2nd Squadrons Imperial Mounted Infantry, which had been formed in 1877 and 1878. Each was about 120 strong and was divided into two troops. Officers and men were drawn from various infantry regiments, wore buff cord riding breeches, were armed with Swinburne-Henry carbines and had bandoliers instead of ammunition pouches. In 1875, Chelmsford's predecessor, Sir Arthur Cunynghame, had declared that 'experience has always shown me that picked officers and men from foot regiments can in a very short time be turned into mounted riflemen of the very best description'.

The Imperial Mounted Infantry were supplemented by men from the Natal Volunteer Corps which consisted of various settler units whose weapons and uniforms were provided by the government, although the men provided their own mounts. All were part-time units, with the exception of the 110-strong Natal Mounted Police. Another fine unit was the Frontier Light Horse, commanded by a British officer, Major Redvers Buller of the 60th Rifles, which had just seen service in the Frontier War. The colonial irregulars were armed with a rifle or carbine and had bandoliers.

At the beginning of the Zulu War, Chelmsford's artillery arm consisted of N Battery, 5th Brigade, Royal Field Artillery, and 11th Battery, 7th Brigade, Royal Garrison Artillery. Moreover, a number of guns were provided for land operations by the Royal Navy. The batteries' guns were 7-pounders which had a maximum range of 3100 yards and were capable of firing shrapnel, common shell, double shell or case-shot. One of the batteries that arrived during the course of the war, and also a detachment from the navy, used 9-pounders, capable of projecting a shell up to 3500 yards.

The Gatling gun was also employed during the war. It was mounted on a carriage (like the field guns) and consisted of ten rifled barrels revolving around a central shaft which were fed from a cylindrical magazine. It was fired by rotating a crank handle. It propelled a .45 inch calibre round up to an effective range of 1200 yards and was capable of firing about 300 rounds a minute. It was prone, however, to jamming.

Hale's rockets, invented by William Hale in the 1860s, were also used, with 9-pounders and 24-pounders respectively being employed by the Royal Artillery batteries and the Naval Brigade. The rockets possessed either an explosive or an incendiary warhead and had an effective range of approximately 1300 yards. Accuracy was not one of their strengths, but they could nonetheless be effective against a massed target, and their high-pitched shrieking sound in flight was calculated to disconcert the Zulus, who were unfamiliar with such a weapon.

Chelmsford could also use the services of two field companies of Royal Engineers. One of these companies and the advance party of the other were present at the outset: the rest of the second company was making its way up from Durban. If occasion demanded, sappers, too, could act as infantry if they could be spared from their normal duties.

The Royal Navy's contribution to the forces at Chelmsford's disposal consisted of detachments of officers and seamen, Royal Marine Artillery and Royal Marine Light Infantry. The Naval Brigade's initial strength was a mere 230 men, but this was to rise to just over 800 men.

Of the black troops, 7630 belonged to the Natal Native Contingent which was divided into three regiments, one with three battalions and the others with two. Each battalion comprised ten companies with nine white officers and NCOs, and 100 natives, and three companies of the 1st Battalion 3rd NNC consisting of dissident Zulus resident in Natal who had opposed Cetshwayo's succession. No uniforms were issued to members of the NNC. Their only means of identification was a red rag tied around the head. Moreover, some wore the occasional item of European clothing. Firearms were noticeably absent. Only one man in ten possessed a gun, many of which were old-fashioned, and consequently the bulk of the NNC were armed with spears and shields. The quality of the officers and NCOs was not high, for the many were unsavoury characters: the majority of the best colonials were serving in the irregular mounted units. The 1st regiment of the NNC had the best officers and NCOs, thanks to its commander, Colonel Anthony Durnford of the Royal Engineers, who had been stationed in Natal for several years and had lost an arm in action. Durnford admired and respected blacks and managed to obtain white subordinates of a better calibre than the majority of those in the other regiments of the NNC, and he enjoyed the esteem of his men.

The NNC formed the bulk of the native levies who were to participate in the war. Others belonged to the Natal Native Horse (which contained five troops of men who were well mounted and armed with carbines), and two companies of Natal Native Pioneers, equipped with picks and shovels, who were intended to supplement Chelmsford's limited number of sappers.

Cetshwayo's army

It was Cetshwayo's aim to fight a defensive war. He thus forbade his warriors to cross the border, in the hope that a purely defensive strategy would reap political dividends. He knew, for example, from white advisers such as Dunn that Britain's resources were far greater than his own and that a violation of British territory would doubtless provoke a response of such magnitude that victory for the Zulus would become unattainable.

Cetshwayo's spies informed him that the Centre Column was the strongest of the invading forces, and so he decided to send the bulk of his army against it. The warriors were told to conserve their energy by advancing slowly, and were to refrain from attacking entrenched positions. Furthermore, they were to avoid night attacks and, after driving back the enemy, were, as noted, not to follow them across the border.

The exact number of warriors Cetshwayo had at his disposal is unknown. The army's nominal strength was probably about 40,000, but some of the regiments consisted of men who were very advanced in years and thus of little worth, so that the number of effective warriors available was about 29,000.

As in the past, the majority of regiments consisted of individuals of the same age drawn from different parts of Zululand. In the north-west, however, the Qulusi, who enjoyed a close relationship with the Zulu royal house, formed their own regiment drawn from their specific locality centred on an *ikhanda* founded by Shaka.

During Mpande's reign it had become common for warriors to marry earlier than was normal, and white shields, which had distinguished senior unmarried *amabutho*, now signified married men. The latter generally lived in their own homesteads and only mustered for exceptional occasions, but some of these regiments continued to serve in the *amakhanda*, although the men were often accompanied by their wives and were free to come and go as they pleased. In Cetshwayo's reign, one such 'white assembly' was the uThulwana regiment, together with other married regiments that had been incorporated with it to keep it up to strength, all of them based at oNdini.

The average strength of regiments in the late 1870s was around 1500 men, but some of the younger *amabutho* were much stronger. For instance, Cetshwayo's favourite regiment, the iNgobamakhosi, numbered perhaps 6000 warriors. Moreover, although it was the norm for newly established regiments to found their own barracks at a specified location, occasionally a new regiment was incorporated into an older one or was assigned to an existing barracks. The uVe, for example, formed shortly before the Zulu War, was a 4000-strong *ibutho* which was incorporated into the iNgobamakhosi.

Lavish uniforms were still sported for ceremonial occasions but it was no longer customary to wear full dress into battle (if indeed it had ever been the practice), although adornment such as stuffed headbands of animal skin or the bushy parts of cows' tails around the arm and leg was frequently on view. Men of rank and members of older regiments generally wore the most elaborate regalia into battle.

Warriors' traditional arms consisted of spears, knobkerries and shields. Men of status sometimes carried battleaxes, though these appear to have been confined principally to ceremonial occasions rather than used as weapons of war.

The standard spear was still the stabbing spear, but by 1879, types with shorter and narrower blades (approximately 12 inches long by 1¼ inches wide) had come into vogue at the expense of the larger weapon employed in earlier days, although the latter was still used by some. As mentioned, however, the throwing spear had been reintroduced by Dingane. The most popular type had a blade about 7 inches long, attached by a shank to a shaft of up to 3 feet in length; such a weapon could be thrown with some degree of accuracy up to about 50 yards, and many of the warriors in 1879 would have possessed one or two such spears.

By this date, of course, firearms supplemented traditional weapons. Indeed, as has been noted, they had been acquired in substantial numbers, and the majority of warriors therefore had access to guns. Most were old-fashioned weapons such as Brown Bess muskets. This fact, combined with a lack of training, absence of spare parts, and irregular supplies of ammunition, rendered guns less deadly than would otherwise have been the case. Zulu fire was notable for its volume and inaccuracy.

In the mid-1850s Cetshwayo had introduced a new type of war-shield among his followers. It was about 3½ feet long and less than 2 feet wide, and thus smaller than the traditional type, making it lighter and easier to wield. Both types were carried during the Zulu War, often by warriors within the same regiment, though the smaller shield was evidently the more popular. Furthermore, the colour-coding of shields was no longer as precise as it had once been and there was less variety: grey and dun colours seem to have passed out of use. Black, however, was still viewed as a sign of youth and white as one of experience. Additionally, in at least some regiments (the iNgobamakhosi for one) warriors had shields that differed in colour from those of fellow members of the same regiment. At the beginning of Cetshwayo's reign, Zululand's cattle had been decimated by an epidemic of bovine pleuro-pneumonia and this perhaps made it impossible to maintain the colour-matching system of previous years.

Tactically, the Zulu army still utilised the 'beast horns' manoeuvre, hoping to overcome the enemy by speed, ferocity and numbers. The warriors moved towards the enemy in open order, skilfully exploiting any cover, then fired a volley and closed up to charge at speed. When about 30 yards off, they hurled their throwing spears if they had them, before pressing home to engage in hand-to-hand combat. Despite a number of obvious limitations, the Zulu army was a highly mobile force (in marked contrast to that of Chelmsford) and enjoyed a high degree of morale and strong motivation, with many of the young warriors, in particular, itching for a fight. It was a potent army operating on familiar terrain, and one that enjoyed significant numerical superiority.

CHAPTER 5

'THEY FELL LIKE STONES' – THE BATTLES OF ISANDLWANA AND RORKE'S DRIFT

'We went to see the dead people at Isandlwana. We saw a single warrior dead, staring in our direction, with his war shield in his hand.... We saw countless things dead. Dead was the horse, dead too, the mule, dead was the dog, dead was the monkey, dead were the wagons, dead were the tents, dead were the boxes, dead was everything, even to the very metals.' *Recollections of a Zulu boy*

The British Centre Column, against which Cetshwayo sent the bulk of his warriors, numbered approximately 4700 officers and men, and it began to cross the Mzinyathi at Rorke's Drift, enveloped in a thick mist and drizzling rain, at about 4.30 a.m. on Saturday 11 January 1879. No opposition was encountered during the crossing, which continued throughout the day, and a camp was established on the Zulu bank.

On the following day Chelmsford advanced from Rorke's Drift against a nearby kraal, none other than Sihayo's homestead, which was located in the Batshe Valley, an area crossed by the track along which Chelmsford planned to advance. Sihayo was at oNdini, but a small Zulu force under one of his sons opened fire from a sheltered position and a brief skirmish ensued in which the Zulus were put to flight, leaving behind about 30 dead, one of whom was their leader. Sihayo's abandoned homestead was then set alight and livestock seized, after which the soldiers returned to camp, having lost few of their own number. In subsequent days, work was undertaken to improve the track at several points along the Batshe Valley – in some places, for instance, it crossed marshy ground – while mounted troops scouted eastward. They duly reported having located a suitable camp-site where the track skirted a prominent hill called Isandlwana, at the west end of a vast plain. The site had a good provision of fuel and water, so Chelmsford decided to establish an advanced base there and to unload some of the wagons before they were sent back to Rorke's Drift to bring on further supplies.

On 20 January, the Centre Column thus advanced to Isandlwana. A short distance to the north of the sphinx-like hill, a spur leads up to a plateau (the Nyoni Heights) which has an east-west axis and whose southern edge forms an escarpment intersected at various places by the courses of streams that flow down to the plain. The plain itself runs east from Isandlwana for several miles; four miles or so wide in places, it is bisected on a north-south axis by dongas formed by the streams. A short distance to the south of Isandlwana is a hill known as Mahlabamkhosi,

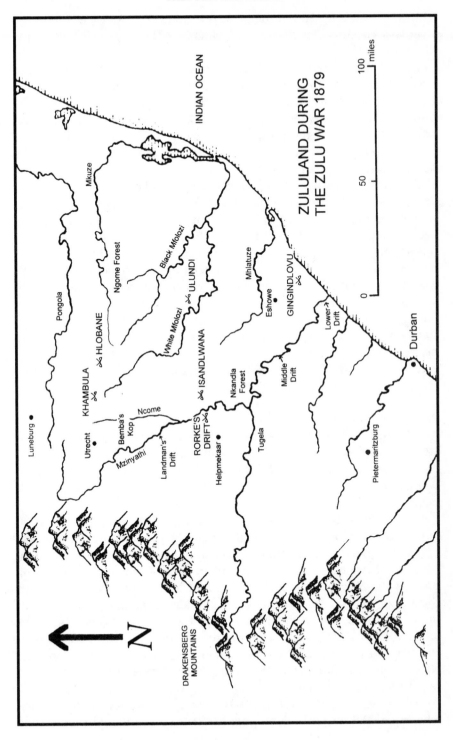

while the southern flank of the plain is bounded by a range of hills – the Hlazakazi Heights – to the east of which are the upper reaches of the Mangeni River.

The column crossed a nek or saddle-back ridge between Isandlwana and Mahlabamkhosi and encamped beneath the eastern face of Isandlwana. The 2/3rd Natal Native Contingent was the northernmost unit, then came the 1/3rd NNC, the 2/24th, N/5 Royal Artillery, the mounted troops and, on the south side of the track, the 1/24th. The Headquarters Staff were located behind the centre of the line, while the wagons were parked on the nek and behind each unit's camp.

Colonel Glyn wished to form a laager but Chelmsford overruled him. Doing so would be time-consuming and, in any event, most of the wagons were going to be sent back to Rorke's Drift for supplies. Doubtless partly because of the stony nature of the ground, the camp was not entrenched; nor was any attempt made to impede an enemy approach by using thorn-bushes and broken bottles. Lieutenant Teignmouth Melvill of the 1/24th was one of a number of officers who felt concerned about the omission of such defensive features: 'These Zulus will charge home,' he said, 'and with our small numbers we ought to be in laager, or, at any rate, be prepared to stand shoulder to shoulder.' On the other hand, infantry picquets were placed out in an arc half a mile by day and a quarter of a mile at night, extending up from Mahlabamkhosi on to the spur, while vedettes were sent up to the surrounding heights during daylight.

Preliminary moves
At dawn on 21 January, Chelmsford sent Major John Dartnell and about 120 irregulars to reconnoitre to the east and south-east, while Commandant Rupert Lonsdale and the 3rd Regiment NNC were despatched to sweep ground to the south and south-east of the camp before joining Dartnell.

Late in the afternoon, Dartnell came across perhaps as many as 2000 Zulu warriors who emerged on high ground just to the north of the head of the Mangeni. The Zulus were under a local chief, Matshana kaMondisa, who had been detached from the main impi – which was marching towards the Ngwebeni Valley north-east of Isandlwana – evidently with the aim of splitting the British forces. In addition to men from the main impi, Matshana's force included his own adherents. When the Zulus failed to attack, Dartnell withdrew to the east end of the Hlazakazi Heights and proceeded to encamp for the night with his men and the NNC, about nine miles from the camp at Isandlwana, to which he sent a request for reinforcements.

The messenger arrived at about 1.30 a.m. on Wednesday 22 January, whereupon Major Clery (Glyn's principal staff officer) took the message to

Chelmsford. Clery states that the general responded thus: 'Order the 2nd Battalion 24th Regiment, four guns, and all the mounted troops to get ready and start at daybreak.' Chelmsford intended to accompany the men moving to Dartnell's assistance; and to strengthen the force he was to leave at Isandlwana, he sent a message to Durnford, commander of No. 2 Column, ordering him to come up post-haste. Durnford, in obedience to an earlier command, had moved with approximately 500 of his men from an escarpment overlooking the Middle Drift on the Tugela, and was now at Rorke's Drift. At about 4.30 a.m., Chelmsford and Colonel Glyn rode out of the camp, evidently expecting a stiff fight, leaving Lieutenant-Colonel Henry Pulleine of the 1/24th in charge.

Although aged 40, Pulleine had never commanded a force in action – he had served on the staff during the recent Frontier War. The core of his force consisted of regular soldiers, most of whom belonged to the 1/24th (there was one company of 2/24th), while the irregular troops included companies of the 3rd NNC. In addition, Pulleine had two 7-pounders from N/5 Battery.

Chelmsford and Glyn made their rendezvous with Dartnell at about 6.15 a.m., having pressed ahead of the infantry and guns. Chelmsford then gave orders to sweep the ground to the east and north-east of the Hlazakazi Heights. In so doing, Dartnell killed some 60 Zulus in a heavy skirmish. Another body of warriors conducted an orderly withdrawal north-east towards Siphezi Mountain, drawing Glyn after them. Chelmsford watched some of the skirmishing and ate breakfast from a commanding position on a nek between two hills north of the Mangeni.

At 9.30 a.m. a galloper arrived post-haste from Pulleine with a message timed 8.05 a.m. It read: 'Report just come in that the Zulus are advancing in force from left front of the camp.' Chelmsford believed that Pulleine was in command of a sufficiently strong force to hold the position. Furthermore, he realised that even if he did move to Pulleine's aid, it would be about 12.30 p.m. before he could arrive, well over four hours after the message had been despatched. He thus sent an officer to view the camp through glasses, but little could be made out at a range of twelve miles.

Concluding that all was well, Chelmsford proceeded to send another officer, Captain Alan Gardner of the 14th Hussars, to Pulleine with orders to strike camp and move towards the Mangeni. Moreover, Commandant George Hamilton-Browne and the 1/3rd NNC were recalled from the skirmishing and likewise sent back towards Isandlwana with (states Hamilton-Browne) orders to assist Pulleine in striking the camp and moving up. Chelmsford then rode forward to locate the best camp-site.

At Isandlwana, meanwhile, shortly before 8.00 a.m., as the men in the camp were having breakfast, a trooper could be seen descending from the plateau, moving at speed, and soon reported that a large force of Zulus was approaching from the north-east across the plateau. Pulleine reacted by dashing off the message that Chelmsford was to receive an hour and a half later. He did more. The 'fall in' was sounded and all the 24th and companies of the NNC were deployed in front of the camp, while a party under Lieutenant Anstey of the 1/24th, doing repair work on the track, was called in. The men eagerly scanned the crest of the plateau but no Zulu assault materialised.

Durnford arrived on the scene at 'about ten or ten thirty a.m.', according to an officer who accompanied him, Lieutenant William Cochrane of the 32nd Regiment, having ridden up from Rorke's Drift with five troops of the Natal Native Horse, approximately 250 men. Coming on behind were a rocket battery under Major Russell, two companies of the 1/1st NNC and transport wagons. Durnford, who was 48 years old, enjoyed seniority over Pulleine, and Cochrane tells us that Pulleine declared: 'I'm sorry you have come, as you are senior to me and will of course take command', whereupon Durnford replied, 'I'm not going to interfere with you. I'm not going to remain in camp.' In all, there were now 1768 officers and men at Isandlwana, about half of whom were black.

Hamilton-Browne, in the meantime, was on his way back to Isandlwana. At about the time Durnford joined Pulleine, he captured a Zulu boy 'frightened out of his life', who told him that the main impi was to the north-east of Isandlwana. Hamilton-Browne promptly sent a lieutenant to report this to Chelmsford and pressed on.

By now the sound of firing could be heard from the Mangeni area. But as the camp itself appeared in no danger, the men at Isandlwana were allowed to fall out for their midday meal, though they were to eat it as quickly as possible. While having lunch, Durnford told Pulleine that he intended to ride out eastward across the plain for he was concerned that a Zulu force, about 600 strong, which had been seen on the plateau retiring in that direction, might have been intent on circling and cutting off Chelmsford.

Durnford set off at about 11.15 a.m., shortly after Pulleine had sent a company of the 1/24th under Lieutenant Charles Cavaye up to the plateau. Durnford said that he expected support if he encountered trouble. He moved across the plain at the head of two of his troops of Natal Native Horse, as well as with the rocket battery and a company of the NNC, both of which had just arrived at Isandlwana: two of Durnford's other troops of NNH had been despatched on to the plateau under Lieutenants Raw and Roberts, while a third had been sent back to help escort the wagons. Durnford had asked for two companies of the 24th, but had agreed that they should remain, following protests against any further reduction of the camp's strength.

At about noon, members of Lieutenant Raw's troop (accompanied by Captain George Shepstone, a son of Theophilus and effectively Durnford's staff officer) caught sight of cattle being driven by Zulus off to the north-east and gave pursuit. The Zulus vanished over the crest and the pursuing troopers rapidly reined in as they reached the spot, finding themselves on the edge of a deep valley through which flowed the Ngwebeni stream. They found more: a sea of black faces, a mass of Zulus sitting silently in serried ranks, crammed into the valley and up its slopes – the main impi, which had so far eluded detection. It was about five and a half miles north-east of the camp at Isandlwana, much closer than was Chelmsford.

The impi numbered at least 20,000 warriors and was under the joint command of Chief Ntshingwayo kaMahole, a renowned warrior in his 70s – who evidently enjoyed precedence – and Chief Mavumengwana kaNdlela, who was in his mid-40s. He was a son of Dingane's principal induna, and a close friend of Cetshwayo. Among *amabutho* known to have been present in significant strength were the iNgobamakhosi, uMcijo, (also known as the uKhandempemvu) uDududu, iSangqu, iMbube, uMbonambi, uNokhenke, uVe, uThulwana, iNdlondlo, uDloko and iNdluyengwe, as well as elements of the uMxhapho.

They had set off from Nodwengu late on the afternoon of Friday 17 January and had encamped beside the White Mfolozi after marching some six miles. The impi covered about nine miles on each of the following two days and, on the 19th, divided into two columns, 'marching parallel to and in sight of each other'. A few mounted scouts belonging to Sihayo went on ahead. On the 20th, the impi saw to its left a body of white horsemen, no doubt a reconnaissance patrol that Chelmsford had sent out that day. After spending that night on the northern slopes of Siphezi Mountain, the Zulus proceeded to occupy the Ngwebeni Valley on the evening of the 21st, although stragglers continued to arrive the following morning. The warriors had conserved their strength in accordance with Cetshwayo's instructions and were well fed, for foraging parties had brought in grain, cattle and goats.

On the basis of Zulu evidence, it is generally held that owing to superstitious custom there was no intention of attacking the British on 22 January: it was the day of the new moon, which was to begin her new life at 1.52 p.m. and hence the Zulus were waiting to attack on the 23rd. John Laband, however, argues that the impi's commanders were planning to launch their attack later on the 22nd:

After all, its being the day of the new moon had not hampered Matshana's remarkably successful diversionary operations, which were clearly part of a concerted strategy. The Zulu commanders, moreover, were in council   that day, considering their next move, and they knew their enemy to be at a fatal disadvantage, which could not be expected to persist indefinitely. Nor, as events proved, was it likely that so large a force as theirs could maintain the advantage of surprise by keeping its presence hidden for a further twenty-four hours until the dawning of a more auspicious day.

The battle of Isandlwana

What is certain is that the Zulus' detection by Raw's troop of Ngwane brought matters to a head. The troopers dismounted, fired a volley and then fell back, as did Roberts's troop (again consisting of Ngwane) to Raw's left. While both troops made a fighting retreat in the face of pursuing Zulus, a company of NNC that had been in close support of Raw took to its heels. The first of the Zulu regiments to give chase was uMcijo, which had been located closest to where Raw's men caught sight of the impi. It surged forward without being ordered to do so either by Ntshingwayo or Mavumengwana, and other regiments rapidly followed suit. Soon a huge wave of warriors was on the plateau advancing at a very fast walking pace and forming up into the 'beast's horns' formation. The right horn was made up of the uDududu, iMbube, iSangqu and the uNokhenke. uMcijo, and elements of the uMxhapho formed the chest, with the uMbonambi, iNgobamakhosi (Cetshwayo's favourite *ibutho*) and uVe on the left. The loins consisted of the uNdi Corps, namely the uThulwana, iNdluyengwe, iNdlondlo and uDloko regiments, following on at the right rear, although some members of these regiments broke away and followed the chest.

Durnford, of course, was making his way across the plain. He had pressed on with his mounted troops, leaving the rocket battery and its NNC escort lagging behind. Cochrane tells us that Durnford had gone several miles when 'a mounted man ... reported that there was an immense impi behind the hills to our left'. No sooner had he done so than the 'Zulus appeared in force in front of us and to our left.... They opened fire at ... about 800 yards, and advanced very rapidly.' Durnford halted, fired a volley, and began falling back 'steadily in skirmishing order, keeping up a steady fire'.

Meanwhile, Major Russell and his rocket battery had just passed Amatutshane, a conical kopje on the plain, and was thus about a mile and a half from the camp, when he became aware of the Zulu advance. He rapidly wheeled left towards the Nyoni Heights and just below Itusi peak encountered the advance-guard of either the iNgobamakhosi or the uMbonambi. Desperately, the battery fired off a 9-pounder rocket. It burst near the Zulus but to little or no effect: the warriors kept on coming, descending the escarpment. Russell's NNC escort took to their heels, leaving him and the handful of men of his battery to fight it out. They

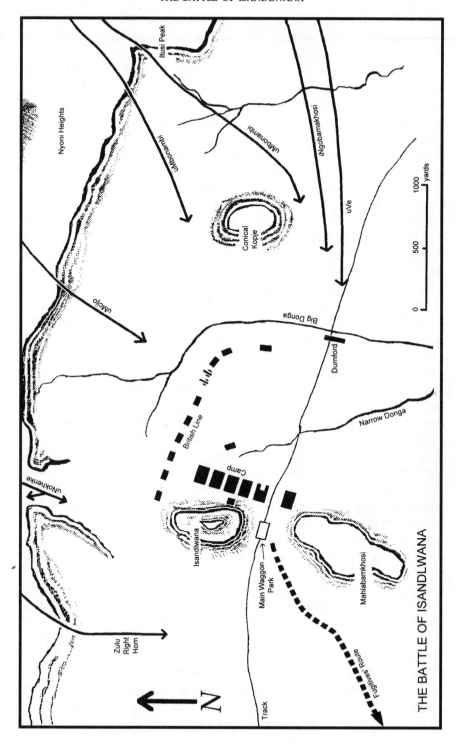

THE BATTLE OF ISANDLWANA

were engaged in hand-to-hand combat when the retreating Durnford arrived on the scene. He then pressed on towards Isandlwana with his men and the survivors of the battery, leaving Russell behind among the dead.

At about 12.15 p.m. Shepstone galloped into the camp – by which time the firing on the plateau had already been heard – and reported to Pulleine. Coincidentally, Captain Gardner arrived simultaneously with Chelmsford's order to break camp. Pulleine hesitated for a moment, before sending word to Chelmsford, 'Heavy firing to left of our camp. Cannot move camp at present.' The 'Alarm' was sounded and the men again began forming up in columns in front of the position.

As the Zulu attack seemed to be developing to the north of the camp, Pulleine sent Mostyn's F Company 1/24th up the spur to plug a gap between the bulk of Captain Cavaye's E Company 1/24th (which was beyond the skyline and to the west of the spur) and a detached section of it under Second Lieutenant Dyson, located even further west. Cavaye and Dyson were in extended order and firing at the bulk of the Zulu right horn which was crossing their front about 800 yards away and intent on outflanking the soldiers. A company of NNC (whose identity is uncertain) was also in the vicinity, to the right, and 'blazing away at an absurd rate', according to a regular officer who witnessed the spectacle.

Further to the right were Raw's and Roberts's Ngwane, conducting their fighting withdrawal against the Zulu centre. In due course they fell back to the foot of the escarpment where they found themselves reinforced by another troop of NNH (again composed of Ngwane) commanded by Lieutenant W. Vause. The troop, which Durnford had sent back to escort the wagons, had just arrived at the camp, and Vause had been ordered by Shepstone to reinforce Raw and Roberts. The Ngwane dismounted and began moving up the slope in skirmishing order, inflicting heavy losses on the uMcijo, and re-emerged on the heights. At about the same time, around 50 men of Captain Stafford's E Company, 1/1st NNC (which had likewise escorted the wagons into the camp), also ascended the escarpment, and took up a position on the extreme left of the ridge. Shepstone was involved in the fighting, for he had returned to join the fray after reporting to Pulleine.

In front of the camp itself, Pulleine had four companies of the 24th (Porteous's A, Younghusband's C, Wardell's H company of the first battalion, and Pope's G Company of the second) as well as a number of unattached men of the 2/24th. There was also at least one company of NNC. Perhaps also present was a mixed force of white mounted irregulars under Captain Robert Bradstreet of the Newcastle Mounted Rifles; but it is more likely that the men in question were also engaged, for a member of a company of NNC under Captain J. F. Lonsdale (located on a low stony ridge about 1000 yards to the east of the camp between two dongas) recalled seeing them ascending the escarpment to his left to help check the Zulu advance.

In due course, Pulleine caught sight of Zulu warriors pouring over the escarpment well to the north-east, i.e., to the right of those of his men who were engaged on the escarpment and whom he decided to recall, for they were in danger of being cut off. Hence the escarpment was abandoned.

Furthermore, Pulleine ordered Major Stuart Smith RA to deploy the two 7-pounders on a rocky crest due east of the NNC camp and about 600 yards from the base of Isandlwana. From this piece of rising terrain, Smith commanded the dead ground of the larger, more easterly of the two afore-mentioned dongas. He then opened fire over the heads of the Ngwane, shelling warriors as they appeared on the skyline.

Infantry companies soon moved up in support, and Smith found himself flanked to the left and right by the companies of Porteous and Wardell which fell in beside him, deployed in skirmishing order, with the men kneeling or lying behind the boulders. Evidently Pope's G Company of the 2/24th (which had likely been augmented by unattached members of the battalion in the camp) took up a position some way off to Wardell's right and again facing in a northerly direction. Roughly to the south of Wardell and Pope was Lonsdale's company of NNC, still in place on the ridge between the two dongas. And what of the left of the line? Apparently, next to Porteous's company were the Ngwane and then a company of the NNC. Beyond were Mostyn's and Cavaye's companies and, finally, Younghusband's company, which Pulleine had evidently sent to cover their retreat.

As the Zulus swarmed forward against Pulleine's extended line, the camp's defenders opened up with their rifles, supported by Smith's guns. A heavy toll was taken of the uNokhenke regiment as it charged down the spur against the left-hand companies: so much so that it turned and began making its way back up the slope before following the uDududu, iMbube and iSangqu, which, as mentioned, were heading westward in an encir-cling movement that would enable them to take the British from the flank and rear.

Many warriors were also killed to the left of the uNokhenke where the uMcijo, elements of the uMxhapho and members of the reserve who had thrown in their lot with the chest, found themselves subjected to with-ering fire in the hollow between the plateau and the rocky ridge where the British firing line was most concentrated. Thus, when some 400 yards from their opponents, the chest came to a halt as the warriors took cover by throwing themselves on the ground. It was now about 1 p.m. Zulus armed with guns tried to answer in kind: but the volume of their fire was only matched by its lack of effect. True, some shots struck home, but the majority of rounds simply passed overhead and landed in the camp area.

One of these, however, killed Quartermaster Edward Bloomfield of the 2/24th, evidently quite early in the battle, according to an eye-witness account written four days later. In contrast, General Smith-Dorrien (who at this date was a subaltern on the staff of the column) recalled of the 24th that it consisted of 'war-worn men.... Possessed of a splendid discipline and sure of success, they lay on their position making every round tell.' Whenever the Zulus rose from cover, they were compelled to get down again.

Further to the Zulu left, the uMbonambi regiment, or at least sections of it, evidently clashed with Pope's exposed company. In 1882, a warrior of the uMbonambi told Bertram Mitford that as the regiment descended the escarpment, redcoats close to the conical kopje 'kept up a heavy fire upon us', with the result that the *ibutho* 'lost a lot of men' who 'kept tumbling over one upon another'. Even so, Pope was eventually constrained to fall back and take up a position between Wardell and Lonsdale on the right of the British line.

Meanwhile, the rest of the Zulu left horn was closing, having swung west around the southern face of the conical kopje, in pursuit of Durnford's command and the survivors of the rocket battery. In due course, Durnford reached the more easterly of the two dongas, about a mile from the camp, where his men made a determined stand, supported by Bradstreet and his command who had either already taken up a position in the donga or now proceeded to do so: from somewhere out on the British left, they had been moved to help defend the camp against the left horn by Captain Gardner of the 14th Hussars. Between them, they poured sufficient fire into the uVe to halt the young regiment in its tracks. Indeed, it was repulsed until reinforced by the older and slower-moving iNgobamakhosi who were in turn brought to a standstill in a dense mass beneath the kopje.

Sooner or later, Smith briefly repositioned one of his 7-pounders so that it could fire against the Zulu left, thus adding to the toll of Zulu dead and wounded in this sector, before it was returned to its original position. Among the Zulus evidently affected by the shelling and rifle fire of their opponents were members of the uMbonambi, on the right of the iNgobamakhosi, who proceeded to move to their left, behind and beyond the iNgobamakhosi and uVe, and thereby found themselves on the extreme left of the Zulu line at about the time the attack of the centre was brought to a halt. The uMbonambi continued to advance on the camp under cover of a herd of cattle which had been grazing on the slopes of Mahlabamkhosi.

Seeing that he was being outflanked, Durnford ordered his men to mount up and abandoned the eastern donga. He rode back towards the camp and took up a new position, perhaps in the westernmost donga. His withdrawal exposed the right of Pulleine's line, and the latter evidently responded by ordering his men to fall back and take up a close defensive position nearer the camp.

As the 24th companies retreated, firing as they went, the Zulu centre began to move forward again. The Zulu commanders, who were overlooking the chest from the plateau, despatched an induna to encourage its advance. He was a member of the uMcijo and as he ran down towards his colleagues he shouted: 'You did not say you were going to lie down!' and exhorted them to action. He paid with his life – he was shot through the head – but the uMcijo (and the rest of the chest) rose in pursuit of the retiring British. At first they trotted forward at little faster than a walking pace, but then, shouting the national cry, 'uSuthu!', they charged, hurling a shower of throwing spears. Some of the warriors reached N/5 before the guns, which had been firing case-shot, could be limbered up, and fierce hand-to-hand fighting took place. But Smith nonetheless managed to have the guns driven off towards the camp.

Fighting at close quarters also occurred elsewhere as the soldiers fell back, for the iNgobamakhosi and members of the uVe who had not joined the uMbonambi's outflanking manoeuvre, surged forward against the retreating enemy: among the withdrawing units was Lonsdale's company of NNC, which was intent on quitting the field. A Zulu named Uguku, who was a member of uMcijo, was to recall that fighting occurred 'all the way' and that as the soldiers 'got into the camp, we were intermingled with them'.

It was the uMbonambi of the left horn who entered the camp first, followed by the iNgobamakhosi and uMcijo. As the battle approached its climax, the uNokhenke burst into the camp from the north-west to participate with the left horn and centre in the slaughter. The rest of the right horn had made its way down to ground west of Isandlwana, intending to effect a junction with the left horn and cut off the British line of retreat along the road to Rorke's Drift.

The reserve was not involved in the battle. It had followed the right horn along the plateau, though well to the rear, and upon arriving behind the camp, and seeing that it was being overwhelmed, headed off in the direction of the British post at Rorke's Drift.

Isandlwana was a scene of desperate conflict, for the fighting had reached fever pitch as the 24th and some of their colleagues fought desperately against the engulfing mass of determined warriors. Shots and screams rent the air which became thick with smoke and dust. Moreover, a partial eclipse of the sun, which was at its greatest extent at 2.29 p.m., cast darkness over the carnage. Bayonets plunged home; spears were thrust through scarlet tunics. Confusion, fear and death were everywhere. In the hand-to-hand fighting, the Zulus learned a bitter lesson – a long bayonet at the end of a rifle thrust proved far more effective than an assegai. As Mehlokazulu kaSihayo of the iNgobamakhosi later recalled: 'Any man who went to stab a soldier was fixed through the throat or stomach, and at once fell.' Some warriors therefore responded by throwing their spears. Gradually, Zulu numerical superiority told, and remorselessly the number of dead and dying soldiers increased. Mpatshana kaSadondo of uVe subsequently told James Stuart that it often took more than one warrior to finish off an opponent: 'It was recognised that fighting against such a foe and killing some of them was of the same high grade as lion hunting'.

Many of the soldiers fell as they withdrew through the camp, fighting as they went. Some managed to escape across the nek through a narrow gap in the Zulu encirclement – which was soon closed – but the majority of the British regulars who died lost their fight for survival on and near the nek, as did many of the irregulars. Captain George Shepstone, for instance, perished at the south-western foot of Isandlwana, evidently accompanied by a fairly substantial number of black troops, in what appears to have been a last stand against members of the Zulu right horn moving in to help the chest and left horn destroy the enemy.

More fleet-footed members of the camp's overwhelmed garrison, or those who possessed mounts or had taken to their heels before the battle reached its climax, were dashing for their lives south-west towards the Mzinyathi, for escape by way of the road to Rorke's Drift had been rendered hopeless by the sight of the right horn closing in behind Isandlwana. As they fled, the fugitives were harried from both sides over difficult ground by warriors of the right and left horns as far as the valley of the Manzimyama stream, while some Zulus kept up the chase even further, particularly intent, it would seem, on killing Europeans.

Among those who died were Lieutenant Teignmouth Melvill and Lieutenant Neville Coghill. The former was carrying the Queen's Colour of the 1/24th, perhaps having been ordered by Pulleine to carry it to safety when it was clear that the day was lost. Evidently, during his flight he met up with Coghill, who was likewise mounted and moreover unable to walk, having damaged his knee two days earlier. Upon reaching the Mzinyathi, which was in flood, Coghill (like other fugitives) managed to make his way across a drift – known ever since as Fugitives' Drift – but Melvill was unhorsed in mid-stream, whereupon Coghill rode back into the water to help him. The men managed to reach the Natal bank, although Coghill's horse was killed by enemy fire, but by then were too exhausted to continue. They were soon killed, either by Zulus who crossed the Mzinyathi or by Africans living on the Natal side of the river. Both officers were posthumously awarded the Victoria Cross years later for endeavouring to save the Colour.

Within a few hours, Isandlwana and much of the countryside within its vicinity had been transformed into a scene of desolation, littered with the wreckage of war. Fifty-two officers, 727 white soldiers and 471 Natal blacks had perished. It is said that little drummer boys present had been hung up and butchered, though doubt has been cast on the veracity of this claim, which was made by some European soldiers who subsequently arrived on the scene with Chelmsford.

Zulu losses had also been heavy (the chest suffered the most severely), but how heavy? To this there is no definite answer. A high proportion of the Zulu dead consisted of injured individuals who subsequently died of their wounds, in some cases far from the scene of battle. The rudimentary state of Zulu medicine was such that even many of the relatively lightly wounded succumbed; there was more hope for those who had been bayonetted than struck by bullets, a fact that led the Zulus to conclude that the latter had been poisoned. Probably between one and two thousand warriors in all must have died.

It was during the momentous afternoon of the 22nd that Chelmsford began returning to Isandlwana, escorted by Mounted Infantry. En route he encountered Hamilton-Browne and his battalion of NNC, whom he had ordered to return to Isandlwana that morning. Seeing the camp being overrun, however, Hamilton-Browne had taken up a defensive position on a ridge from where he had watched the horrific events unfolding. He told Chelmsford that the camp had fallen. The general reacted with angry incredulity, but soon sent an officer to recall Glyn and the rest of the men in the Mangeni area.

Following the arrival of Glyn's column, Chelmsford delivered a short speech and began moving towards Isandlwana, with the 2/24th around the guns in the centre and flanked by the other units. As they drew near, they saw large numbers of Zulus on the escarpment, to which they had retired from the camp that they had thoroughly looted.

Darkness had fallen by the time Isandlwana was reached. Upon ascertaining that all the Zulus were gone, Chelmsford and his men bivouacked for the night in a position of all-round defence. Shock, sadness and fear were the dominant emotions. There was also a sense of foreboding. A dull red glow and the sound of distant gunfire could be seen and heard from the direction of Rorke's Drift.

The battle of Rorke's Drift
Instead of engaging at Isandlwana, the Zulu reserve, as noted, headed off in the direction of Rorke's Drift. It consisted of the uThulwana, iNdlondlo, uDloko and iNdluyengwe regiments and totalled approximately 3500 warriors. It was under the command of 40-year-old Prince Dabulamanzi kaMpande, a half-brother of Cetshwayo who was vexed at having missed the action at Isandlwana, as were many of his warriors. On the way it split into three contingents, and the youngest regiment, the iNdluyengwe,

whose warriors were on average 33 years old, in contrast to those of the other regiments, who were all in their 40s, was foremost.

The iNdluyengwe forded the Mzinyathi just above Fugitives' Drift (having killed some of the survivors from Isandlwana) while the other contingents crossed further upstream near the confluence of the Mzinyathi and the Batshe. After crossing, the contingents rested and took snuff. The iNdluyengwe then recommenced marching, heading north-west (some detached sections ravaged the plain towards Helpmekaar) and in due course the other contingents began to move in the same direction.

Meanwhile, at about 3.15 p.m., fugitive horsemen from Isandlwana arrived at Rorke's Drift where Lieutenant John Chard RE (a 31-year-old charged with supervising the ponts at the drift and preparing an entrenchment on the Natal bank to protect the crossing) was writing home after eating lunch. In Norman Holme's compilation, *The Silver Wreath*, Chard is quoted as saying that his attention was caught by 'two horsemen galloping towards [him] from the direction of Isandlwana. From their gesticulation and their shouts ... we saw that something was the matter.' One of the men, Lieutenant Adendorff of the 1/3rd NNC, told Chard that the camp at Isandlwana had been annihilated and that a force of Zulus was advancing on Rorke's Drift.

When the Centre Column had crossed into Zululand at Rorke's Drift on the 11th, B Company of the 2/24th had been left behind, together with a company of the 2/3rd NNC and several detached personnel. It was stationed in an abandoned Swedish mission about a quarter of a mile south-west of the drift. B Company's commander was 33-year-old Lieutenant Gonville Bromhead, handicapped by increasing deafness. He, too, had just received word of the Zulu approach, for Chard relates that while he himself was talking to Adendorff, a messenger arrived from Bromhead asking him 'to come up at once'. Upon arrival at the post, he found that preparations for its defence were already in hand:

> Lieut. Bromhead had, with the assistance ... of other officers present, commenced barricading and loopholing the store building and the Missionary's house, which was used as a Hospital, and connecting the defence of the two buildings by walls of mealie bags [and biscuit boxes], and the two wagons that were on the ground.

In the absence of Major Spalding, the post's commander, who had ridden off to Helpmekaar hours earlier, Chard, slightly senior to Bromhead, now assumed command of the defence. The total number of men at the post, including the sick and wounded, is uncertain. Ian Knight, a leading authority on the battle, states that 'the most convincing estimate appears to be 152, excluding Stevenson's 2/3rd NNC', which probably numbered about 100 men, and Chard himself. A withdrawal towards Helpmekaar,

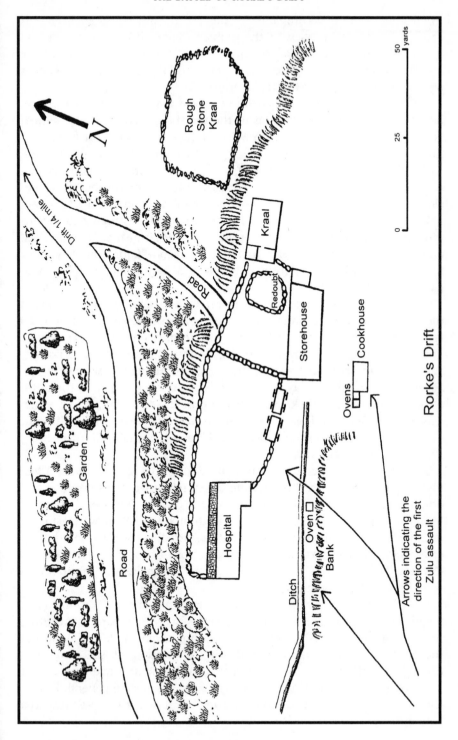

Rorke's Drift

N

Rough Stone Kraal

Drift 1/4 mile

Road

Kraal

Redoubt

Road

Storehouse

Cookhouse

Ovens

Garden

Hospital

Oven

Ditch

Bank

Arrows indicating the
direction of the first
Zulu assault

0   25   50   yards

95

where there were two companies of the 1/24th, was considered but this course was rejected in view of the problems entailed in trying to defend two cumbersome wagons laden with the sick and wounded while on the march. The only viable option was to stand and fight. Hence, as rapidly as possible, they continued to prepare for battle.

The principal buildings attached to the post were a hospital and a storehouse. The hospital was located in the Oskaberg Mission House, which belonged to the Reverend Otto Witt. It had stone and brick walls, a thatched roof, and a verandah running along the north front, just beyond which the ground, covered by bush, sloped away towards a road that ran to the drift. Mud-brick walls divided the interior of the building into eleven rooms, some of them little larger than cupboards. On 22 January 1879, the hospital had 35 sick and injured patients belonging to various units, three of whom had been wounded in the skirmish at Sihayo's kraal on the 12th. The inmates were cared for by Surgeon-Major James Reynolds, three men of the Army Hospital Corps and a chaplain, the Reverend George Smith.

Some 35 yards to the east of the hospital, and slightly to the rear, stood the storehouse, a larger stone-built structure measuring some 80 feet by 20 feet, with a thatched roof. It had previously functioned as Witt's chapel. The stores were presided over by Acting Assistant Commissary J. L. Dalton, aged 50, an ex-Sergeant-Major of the 85th, and Acting-Storekeeper Byrne. South of the storehouse lay the cookhouse, and in front, just to the right, of the stores was a cattle kraal, with stone walls 4 feet high, below which was a large, rough-and-ready cattle enclosure with lower walls. The post was overlooked, to the south-east, by Shiyane Mountain, 500 feet high, and some 300 yards away.

Mealie bags and biscuit boxes were used to form a rampart about 4 feet high. On the south side, this ran from the storehouse to the south-east end of the hospital, incorporating the two wagons in the defences. It then ran from the north-west end of the hospital (though the defences here appear to have been incomplete when the battle started) eastward along the top of a rocky terrace – extending along the front of most of the station – towards the smaller of the cattle kraals, and from here it continued to connect with the storehouse.

Firing positions around the perimeter were allocated by Bromhead to members of his company and to anyone else with firearms, including some members of the NNC company. Loopholes were made in the walls of the hospital, which was provided with a garrison of six men of B Company. Furthermore, rifles were issued to hospital inmates capable of using them, and ammunition made ready for the men in general. Private Hitch of B Company was stationed astride the roof of the storehouse as a look-out.

Shortly after 3.30 p.m., while the preparations were in progress, Chard received reinforcements when a white officer, whose identity is uncertain, rode up with a detachment of NNH, perhaps about 100 strong, after escaping from Isandlwana. Chard asked him to deploy part of his command at the drift, while the rest were to act as outpost 'in the direction of the enemy, and check his advance as much as possible'.

Chard also relates that several more survivors of Isandlwana appeared on the scene and 'tried to impress upon us the madness of an attempt to defend the place'. In so doing, they hindered preparation work on the defences, for it was 'impossible to prevent the men getting around them in little groups to hear their story'. They then left the tiny garrison to its fate.

At about 4.20 p.m., the garrison heard the sound of firing coming from behind Shiyane Mountain. The NNH had become engaged in skirmishing with advancing Zulus. Soon their white officer (whom Knight believes was almost certainly Lieutenant A. F. Henderson, the commander of a troop of BaSotho belonging to Durnford's No. 2 Column) galloped up after disengaging, reported the proximity of the Zulu force, and then rode away towards Helpmekaar in the wake of his fleeing men. Their flight alarmed the NNC, who likewise made off, as did their European commander, and some of the enraged garrison fired at them as they did so. Hence the strength of the garrison was rapidly depleted.

The perimeter was now too long and Chard immediately withdrew men from the line to erect an inner barricade of biscuit boxes between the western end of the storehouse and the northern rampart. This task was still underway when Hitch shouted from the roof as Zulus skirting the southern side of Shiyane began to come into view to the south-east. It was about 4.30 p.m.

The Zulus in question were the iNdluyengwe. Only a few appeared at first, but soon they numbered between 500 and 600 and formed up into the classic crescent formation. They advanced at a steady trot towards the south wall, firing ineffectively as they did so. Many were cut down when the British opened fire. Nonetheless, their colleagues pressed on. Chard comments:

> We opened fire on them, between five and six hundred yards, at first a little wild, but only for a short time.... The men were quite steady, and the Zulus began to fall very thick. However, it did not seem to stop them at all.... It seemed as if nothing would stop them.

When within 50 yards of the south wall, however, they were subjected to such heavy cross-fire from the hospital and storehouse that they veered left to find a more vulnerable sector, though some took cover and proceeded to fire at the defenders.

Their colleagues surged around to attack the hospital, from the west and north, and the west section of the northern perimeter defences. Here there was less chance of being caught in cross-fire. Moreover, there was more cover provided by bush and trees, cover that extended eastward to about the point where the cross-wall of biscuit boxes ran southward from the northern perimeter. So the warriors managed to engage in ferocious hand-to-hand fighting. Even so, they were soon repulsed and took shelter. Private Hitch recalled:

> Had the Zulus taken the bayonet as freely as they took the bullets, we could not have stood more than fifteen minutes, but they seemed to have a great dread of the bayonet, which stood to us from beginning to end.

Meanwhile, the two other Zulu contingents had evidently joined forces to the east of Shiyane and they now emerged round the southern side of the mountain, following in the footsteps of the engaged younger regiment. Some of them took up positions among rocks near the foot of Shiyane, from where they were to harass the British with gunfire, but the majority moved north-west of the post and occupied the garden, the sunken road and the nearby area of bush.

Reinforced, the iNdluyengwe, together with the new arrivals, renewed their attack against the hospital and northern perimeter wall, partially screened by the thick bush. After some fierce fighting, the Zulus were forced back, only to come on again in a series of determined assaults. The uThulwana seem to have borne the brunt of Zulu losses during this phase of the battle.

Casualties were, of course, also sustained by the defenders. Some of the troops manning the north wall, for example, were hit in the back by fire from the Zulus on Shiyane. The British wounded were tended in the store-house, which had been transformed into a makeshift surgery. A constant stream of men was to require Reynolds's attention.

The ammunition of the defenders was being expended rapidly by the ferocity of the Zulu onslaught. Fresh rounds, however, were supplied by Chaplain Smith, assisted by wounded men no longer able to fight.

Chard, Bromhead and Dalton were also playing their part, constantly moving back and forth along the line, giving encouragement and engaging in the fighting whenever occasion demanded. Of Bromhead, Chaplain Smith comments:

> As long as we held the front wall, the Zulus failed in their repeated attempts to get into the far-end room of the hospital, Lieutenant Bromhead having several times driven them back with a bayonet charge.

At around 6 p.m., in failing light, the Zulus began to fan out to their left, attacking further along the north perimeter. In response, Chard ordered his men to fall back to the line of biscuit boxes, realising that they could not defend the entire perimeter. He thus reduced it to a circumference of about 170 yards, in which the storehouse's back wall formed an impenetrable barrier. The Zulus immediately occupied the outside of the defensive wall that Chard had abandoned and opened fire from it.

The hospital's defenders evacuated the building under severe pressure. While some of those inside continued firing through the loopholes, others began tunnelling eastward through the partitions of unconnected rooms at the rear – a task that became more desperate when Zulus forced their way into the building and set alight the thatched roof. The warriors were held at bay by two or three men who afforded protection to those digging frantically with their bayonets and helped patients on and through the resulting gaps to the yard beyond. It was an exhausting, laborious, frightening task. Upon emerging from the hospital, the survivors had to cross the yard to rejoin their colleagues behind the biscuit boxes. Some failed to make it, cut down by Zulu fire or by warriors who dashed forward, spear in hand. Chard relates the fate of Trooper Hunter of the Natal Mounted Police after he emerged from the hospital:

> He stood still for a moment, hesitating which way to go, dazed by the glare of the burning hospital, and the firing that was going on all round. He was assegaied before our eyes, the Zulu who killed him immediately afterwards falling.

With the onset of darkness, the garrison found itself completely surrounded as the Zulus shifted the focus of their assault to the east side of the station (while keeping up the pressure elsewhere) and launched an attack from the north-east, intent on breaking their way in over the stone kraal that formed the defenders' eastern perimeter. Being further from the burning hospital, this sector was less well lit and thus offered the Zulus more cover. A desperate struggle ensued in which the Zulus finally succeeded in driving their opponents from the kraal. Furthermore, some warriors moved against the storehouse, bent on setting it alight, but were shot down by the men charged with its defence.

As the battle raged, some of the defenders set to work making an 8 feet-high redoubt of mealie bags within the reduced defences. The most seriously wounded members of the garrison sheltered in the redoubt, which provided a second and elevated field of fire and could serve as a final line of defence should this be necessary – by now a distinct possibility.

The weary Zulus made their last charge at about 10 p.m. at the latest. Nonetheless, they kept the garrison on tenterhooks into the early hours by shouting 'uSuthu!' from one quarter or another, and by firing in a desultory manner. From about 4 a.m. silence ensued, though the garrison remained alert.

Dawn came about an hour and a half later. The Zulus were no longer in sight, for the majority had fallen back the way they had come. As a precaution, however, the garrison hurriedly strengthened its defences in the event of further attack. Then, at about 7 a.m., hearts in the camp sank when a large body of Zulus appeared on a hill to the south-west of their position and the weary soldiers hurriedly manned the defences. A huge amount of ammunition, some 20,000 rounds, had been expended, and little remained, no more than one and a half boxes, although each man had an ample supply in his pouch. With an acute sense of foreboding, the soldiers watched, expecting the Zulus to come on again. They did not. They stood looking at the post for a while, brave men looking at brave men, before at last disappearing at around 8 a.m.

Tension thus eased in the camp and soon turned to elation when mounted troops were seen galloping towards the battered post. They were Russell's Mounted Infantry, and they were followed by Chelmsford's and Glyn's column, who had left Isandlwana before dawn so that the ghastly remains of the previous day's battle would not be seen by the young men of the 2/24th. En route Chelmsford had come across the majority of the Zulus who had been engaged at Rorke's Drift, now moving in the opposite direction. Both sides had refrained from attacking.

Chelmsford feared that the garrison at Rorke's Drift had been annihilated and his sense of relief upon seeing that this had not occurred can well be imagined. He interviewed those who had distinguished themselves in the post's defence and must have been struck by the decisive role the hastily erected defences had played in its survival.

Zulu dead lay scattered in and around the virtually demolished defences, heaped along the northern face of the perimeter. According to Chard, burial parties soon disposed of 351 Zulus, but for months to come bodies of scores of others who had been mortally wounded were found strewn about the surrounding countryside – there is reason to believe that many were finished off on the day after the battle by British patrols – while others must have died of their injuries after reaching their homesteads. Total Zulu losses may have been in the region of 600 dead. Dabulamanzi's men undoubtedly paid a high price for the courage they had displayed, and subsequent jeers made against the survivors by their countrymen that they had fought like women were cruelly misplaced. As for the British, fifteen members of the garrison had been killed outright, two mortally wounded, and sixteen others less seriously injured.

The heroic defence of Rorke's Drift presented Chelmsford and others such as Frere with a propaganda coup that was exploited to the full in an effort to redeem the fiasco of Isandlwana. It was portrayed as a major strategic reverse for Cetshwayo, an action that thwarted a Zulu invasion of Natal. The magnificent stand of Chard and his men did not go unrewarded. Indeed, eleven Victoria Crosses were awarded to members of the post, an unprecedented number for a single action, and among the recipients were Lieutenants Chard and Bromhead.

Even so, Isandlwana itself had been a grievous blow. As a result of the heavy losses sustained, Chelmsford had no alternative other than to ride off towards Pietermaritzburg shortly after reaching the post to begin preparations for a renewal of the campaign.

On 11 February the news of the battle of Isandlwana reached London and was discussed at a cabinet meeting that afternoon. The Prime Minister, Benjamin Disraeli, and his ministers were horrified by what had happened (as was the nation when the news appeared in the press) and arrangements were made to send out substantial reinforcements post-haste. The government, which was preoccupied by a conflict in Afghanistan, had suddenly found itself entangled in a costly and essentially disastrous war it had not wanted, a war brought about by the wayward Sir Bartle Frere. In parliament, the opposition demanded his recall. The government declined to do so, but censured him instead. Frere was informed bluntly that neither he nor Chelmsford had 'authority either to accept a cession of territory nor to proclaim the Queen's sovereignty over any part of the country [Zululand]'.

And what of the Zulus? Dabulamanzi returned to oNdini under a cloud. He had disobeyed orders by moving against Rorke's Drift and had only succeeded in squandering the lives of many of his men. Cetshwayo was not impressed and Dabulamanzi soon left oNdini in disgrace. The king was also angered by the failure of many warriors to make their way back to oNdini for purification ceremonies. Instead, they had returned to their homes. Above all, however, he was shocked by the losses that had been inflicted on his army at Isandlwana and Rorke's Drift: 'An assegai has been thrust into the belly of the nation,' he lamented, 'there are not enough tears to mourn the dead.'

Worse was to come. Britain was determined to avenge Isandlwana.

CHAPTER 6

'WE ARE THE BOYS FROM ISANDLWANA!'

'What have I done? I want peace – I ask for peace.'
Cetshwayo kaMpande

When the main impi left Nodwengu on 17 January on the way to confront the Centre Column, it was accompanied by a smaller and qualitatively inferior force charged by Cetshwayo to deal with the threat posed by Colonel Pearson's No. 1 Column of 4750 officers and men in the south-east. In command was Godide kaNdlela, a 70-year-old whose younger brother Mavumengwana was joint commander of the main impi.

On the 18th, Godide and his command separated from the warriors en route to Isandlwana and headed off south-east. The best fighting material in Godide's impi consisted of the bulk of the uMxhapho regiment who were in the prime of life and some of whose colleagues were with the main army. In contrast, the warriors belonging to the accompanying uDlambedlu and izinGulube regiments were in their mid-50s.

After nightfall on 21 January, the impi arrived at Gingindlovu, the royal homestead in south-east Zululand built by Cetshwayo after defeating his brother Mbuyazi in 1856. They found it a smouldering ruin. It had just been put to the torch by members of Pearson's No. 1 Column which was encamped in the neighbourhood, having recently advanced from the Lower Drift of the Tugela. Godide therefore chose to ambush the British the following day on suitable ground just to the north.

Colonel Pearson's column had crossed into Zululand following the expiry of Frere's ultimatum and had established a fort called Fort Tenedos on the north bank of the Tugela. This was to complement one that had already been erected on the Natal side and which bore the name of the column's commander.

Pearson had orders to establish a base at an abandoned Norwegian mission station at Eshowe some 37 miles into Zululand, prior to advancing on oNdini. He decided to split his force into two mutually supporting divisions and set off early on 18 January at the head of the first division which was 2400 strong and included five companies of his own battalion, the 2/3rd Buffs. The division's armament included two 7-pounders, rockets and a Gatling gun belonging to the Naval Brigade. Lieutenant-Colonel Welman of the 99th was to bring on the second division.

Pearson marched early on the 22nd and paused for breakfast at about 8 a.m. after crossing the Nyezane River with the head of his division. He halted in an area of flat scrubland just to the north of the Nyezane. To his

102

front was a steep ridge, with three spurs running down towards the river, divided by gullies with thick growth. The track climbed the central spur, the lowest, passing a prominent knoll on the way and a small kraal on the left, near the crest.

Unbeknown to Pearson, Godide and his men were concealed on the ridge, intent on ambushing and encircling the British as they ascended the central spur. Since separating from the main impi, Godide had been augmented by several contingents of local warriors and his force now probably numbered between 4000 and 6000 men.

Things did not go to plan. Pearson soon caught sight of a number of Zulu scouts ahead and sent a company of NNC to disperse them. But as the NNC were moving up Wombane, the easternmost of the spurs flanking the track, concealed Zulus suddenly leaped to their feet, shouted 'uSuthu!', opened fire and charged, thereby routing the NNC.

Pearson rapidly responded by sending forward the men at the head of his division, two companies of the 2/3rd Buffs and two companies of the Naval Brigade, with two 7-pounders and a rocket tube, to occupy the knoll near the road. The warriors streaming down Wombane thus came under heavy flanking fire. Nevertheless, they pressed on and proceeded to swing to their right, attempting to close, dashing from bush to bush, skirmishing in extended order. Two further companies of the Buffs formed up on the right of the road and advanced determinedly against them. The Buffs were soon supported by other units (including men rushed up by Welman) and succeeded in repulsing the left horn, which nonetheless fell back in an orderly manner, only to be severely mauled when on the open hillside by a fusillade from the knoll and by fire from a Gatling gun which had been manhandled up on to the central spur from the rear.

Meanwhile, the rest of the impi had advanced. The chest had moved forward and had massed at the homestead on the central spur, from where its fire was seriously threatening Pearson's position on the knoll, while the right horn had tentatively advanced the western spur. The chest, however, was driven back, principally by members of the Naval Brigade and a company of the Buffs, who advanced up the spur. Seeing that the battle was lost, the right horn likewise retired. Hostilities ended at about 9.30 a.m., an hour and a half after they had commenced.

Pearson's losses were slight: two officers and six men of the NNC and three men of the Buffs were killed, while fifteen men were wounded. The British officially estimated Zulu dead at about 300, but the real number likely exceeded this figure. Despite their numbers and advantageous position, the Zulus had been soundly defeated, and the morale of the surviving warriors badly dented.

Pearson continued towards Eshowe at noon and arrived the following day, having burnt homesteads en route, annoyed at having been attacked.

On the 24th he was joined by Welman whose advance had been without incident.

On 28 January, by which time work on fortifying Eshowe had commenced, a runner arrived with word from Chelmsford, who had, of course, been defeated at Isandlwana hours after the battle of Nyezane. Pearson was told that all previous orders were now void and that he could withdraw if he wished, although if he did so he should try to hold on to the Lower Drift. The colonel consulted his subordinates and a decision was made to stay put. However, to ease the burden on supplies, it was decided to send back most of the mounted men and the majority of the 2nd NNC. Pearson's force – which was to endure a long siege – was therefore reduced to 1339 whites and 355 blacks plus non-combatants.

The invasion of No. 4 Column
Meanwhile, on 18 January, Colonel Evelyn Wood and his column of 2278 men had marched from their encampment at Bemba's Kop on the Ncome, north-east towards the upper reaches of the White Mfolozi. Since the expiry of the ultimatum on 11 January, much of the countryside to the south, east and north of Bemba's Kop had been scoured by mounted patrols belonging to Wood's column, routing minor Zulu forces encountered and seizing livestock. In so doing, Wood had eased the pressure on the Centre Column, which had crossed into Zululand at Rorke's Drift on the 11th.

On 20 January, Wood reached the White Mfolozi and began to establish a base called Fort Thinta, while a patrol under Lieutenant Colonel Redvers Buller, who was in command of Wood's mounted troops, rode off across the river to reconnoitre. Upon reaching Zungwini Mountain, the westernmost of a chain of flat-topped mountains, Buller encountered stiff opposition from a force mostly consisting of Qulusi and was compelled to conduct a fighting retreat across the White Mfolozi.

On the 22nd, Wood himself led a strong patrol, including infantry, towards Zungwini, and reached the summit after forcing back several hundred Zulus. From his vantage point he saw about 4000 warriors drilling on the next mountain in the chain, Hlobane.

Wood spent the 23rd resting at Fort Thinta, before advancing towards Hlobane at dawn on the 24th, intent on dealing with the large Zulu impi he had seen. Skirmishing ensued, during which Wood received a bombshell – a messenger arrived with news of the Centre Column's defeat at Isandlwana.

Wood therefore headed back to Fort Thinta, before withdrawing north-westward on 31 January to establish a fortified camp on Khambula Hill, fourteen miles or so due west of Zungwini. From here he could keep an eye on the Zulus around Hlobane and cover the approaches to Utrecht and Luneburg, the latter being the base of Colonel Rowland's No. 5 Column.

From Khambula, Wood sent Buller on raids against the Qulusi. The first of these occurred on 1 February when Buller destroyed their *ikhanda*, ebaQulusini, near Hlobane, without opposition.

Wood continued, too, in his endeavour to exploit the semi-independent status of the clans of north-western Zululand, hoping to get them to forsake Cetshwayo. With a view to weakening their resolve and securing their submission, he despatched Buller with the mounted troops to raid outlying homesteads and seize cattle. Buller was also charged with finding Prince Hamu, who, it will be recalled, had promised to desert to the side of the British and was being kept by Cetshwayo at oNdini. Furthermore, Buller rode north to assist Colonel Rowlands by attacking marauding bands of Zulus raiding across the border into the Transvaal.

In late February, Rowlands was required to move to Pretoria, where Boer republican elements were stirring in the wake of Isandlwana. No. 5 Column therefore came under Wood's command, and its mounted men were ordered up to Khambula.

On 12 March, the British experienced a reverse beside the Ntombe River north-east of Luneburg. A convoy carrying ammunition and rations to the garrison there, and a company of the 80th Regiment which had been sent out from Luneburg to help bring it in, were attacked by a mixed force of at least 800 Swazi and Zulu warriors under a warlord named Mbilini Mswati, a renegade son of the Swazi king who had fled to Zululand in 1866. The toll of British dead was one officer and sixty men, a civil surgeon, two white wagon conductors and fifteen black drivers, while the bodies of only thirty of Mbilini's warriors were found among the dead.

Cetshwayo's position, nevertheless, had just been seriously weakened, for Hamu, who had managed to slip away from oNdini, defected to the enemy and turned up at Khambula on 10 March, where he was soon joined by up to 1300 or so of his adherents. The fighting men were drafted into an existing unit known as Wood's Irregulars, while Hamu and the non-combatants were located near Utrecht.

Cetshwayo, meanwhile, had summoned the bulk of his warriors to reassemble at oNdini by 22 March for another major campaign. Even so, he and his council hoped to avoid further bloodshed and, during the course of the month, made peaceful but unfruitful overtures to the British. Eventually the king and his advisers decided that the majority of the assembled warriors should march north-west under Mnyamana to the assistance of the hard-pressed Qulusi, while the remainder were to reinforce the warriors in the vicinity of Eshowe – where Pearson had been under siege since early February – and prevent any relief force from breaking through.

The main impi, which was little inferior in strength to that of the Isandlwana campaign and once again included warriors from all the crack regiments, set off from oNdini on 24 March and by the afternoon of the 27th was nearing the Qulusi stronghold and cattle depot of Hlobane.

Unaware of the impi's advance, Wood set out that very night with his mounted troops and levies to attack Hlobane, having been instructed by Chelmsford (who was planning to march to the relief of Eshowe) to create a diversion in the north-west and thus draw off some of Cetshwayo's forces.

Wood decided to assault Hlobane by means of a pincer movement, whereby 640 men under Lieutenant Colonel John Russell would ascend a plateau adjoining the mountain's west end, while Buller and 675 men would climb the eastern slopes of Hlobane itself. Before dawn on the 28th, both parties began their respective ascents.

As Buller moved up Hlobane, a severe thunderstorm broke overhead and flashes of lightning illuminated the scene, betraying his presence to Zulus in caves above who opened fire, causing a few casualties. Nevertheless, Buller managed to come out on the summit, driving a small number of Zulus before him. He then swept westward across the extensive and gently undulating summit, rounding up about 2000 Zulu cattle, and clashing with an increasing number of Qulusi and Mbilini's men who were expecting the arrival of the main impi.

The force despatched from oNdini was indeed approaching and, between 10 a.m. and 11 a.m., Buller suddenly caught sight of it drawing near from the south-east. He was thus forced to quit Hlobane as fast as he could by descending the Devil's Pass, difficult ground falling steeply away for about 200 feet in a narrow series of giant steps strewn with boulders down on to the Ntendeka plateau, which Russell had abandoned after likewise spotting the main impi.

The descent proved a nightmare. Some horses lost their footing and plunged to their deaths, while a number of the men were killed by the Qulusi and adherents of Mbilini. Buller, however, once again proved himself an inspiring leader, for amid the fear and confusion he moved back and forth encouraging his men, saving some who had got into difficulties. He was to receive the Victoria Cross for his gallantry.

The British then withdrew in disarray to Khambula, having lost fifteen officers, seventy-nine men and over a hundred black levies. The Zulus, who numbered at least 20,000 warriors, proceeded to bivouac beside the White Mfolozi a few miles west of Hlobane and about fifteen miles from Wood's camp, the Qulusi and Mbilini's followers having joined the main impi.

The battle of Khambula

Shortly after dawn on 29 January 1879, Wood sent Commandant Pieter Raaff and his Transvaal Rangers from Khambula to locate the impi. En route Raaff came across a Zulu who had slipped away from the enemy. He was one of Hamu's men and had fought on the British side at Hlobane where, to save himself, he had discarded his British insignia and temporarily thrown in his lot with his former colleagues. He was sent on to report to Wood, and warned him that the impi would probably attack at 'dinner time'.

Meanwhile, Raaff had pressed on and at about 10 a.m., after reaching the edge of the Zungwini plateau, caught sight of the warriors cooking beside the White Mfolozi and a tributary stream, having moved a few miles north from their overnight encampment. At 11 a.m. Raaff returned to the British camp to report that the Zulus were advancing north-west on Khambula, and outlying units were hurriedly called in.

The Zulus were soon spotted when about five miles away, heading westwards in five columns. Wood feared that instead of moving against him, the impi would continue towards the settlement of Utrecht. When they reached hills approximately four miles south-east of his position, the Zulus halted. For over an hour they remained stationary, watched anxiously by the British.

Cetshwayo had given orders that no fortified positions were to be attacked. His commanders were to seize British cattle and lure the enemy from their positions into the open. Failing that, they were to march on into the Transvaal and force the British to follow them, and there hopefully surprise attack the pursuing British. But Zulu spirits were high following Hlobane. Many warriors, especially the younger *amabutho*, were itching to come to grips once again. Indeed, it is said that Mnyamana simply lost control of his army. He was to watch the battle from a hill about three miles from the British position, while Ntshingwayo, the senior commander at Isandlwana, directed the warriors from about 700 yards east of Wood's position.

In due course the left horn, the uMcijo regiment, recommenced marching. It was indeed heading for Utrecht. But at about 1 p.m. it changed course, suddenly veering right, directly towards the British camp. The pace also changed. Now it came on fast, before halting about three miles from Wood's position.

In the meantime, the right horn which, despite what is sometimes maintained, consisted entirely of the iNgobamakhosi regiment, had likewise begun to move. It circled around to the north of Khambula until it reached a point about a mile and a half from the enemy. Meanwhile, the chest edged forward towards Wood, but was nevertheless much further from the British position than the right horn.

And what of the British? At around 12.45, after dinner had been eaten, the tents were struck and the defences manned. Wood was in command of 669 mounted troops and 1238 regular infantry belonging to eight compa-

nies of the 90th Light Infantry and seven companies of the 1/13th Light
Infantry. Moreover, there were 58 of Wood's Irregulars present (the
remainder had deserted following Hlobane), eleven Royal Engineers, and
the 110 men of No. 11 Battery, 7th Brigade, Royal Artillery, with their six
7-pounders. In all, 2086 officers and men, of whom 88 were unfit for
service due to illness.

Wood's defences on Khambula included a hexagonal main laager with
the wagons locked tightly together and with sods thrown up beneath the
wagons to form a rampart. The southern side of the laager overlooked
ground that fell away gently before descending sharply into a valley that
ran along the southern side of the position. To the north, in contrast, the
ground fell away gently, providing a better field of fire. About 306 yards to
the east of the laager, and in a more elevated position on a narrow ridge of
tableland, was an earthwork redoubt in which two of the 7-pounders were
placed, facing north-east. The other four guns were placed between the
redoubt and the laager to cover the northern approaches. To the
south-west, the redoubt was connected by a palisade to a smaller laager on
lower ground, on the edge of the ridge's southern face: this held the
column's 2000 cattle. About 200 yards to the west of the main laager and
on the lip of the valley was the garrison's refuse tip, on which clumps of
mealies and long grass had grown rapidly amidst the horse manure.

One company of the 90th Light Infantry was in the redoubt, while one
and a half companies of the 1/13th were stationed in the cattle kraal. The
rest of the infantry manned the main laager, which also contained the
mounted troops. Range markers had been set up around the camp to
enhance the effect of the defenders' fire. The gun crews manning the guns
between the main laager and the redoubt were told to fall back to the
former if the Zulus got close.

At about 1.30 p.m., the right horn, after taking up its new position,
began to advance towards the British camp. To goad the oncoming
warriors into launching a full-scale attack, Wood sent Buller and about 100
mounted men, some of who were black, towards the Zulus. Buller and his
men rode out from the main laager when the right horn was less than a
mile away. When within range, he ordered his men to dismount and fire.
This spurred on the iNgobamakhosi. Buller's force then rode back towards
the laager, dismounting and firing again as it did so, while the Native
Horse rode off to the west, from where they were to harass the flanks of the
enemy during the course of the battle.

At approximately 1.45 p.m., the artillery opened fire over Buller's
retiring men at the oncoming iNgobamakhosi, who were taunting the
withdrawing horsemen by shouting 'We are the boys from Isandlwana!'
Then, when the right horn was about 300 yards from the British position,
the 90th Light Infantry opened fire. This, combined with flanking fire

from the redoubt, severely mauled the Zulus, whose advance was checked– for, as a Zulu named Sihlahla recalled shortly after the battle, they 'could not face the bullets'. A few managed to reach the main laager, only to be slain. Consequently, within 45 minutes or so of the battle's commencement, the right horn began falling back north-east to the cover of some rocky ledges where it was to remain for much of the rest of the engagement.

At about 2.15 p.m., as the right horn was withdrawing, the rest of the impi began advancing to the attack, the chest from the east and the left horn from the south. As the chest approached at a steady trot across the open ground, it was subjected to artillery fire that cut swathes through its ranks. It thus veered left towards the dead ground of the valley, to which the left horn was advancing.

In due course the first wave of warriors of the left horn surged out of the dead ground, only to run into withering cross-fire from the southern sides of the main laager and the cattle kraal. But the hordes of warriors continued to swarm up the gentle slope leading to the British camp, funnelling into the gap between the kraal and the laager. The narrowest part of the slope was in front of the kraal and the Zulus there, most notably the uNokhenke regiment, soon forced their way into the kraal and engaged hand-to-hand with the 1/13th deployed there, both sides being hampered by the terrified cattle. The outnumbered soldiers managed to extricate themselves and fell back towards the redoubt, while Zulus with rifles opened fire from the wagons on the main laager.

Following the capture of the cattle kraal, some 1000 to 1500 Zulus – evidently the uMbonambi regiment – began to form up to the west of the kraal in preparation for an assault on the main laager. In response, at about 3 p.m., Wood ordered Major Hackett to counter-attack with two companies of the 90th. To the consternation of the Zulus, Hackett and his men moved out of the laager, fixed bayonets, and advanced towards them, supported by case-shot from the artillery. They threw the Zulus on to the defensive and back over the rim, from where Hackett's men poured fire down into the valley. The Zulus were also forced to abandon the cattle laager under stiff fire from the redoubt and the guns.

In turn, however, Hackett came under heavy fire from warriors armed with Martini-Henry rifles deployed in the vacated huts of Wood's Irregulars to the east, and from behind the camp's refuse dump to the west. The Zulus behind the rubbish heaps belonged to the uMcijo *ibutho* which had been driven back by a company of the 1/13th that emerged from the south-west corner of the main laager (at about the time of Hackett's sortie) with the aim of repulsing the regiment with the bayonet. Consequently, Hackett's men were forced to withdraw to the main laager, taking with them their wounded commander, who had been shot in the face.

At about this time, with Hackett falling back on the main laager, Wood was forced temporarily to withdraw a company of the 1/13th stationed at the right rear of the principal laager, owing to Zulu fire from behind the refuse dump. Meanwhile, the Zulus among the huts were hit by shells from the artillery, while the warriors sheltering behind the refuse dump were finally killed or put to flight by volleys of rifle fire that flattened the dumps.

Subsequently, the Zulus launched several more assaults. At one point, warriors reached the trenches along the southern side of the redoubt before being driven off. Then, at about 4.30 p.m., they moved against the north and north-east faces of the British position, supported by the iNgob-amakhosi, who moved forward from the rocks where they had been sheltering. Again they were repulsed.

The Zulus' gallantry impressed their adversaries. Sergeant Edward Jervis of the 90th Light Infantry wrote two days after the battle: 'I confess that I do not think that a braver lot of men than our enemies in point of disregard for life, and for their bravery under fire, could be found anywhere.'

By 5.30 p.m. the Zulus were evidently spent and intent on retiring. Wood therefore ordered a company of the 1/13th to clear the cattle kraal, where some warriors were still present, and despatched a company of the 90th to the edge of the valley in front of the cattle-laager. Here, after driving Zulus back with the bayonet, it opened fire on the warriors below as they began falling back eastwards towards Zungwini.

Their orderly withdrawal was turned into a rout when Wood launched his mounted troops against them. The pursuit lasted for over two hours and many of the exhausted Zulus were mercilessly slaughtered. Some simply stood and waited to be shot: others were stabbed with spears that had fallen into British hands. Buller is said to have been 'like a tiger drunk with blood'. He was not alone. For example, Captain Cecil D'Arcy of the Frontier Light Horse exhorted his men: 'No quarter, boys, and remember yesterday!', whereupon they butchered 'the brutes all over the place'. They probably needed little encouragement.

The number of Zulus killed in the battle, or who died during the pursuit or subsequently from their injuries, is unknown: but it was high. During the following two days, 785 Zulu dead were collected from Khambula and its environs; and in a letter to his parents, D'Arcy noted that there were 'hundreds and hundreds' of Zulu bodies 'some miles off, that are being eaten by dogs and vultures'. In short, the official British estimate of Zulu dead as 'nearly 2000' is not likely to have been far wrong. A high percentage of high-ranking men had perished, for as Cetshwayo rightly commented, they had 'exposed themselves a great deal, attempting to lead on their men'.

Wood's casualties, in contrast, were modest. Eighteen British soldiers were killed, and eight officers and fifty-seven men wounded, of whom ten subsequently died. Khambula is frequently said to have been the decisive battle of the war. This is a fair assessment. Not only did the battle inflict heavy losses on the Zulus' crack regiments – causing much lamentation throughout the nation – but it also rammed home a fundamental point. No matter how bravely Cetshwayo's warriors pressed home their attacks, their shields and assegais were no match for artillery and firearms employed effectively by British soldiers in compact positions. Cetshwayo was greatly saddened and angered by the battle's outcome, and understandably so. Barring a miracle, the war was as good as lost.

The battle of Gingindlovu

Not all of the warriors who had assembled at oNdini by 22 March participated in the Khambula campaign. A significant minority of them, as mentioned, were sent south-east to reinforce the warriors around Eshowe, thereby putting further pressure on Pearson's beleaguered No. 1 Column and threatening any British attempt to march to its relief.

The British garrison at Eshowe therefore witnessed a growing enemy presence in the neighbourhood in the closing week of March, and by the beginning of April there were some 10,000 warriors in south-eastern Zululand. Some of them belonged to coastal elements of regiments such as the iNgobamakhosi, uMcijo and uMbonambi. Indeed, it is likely that almost all *amabutho* were represented, but many of the warriors were irregulars, including non-Zulu Tsonga from chiefdoms in the vicinity of St Lucia Bay which had strong cultural and tributary links with the Zulu state.

On 28 March, the day before Khambula, Chelmsford began advancing from the Lower Drift of the Tugela to relieve Eshowe. He headed a force that totalled 3390 Europeans and 2280 Africans, some of its constituent units having recently arrived in South Africa after being sent out by the British government following Isandlwana. Its regular element consisted of the 57th and 91st Regiments, six companies of the 3/60th Rifles, five companies of the 99th and two of the Buffs, Mounted Infantry, and a contingent of the Naval Brigade which included two 9-pounder guns, two Gatlings, and two heavy 24-pounder rocket tubes. John Dunn, the 'White Zulu', was also present, now well and truly on the British side.

Chelmsford did not advance towards Eshowe along the route taken by Pearson, for the nature of the terrain was close and presented the Zulus with the opportunity of setting an ambush. At Dunn's suggestion, he moved up a track along the coast before heading inland. Progress was slow, partly because Chelmsford ensured that the camp was entrenched and laagered after each day's march.

By the evening of 1 April, Pearson's observers at Eshowe could see the approaching column as it moved into laager on the south side of the

Nyezane near burnt-out Gingindlovu. Chelmsford encamped on the summit of a slight knoll more than a mile from the river.

The laager was 128 yards square, thus providing sufficient room for the column's 2000 oxen, 300 horses and the black levies. Some 15 yards in front of the wagons was a trench 157 yards square, and the excavated earth was used to build a waist-high wall on the inner side of the ditch. In the event of combat, it would be manned by many of Chelmsford's white troops who bivouacked between the wall and the wagons so that battle stations could be rapidly manned: and some of the infantry were to be positioned on top of the wagons, thereby confronting the Zulus with a double tier of fire. The north-west face was nearest to the river, and had a Gatling in each corner, while the rear face had the two 9-pounders in one corner and the rockets in the other.

The British spent an uncomfortable night, anticipating an attack. Rain fell steadily and at midnight Chelmsford gave orders for the strengthening of the defences. Then, at 4 a.m., as dawn approached, the soldiers stood to arms.

By this time the Zulu forces in the region had concentrated and were closing in. They were commanded by Somopho kaZikhale, the senior induna of the emaNgweni *ikhanda* and a close friend of Cetshwayo, who had instructed him to minimise Zulu losses as far as possible. Somopho had intended to ambush Chelmsford as the British commander headed towards Eshowe along the inner track, but the general's decision to march through the more open terrain of the coastal route had thwarted him. Now, with Chelmsford only a day's march from Eshowe, Somopho had to strike, for delaying an attack until Chelmsford was closer to Eshowe ran the risk of being taken in the rear by Pearson.

At 5.45 a.m., with the ground enveloped in thick mist, reports from mounted scouts and picquets reached Chelmsford, warning of the Zulus' advance. The mist gradually lifted and warriors were sighted north of the Nyezane, and on Misi Hill to the west of the laager, on the south side of the river. The Zulu concentration to the north divided and proceeded to cross the Nyezane, though reserves stayed on the hills to the north of the river. The left division, or left horn, then headed towards the north-east corner of the British position while the other division, the chest, moved against the northern face of the square. In the meantime, the Zulus on Misi Hill deployed, threatening both the western and southern faces of the laager. Hence, within ten minutes of coming into view, the Zulus were formed into the famed crescent formation and advancing against three sides of Chelmsford's position.

They moved forward in three relatively distinct lines of knots and groups of men, and when some 1000 yards from the laager, came under concerted fire from the Gatlings, the artillery and the rockets. In turn, when about 800 yards from the British position, the Zulus themselves opened fire. As Captain Edward Hutton of the 3/60th Regiment recalled:

> In spite of the excitement of the moment, we could not but admire the perfect manner in which these Zulus skirmished. A small knot of five or six would rise and dart through the long grass, dodging from side to side with heads down, rifles and shields kept low and out of sight. They would then suddenly sink into the long grass, and nothing but puffs of curling smoke would show their whereabouts. Then they advanced again, and their bullets soon began to whistle merrily over our heads or strike the little parapet in front.

In response, when the Zulus were about 400 yards off, the British infantry began firing volleys. The left horn and chest enjoyed cover afforded by the long grass, bush and ant-hills – in places the grass and bush came to within 100 yards of the British – but the right horn was rather more exposed.

It was the warriors of the left horn and chest who first pressed home an attack, charging the northern and north-eastern perimeters of the laager. As they converged on the British, they were cut down in large numbers by the withering fire. Several desperate attempts to close by warriors 'brave to madness' failed – none of the charges came to within 20 yards or so of the north-east corner of the laager – and soon heaps of dead and dying Zulus littered the ground.

At 6.40 a.m. the chest began falling back into the long grass, whereupon Chelmsford sent Barrow, with 120 Mounted Infantry and Natal Volunteers, out against them. But Barrow and his men soon received a nasty shock. The Zulus regained their fighting spirit and began closing round, intent on cutting off their pursuers. Barrow was forced to conduct a fighting withdrawal back to the sanctuary of the laager. The chest then veered to the right and joined in the assault of part of the right horn against the west front of the British position. Here, too, the Zulus failed to make headway, for their ranks were decimated by the impenetrable enemy fire.

Simultaneously with this unsuccessful onslaught against the western front of the laager, around 7 a.m., the other division of the right horn began what was to prove the most determined assault of all against the southern sector of the British position. Here Dabulamanzi, Cetshwayo's brother, urged on the warriors from horseback and sustained a flesh wound above the knee in the process. The ferocity of the attack was partly due to the presence of the NNC in the rear of the laager, which led the Zulus to conclude, mistakenly, that Chelmsford lacked enough British troops to man his entire position. Once more, however, the Zulus were cut down relentlessly; soon, demoralised, they began falling back to low ground to the south.

Seeing this, Chelmsford ordered Barrow to lead all the mounted troops out of the unengaged east face of the laager, partly with the aim of attacking the east flank of the right horn. This sortie proved the final straw for the Zulus in general; they commenced a withdrawal that soon degenerated into a rout when troopers charged home with swords drawn. Some of the warriors were pursued as they headed west towards Misi Hill or southward (their pursuers included members of the NNC who vacated the laager at 7.15 a.m.) while part of Barrow's force wheeled north against the Zulus falling back towards the Nyezane and drove them through the river.

British casualties in the battle were slight – two officers and eleven men killed, four officers and forty-four men wounded. In contrast, Chelmsford reported that 471 enemy dead were found within 984 yards of the laager and that another 200 had been discovered in the vicinity. Other bodies were found at a distance of up to five miles. Chelmsford estimated the total number of enemy dead as 1000, but the War Office was to put the figure at 'nearly 1200' after accepting slightly higher estimates of other officers.

The following day Chelmsford advanced to Eshowe, headed by the 91st Highlanders with pipes playing and colours flying. Two days later, the Relief Column and Eshowe's former garrison began returning to Natal. Chelmsford headed back by the coastal route and arrived in Natal on the 7th where he was to prepare for renewed hostilities, well satisfied with recent developments.

Cetshwayo felt differently. Coming close on the heels of Khambula, Gingindlovu had again depressed his spirits and further undermined national morale.

Prelude to Ulundi

During Chelmsford's absence, the bulk of the reinforcements sent from Britain had arrived at Durban and were becoming acclimatised. Among them were three infantry battalions, the 2/21st Royal Scots Fusiliers, the 58th and 94th. Moreover, the 1/24th had been reconstituted with a draft of 600 men. Additional gun batteries had also arrived, while new colonial mounted units, such as the Natal Light Horse, had been formed. Furthermore, along with the reinforcements had come four major-generals.

Chelmsford now prepared for what he hoped would prove the knock-out blow, using two invading columns. One, the First Division, some 7500 men strong, would advance up the coast from Fort Pearson at the Lower Drift of the Tugela under the command of the newly arrived Major-General H. H. Crealock, destroy important *amakhanda*, and hopefully ease the pressure on the other British forces by compelling Cetshwayo to send part of his army against it. The Second Division, approximately 5000 strong, under Major-General E. Newdigate, would march by way of

114

Landman's Drift on the Mzinyathi, a crossing upstream from Rorke's Drift. The latter was rejected as a point of entry partly because Chelmsford did not wish his men to pass Isandlwana, where the decaying bodies of the soldiers killed on 22 January still lay. After advancing from Landman's Drift, the division would cross the Ncome and then swing south towards Babanango, beyond Isandlwana, before heading towards oNdini along the route the Centre Column would have taken had disaster not overwhelmed it. The division was to link up with Wood's command of 3200 men, henceforth to be known as the Flying Column, currently still at Khambula.

The units that comprised the Second Division, which Chelmsford intended to accompany, began to concentrate at Landman's Drift in early May. Meanwhile, on 5 May, Wood left Khambula with the aim of linking up with the Second Division.

During the course of the month, Chelmsford also sent out a number of patrols and raiding parties from Landman's Drift to reconnoitre and reduce the Zulus' capacity to offer resistance in the areas through which he would march by seizing cattle and destroying homesteads and crops. Little opposition was encountered; much of the countryside had been abandoned. Cross-border raids were also conducted on Chelmsford's orders by forces to the east, who crossed the Tugela.

On 18 May, a patrol of the 17th Lancers reported having located a drift across the Ncome at Koppie Alleen, less than ten miles north-east of Landman's Drift. Beyond it, a track usable by wagons headed east before turning south towards Babanango. Chelmsford had intended crossing the Ncome further upstream, i.e. about twenty miles north of Landman's Drift, and had had supplies transported to the point; but as a shorter route to oNdini was now possible, the supplies were transferred to Koppie Alleen instead.

While this was underway, Chelmsford turned his attention to burying the soldiers who had fallen at Isandlwana. Thus, on 21 May, Major-General F. Marshall, who commanded the Cavalry Brigade attached to the Second Division, arrived at the battle site with a force largely consisting of the 17th Lancers, and having put to the torch surviving Zulu homesteads on the way, commenced burying the British dead. He then returned to Landman's Drift, leaving the task to be completed later.

By the end of May, the Second Division had advanced to Koppie Alleen, and on the 31st its leading brigade crossed the Ncome into Zululand and encamped on the far bank, to be followed the next day by the division's second brigade. It was intended to link up with Wood's Flying Column on 2 June in a valley between the Tshotshosi and Tombokola Rivers.

Crealock's division, on the other hand, was still not ready to advance from Fort Chelmsford (recently established beside the Nyezane, to which the foremost units had advanced from the Lower Drift) and it would not be until 19 June that his entire force was assembled beside the Nyezane.

Chelmsford was in sanguine mood, but he soon received shattering news. On Sunday, 1 June, an observer on his staff was killed in ignominious circumstances while out reconnoitring, after being abandoned by his colleagues following a surprise Zulu attack in the Tshotshosi Valley. The observer was no ordinary mortal. He was none other than young Louis Bonaparte, the Prince Imperial of France, only son of the late Napoleon III, and had been living in exile in Britain since being forced to flee France during the Franco-Prussian War.

The prince's death was a devastating blow which put Chelmsford under even greater pressure to crush the Zulus, for the news of Louis's death was met with horror and incredulity in Britain and France. Indeed, it caused a wave of Anglophobia in the latter country, even among Republicans who had derided the prince's claim to the vacant French throne.

On 3 June, Newdigate's Second Division pressed on. It crossed the Tshotshosi River the following day and encamped on ground just vacated by Wood, whose Flying Column had already crossed the river and now advanced to a new encampment on the far side of another river, the Nondweni.

Early on 5 June, Marshall and the Cavalry Brigade rode east to reconnoitre after hearing that a small Zulu force lay to their front, and in so doing met up with Buller and irregular horse from the Flying Column. A skirmish ensued in the valley of the Ntinini (Phoko) River in which the Zulus forced their opponents to withdraw.

On that same day, Chelmsford, having advanced to the Nondweni, interviewed three envoys from Cetshwayo, who earnestly desired to bring an end to hostilities, a desire shared by the principal men of his kingdom. Chelmsford, however, was determined to prosecute the war to a successful conclusion. Hence the diplomatic overture proved futile, as did others launched by Cetshwayo during this period.

Chelmsford established an intermediate depot called Fort Newdigate beside the Nondweni. Then, on the 7th, he moved on to the Ntinini, where he halted for over a week. He did so to await the arrival of fresh supplies that were brought up, escorted by the Flying Column and half the regular cavalry of the Second Division which had been charged with the task.

During the delay, Chelmsford began working on another post, Fort Marshall, to the south at Siphezi, on the main track to oNdini: like Fort Newdigate, it was garrisoned by two companies of the 21st. Meanwhile, Buller ranged far and wide, successfully clashing with Zulu forces, destroying homesteads and plundering livestock.

On 17 June, the fresh supplies and their escort finally arrived. By this date, Chelmsford had received word that the British government had sent

General Sir Garnet Wolseley, a highly experienced and respected 46-year-old, to South Africa to supersede him. The news gave added urgency to Chelmsford's campaign. He had no intention of sitting back and allowing Wolseley to cover himself in glory.

On the 18th, Chelmsford pressed on past Fort Marshall and reached the Babanango Heights the following day, watched by bodies of Zulu warriors, one of which skirmished with a cavalry detachment in the neighbourhood. On the heights, another post, Fort Evelyn, was built on 23–24 June and garrisoned by two companies of the 58th. Finally, on 27 June, after a painfully slow advance from Koppie Alleen, Chelmsford reached the Mthonjaneni Heights overlooking oNdini, sixteen miles away in the Mahlabathini Plain below. En route from Babanango, Wood had destroyed six *amakhanda* in the emaKhosini Valley on the right bank of the White Mfolozi, a sacred spot for the Zulus as it was the burial ground of Cetshwayo's forebears.

Crealock, for his part, began advancing from the Nyezane on 19 June. His progress, too, was slow, partly due to a shortage of wagons. No opposition of any consequence was encountered and it was clear that much of the region's manpower had made its way to oNdini, where Cetshwayo's forces were once again assembling. After reaching the Umlalazi River, the First Division constructed Fort Napoleon on 25–26 June, while patrols penetrated further, aggressively scouring the countryside towards the Mhlatuze, killing, destroying and plundering in sorties that continued into July, again encountering little or no resistance.

Cetshwayo, as has been noted, had by now begun mustering his forces. Morale was low, but the call to arms was generally obeyed – a rumour that the British would castrate Zulu males and take their wives presumably instilled some waverers with a will to fight – and by the third week of June the bulk of the Zulu army had assembled on the Mahlabathini Plain.

The Zulu king was still anxious to avoid further bloodshed, however, especially given increasing signs of disaffection with the war among sections of his people. Indeed, there were reports of actual defections to the British camp, especially in the south-east of his kingdom. He therefore sent back his original three peace envoys to Chelmsford. They came before the general, on 27 June, on the Mthonjaneni Heights, bearing a letter from their king, 150 of the oxen captured at Isandlwana, and two great elephant tusks. But Cetshwayo was still not prepared to submit abjectly to all Chelmsford's terms, which included a demand that at least 10,000 cattle or 20,000 sheep should be surrendered. Consequently, although Chelmsford agreed to a brief delay in crossing the White Mfolozi to give Cetshwayo a last chance to comply, he knew that such compliance was well-nigh impossible.

117

At 8.45 a.m. on 30 June, Chelmsford advanced from the Mthonjaneni Heights down towards the White Mfolozi, leaving a garrison (partly comprising two companies of the reformed 1/24th) to hold defences that had been prepared on the heights, and in which all the tents and the majority of the supplies were placed. He took approximately 5500 men, each of whom was carrying rations for ten days, a blanket, waterproof sheet and greatcoat. Cavalry reconnoitring ahead soon sighted three large bodies of Zulus heading towards the river, doubtless intent on preventing the British from crossing.

The British found the going difficult, however, and halted at around 3.30 p.m. at the foot of Mthonjaneni, by which time Chelmsford had received further envoys from Cetshwayo. They brought with them the sword taken from the late Prince Imperial and word that Cetshwayo was prepared to hand over more cattle and two 7-pounders taken at Isandl-wana. Chelmsford seemed more amenable than hitherto, declaring, for example, that in lieu of a previous condition, the surrender of one of Cetshwayo's regiments, he would accept 1000 rifles captured at Isandl-wana. Moreover, he announced that Cetshwayo had until noon on 3 July to comply and that the British would remain on their side of the White Mfolozi until that hour. But as John Laband comments:

> This apparent magnanimity had a purpose.... The difficult terrain at the foot of Mthonjaneni made it almost impossible for cavalry to operate, and Chelmsford was naturally concerned that the Zulu might attempt to attack his force while it was strung out on the line of march. Continuing diplomatic exchanges would shield the British until they were more favourably placed.

On 1 July, at 7.30 a.m., Chelmsford resumed his advance, with Buller and his mounted men of the Flying Column to the fore. Buller reached a drift across the White Mfolozi just before 11 a.m. and from a vantage point on a small kopje proceeded to watch Zulu forces drilling on the plain beyond and being doctored for the impending conflict.

Since it seemed that the Zulus were not intent on launching an attack that day, the Flying Column began to form a laager less than a mile from the drift. But around 1 p.m., while work was still in progress, and as the wagons of the Second Division were still on the move, a sudden Zulu movement towards the river occurred, causing consternation among the British, particularly among the less experienced men of the Second Division. In due course, however, the alarm abated, for instead of trying to exploit the evident British disarray, the Zulus began retiring to their quarters later that afternoon.

During the course of the following morning, the Second Division closed up with the Flying Column and likewise laagered. Once again Zulus advanced in strength towards the river before withdrawing, and did the same on the 3rd, before heading off in the direction of oNdini.

On 2 July, Cetshwayo made his final gesture of peace by ordering a herd of a hundred or more of the royal white oxen to be driven to the British camp. However, the proud young warriors of the uMcijo regiment prevented them from reaching their destination. Other *amabutho* were in similar militant mood. On that same day, therefore, Cetshwayo reluctantly issued instructions for battle. No attack was to be launched against the British when they were stationary and thus no doubt entrenched, and if the Zulus did manage to defeat the enemy in the open, they were not to pursue the British across the White Mfolozi, given the defences on the far bank.

It was on 2 July, too, that Chelmsford received a telegram from Wolseley, who had landed at Durban on 28 June and was currently endeavouring to join Crealock. The telegram, sent on the 30th, instructed Chelmsford: 'Concentrate your force immediately and keep it concentrated. Undertake no serious operations with detached bodies of troops. Acknowledge receipt of this message at once and flash back your latest moves.' But Chelmsford was now only five miles from Cetshwayo's principal homestead and had no intention of heeding Wolseley's order to desist from serious operations.

At about 1 p.m. on 3 July, following the expiry of the time Chelmsford had granted Cetshwayo to comply with his conditions, Buller crossed the White Mfolozi with a strong force of mounted men of the Flying Column to reconnoitre ahead and find a suitable location for battle. He moved north-east over the Mahlabathini Plain and approached a stream called the Mbilane, unaware that he had been lured on by Zulus, some of them driving a large flock of goats, charged with this very task. Finally, close to the stream, Buller sensed a trap and called upon his men to halt. He was right. Some 4000 warriors, many of them uMxhapho, emerged from the long grass and opened fire, then charged and forced a retreat. Buller and his men found their return route threatened by other Zulus closing in on both flanks, but managed to make it back across the White Mfolozi, having lost only three men, partly owing to support from other mounted troops. But it had been a close run thing.

That evening, Chelmsford told his subordinates that he would advance at dawn and would then form his infantry into a large square, inviting a Zulu assault. No laager or entrenchments would be used, to show the Zulus that a British square 'could beat them fairly in the open'. At around 11 p.m. on this bitterly cold night, the British heard the unnerving sound of massed singing and dancing from the plain as the Zulus prepared themselves for the rigours of battle. The Zulus did not intend to contest the crossing of the White Mfolozi. They would let the British on to the Mhalabathini Plain and destroy them in the open.

The battle of Ulundi

The 4166 European and 958 black soldiers in the British camp stirred early on the morning of Friday, 4 July, rising at 3.45 a.m. under bright moonlight. At 6 a.m., Buller's mounted irregulars crossed the drift and took up a position on a bluff overlooking the crossing. They were then followed over the river by the remainder of the force minus some 529 white troops (mostly members of the 1/24th) and just under a hundred blacks who were to hold the camp: and the fact that most of the wagons were also left behind persuaded the Zulus that Chelmsford had played well and truly into their hands.

By 7.30 a.m. the column had cleared the rough terrain along the riverside and adopted a rectangular formation. Its front face was manned by five companies of the 80th, its rear face by two companies of the 94th and two of the 2/21st, and the longer side faces by eight companies of the 90th and four of the 94th (on the left), and eight companies of the 1/13th and four of the 58th (on the right). Two Gatlings were in the centre of the front face, while the artillery, consisting of twelve guns, was positioned in the corners and along the sides of the formation.

Within the 'square' were the headquarters staff, the balance of No. 5 Company, RE, now commanded by Chard, the veteran of Rorke's Drift, the 2nd NNC, 50 wagons and mule carts carrying reserve ammunition, as well as a number of hospital wagons. All the mounted men were outside the square.

The advance north-east across the plain then began shortly before 8 a.m. to the sound of the band of the 1/13th and screened by Buller's men. Shortly thereafter, while approaching Nodwengu, the British caught sight of Zulus gathering in numbers.

At approximately 8.30 a.m., Chelmsford halted upon a low ridge with a level summit between Nodwengu and oNdini, which Buller had selected as the site of battle the previous day. The longest sides of the 'square' faced roughly north and south, while oNdini was less than two miles to the south-east. The ground sloped away gently on every side of the position, providing a good field of fire.

Meanwhile, Zulus had appeared in increasing strength to the north and west, and others were then sighted to the east, emerging through mist. By about 8.20 a.m., a vast array of warriors could be seen in a horseshoe formation, the majority of them surrounding the north, east and southern sides of the square, while others moved to complete the encirclement. The official British estimate put the number of Zulus at 20,000; and since, according to Cetshwayo, all his regiments were represented in the army, which he believed was comparable in strength to that at Isandlwana, this total, possibly including some Tsonga, seems more or less correct.

Cetshwayo was not present. He had travelled east from oNdini the previous evening to another of his residences. On the other hand, Mnyamana, Cetshwayo's prime minister, may have been on the scene. The king's favourite brother, Ziwedu kaMpande, was certainly there, and watched the battle from a hill, accompanied by a number of Cetshwayo's other brothers and several great chiefs.

To goad the Zulus into attacking prematurely, Buller's irregular cavalry were sent to draw them into effective range. Meantime, the regular cavalry of the Second Brigade, the 17th Lancers and a squadron of Dragoons entered the rear of the square. Shortly after the British square ceased to advance, therefore, Buller's men became engaged in skirmishing with the oncoming Zulus on three sides of the position, firing and falling back before the *amabutho*. While this was occurring, Shepstone's Horse, attached to the Second Division, opened fire at a range of about 300 yards from outside the left rear of the square against the uMcijo, who were moving towards them in a great column. They then withdrew into the square – the rear face wheeling outwards to let them do so – and soon all the irregular horsemen were likewise within the position, a gap having been made for them.

At 8.45 a.m., the 9-pounders opened up, firing shrapnel over the heads of the retiring mounted men at the Zulus who were well within range, and within a short period the guns on all sides of the formation were in action. At this stage they were located just outside the square. As the Zulus were in skirmishing order, however, little punishment was inflicted – they kept on coming. The two Gatlings then opened fire, as did the infantry, who were in four ranks – the front two kneeling – discharging volleys. The right face of the square (i.e. the southernmost) was the first to be fully engaged, but at 8.50 a.m. fire from the position became general.

Despite the withering fire, the foremost Zulus bravely attempted to charge home, shouting 'uSuthu!' as they ran; but their ranks were decimated and the assault was checked when the warriors were still 70 yards or more from the square. On the other hand, when some 400 yards or more from the right face of the British formation and subjected to medium-range fire, the warriors charging against that face veered left up a depression that ran along the rear of the square, which gave them complete cover to within 150 yards or so of the right rear corner of the British formation.

Some 2000 to 3000 warriors, mostly iNgobamakhosi and uVe, massed in the depression before surging forward, some of them coming as close as nine paces from the square. In general, however, the rush was checked within 30 yards of the corner, as the British in this sector discharged 'a solid and well directed' weight of fire – including seven rounds of case-shot by the 9-pounders of N/6 Battery. A British officer, Captain Slade, later admitted in a letter to his mother that the gallant endeavours of the Zulus to reach the square were something to be marvelled at. The Zulu dead, recalled a corporal of the 58th, 'fell as though they had been tipped out of carts'.

The uMcijo, in contrast, did not subject the left rear corner of the British square to anything like as much pressure. Most of them halted on a ridge when still some 300 yards from the enemy.

The assault against the British left face, on the other hand, was undertaken with such determination that the British expected hand-to-hand fighting to occur and so fixed bayonets. But here, too, as elsewhere, the oncoming warriors were brought to a halt. Like their thwarted colleagues, they took cover in the long grass from where many opened up with sustained and heavy return fire, which proved woefully ineffective.

Seeing that the attack had faltered, the main Zulu reserve, a few thousand strong and evidently composed of men belonging to older regiments, began heading towards the field of battle from oNdini, only to find themselves subjected to accurate shellfire by 9-pounders at the front of the square which forced them to retire. By 9.20 a.m., a general and disorderly withdrawal had commenced. Minutes later, Chelmsford turned to the commander of the 17th Lancers, Colonel Drury-Lowe, and said, 'Go at them, Lowe!' Five troops of the 17th Lancers and twenty-four men of the King's Dragoon Guards under Captain Brewster therefore rode out through an opening made for them, briefly dressed their ranks to the rear of the square, and charged, the Lancers yelling 'Death! Death!'

Some of the fleeing Zulus turned to fight, but the majority pelted towards the overlooking hills as fast as they could. The cavalry were soon assisted by the mounted men of the Flying Column, and the pursuit was conducted as far as the hills, where the Zulus began rallying on ground unsuitable for horses to operate. Wounded Zulus still on the plain or warriors hiding on it, such as in the long grass, were killed with bloodthirsty efficiency, especially by the Natal Native Horse and the NNC, and this continued for hours after the battle had ended. Most of the Zulus who had managed to make good their escape retreated over the hills to the north.

Chelmsford's casualties at Ulundi, as the battle became known to the British, were light: two officers and ten men killed, nineteen officers wounded (one of whom later died) and sixty-nine men wounded. Although disputed, for there was no body-count of the dead following the battle, Zulu losses were certainly much heavier. The official estimate of 'not less than 1500' seems reasonable.

It is sometimes said that the Zulu assault at Ulundi lacked commitment. Colonel Evelyn Wood, for instance, declared in his memoirs that he 'could not believe [the Zulus] would make so half-hearted an attack'. Perhaps he was being somewhat disingenuous, wishing to play down Chelmsford's victory whilst magnifying his own at Khambula; but other veterans of previous battles expressed comparable sentiments, as did some Zulus. For example, in a book by Charles Norris-Newman (published in 1880), Mehlokazulu kaSihayo is quoted as saying that the Zulus did not fight with 'the same spirit' at Ulundi as hitherto 'because [they] were ... frightened'.

That their previous experiences at Khambula and elsewhere had shaken the Zulus' morale, and made many of them reluctant to face British fire-power again, need not be doubted. Nevertheless, many of Cetshwayo's warriors fought with great bravery. Colonel W. A. Dunne, for example, while noting that the Zulus were no longer willing to fight with reckless daring, commented that their courage was conspicuous. In short, as Laband comments:

> There is overwhelming evidence to show that in the initial stages of the battle, before the hopelessness of their task overcame them, the Zulu came on with enormous pluck.... Indeed, many of the British were simply astonished at the 'amazing courage' of the Zulu, who repeatedly and unflinchingly attempted to charge through the withering fire.

Some question whether the British fire was truly withering. The infantry fired approximately 35,000 rounds at Ulundi, and rounds fired were calculated at between 6.4 and 7 per infantryman, depending on his unit: hence the contention that the rate of fire was low, suggesting that the Zulus were easily repelled. But the rate was in fact slightly higher than it had been at Gingindlovu (where the average number of shots fired per regular soldier was 6.2); and as Colonel Callwell noted in his official manual on the conduct of 'small wars', such as the Zulu War, in a typical battle, under ten rounds per man was the norm.

The battle of Ulundi fatally undermined Cetshwayo's already waning authority and rendered Zululand prostrate before the British. On 6 July, in the letter referred to above, Captain Slade voiced the general opinion of the victors when he wrote, 'We all felt at last that the power of the Zulus had been destroyed.' Without doubt it was a sentiment shared by many of the vanquished – an era had passed.

The capture of Cetshwayo

After the battle, the bulk of the victorious force moved to the Mbilane stream where the men rested and had dinner, while their colleagues still scoured the plain, flushing out concealed Zulus and destroying *amakhanda*. oNdini itself was put to the torch at 11.40 a.m., shortly after the square had set off for the Mbilane. During the course of the afternoon, the British returned to their encampment beside the White Mfolozi.

Cetshwayo, on the other hand, soon received word of his army's defeat and fled north across the Black Mfolozi to one of Mnyamana's homesteads in northern Zululand, where he arrived three days after Ulundi. By this date, Chelmsford and his men had returned to the Mthon-janeni Heights where, owing to bad weather, they remained for several days before withdrawing.

During this time, on 16 July, Chelmsford met Wolseley and the First Division roughly midway between Mthonjaneni and the coast. Chelms-ford then said farewell to his men, rode on to Durban, and sailed for England.

Wolseley had been advised by Sir Henry Bulwer to do all he could to convince the Zulu nation that 'we desire nothing from them but a proper security for peace [and] that we do not desire any portion of their territory; that our quarrel was with the King, and not with them.' The apprehension of Cetshwayo was thus central to Wolseley's task of bringing about the 'settlement' of the Zulu question.

It was not long before Wolseley heard reports that Cetshwayo was gathering armed men in northern Zululand. So he decided to reoccupy oNdini with units that had belonged to the First Division and direct oper-ations from there. He made oNdini his headquarters on 10 August, by which time many chiefs had submitted, and the hunt for Cetshwayo commenced with patrols being sent north of the Black Mfolozi.

On the 14th, a party of chiefs and indunas headed by Mnyamana arrived at oNdini, bringing a large number of cattle on the king's instruc-tions. Their object was to intercede on Cetshwayo's behalf, 'We had gone,' recalled Ntshingwayo, 'simply to ask for his head, that he might live and not perish', and continue residing in Zululand. Wolseley assured them that Cetshwayo would not be executed – his continued residence in Zululand was another matter.

Wolseley kept Mnyamana and four other senior members of the party at his camp, and continued to hunt down Cetshwayo, who moved to more inaccessible terrain and from homestead to homestead to elude patrols, his support increasingly ebbing away.

On 20 August Wolseley gave orders to 'burn Kraals & carry off cattle where the King is known to be & to be concealed by the inhabitants'. Furthermore, torture was employed to induce Zulus to betray his where-abouts. For instance, Chief Mbopha kaWolizibi, a royal favourite, was kicked to the ground and burned with firebrands in a futile attempt to extract such information.

Cetshwayo's freedom ended early on 28 August when he was surrounded in a homestead on the fringe of the Ngome Forest, together with a number of his followers. That night – while being taken to Wolseley's camp at oNdini – two of the king's companions were allowed to return home on the grounds that they had not been members of the royal entourage. They took with them secret instructions ordering Mahubulwana kaDumisela of the Qulusi to disband his men, who were still under arms in the north-west where they had clashed with troops charged with pacifying the area.

Cetshwayo arrived by cart at oNdini on the 31st, where he was told that he had been officially deposed as Zulu king for having violated his 'coronation vows', and that he was to be sent into exile and his kingdom split into independent chiefdoms. The following day the distraught Cetshwayo was escorted towards Port Durnford (on the coast above the Umlalazi River) and, on 4 September, sailed for Cape Town, where he was to be confined in the castle.

Three days earlier, Wolseley had assembled prominent Zulus at oNdini to acquaint them with recent events and explain to them the pattern of their future.

CHAPTER 7

CIVIL WAR AND REBELLION

'The rule of the House of Chaka is a thing of the past ... it is like water spilt on the ground.' *Sir Arthur Havelock*

On the afternoon of 1 September 1879, some 200 Zulus were assembled at oNdini, and through the services of John Shepstone – who acted as Wolseley's interpreter – they were told that Cetshwayo had been sent into permanent exile. Furthermore, they heard details of how Zululand was now to be governed, for over the course of the previous weeks Wolseley had devised a settlement scheme after receiving advice from various sources, most notably Sir Theophilus Shepstone and John Dunn. Henceforth Zululand was to be ruled by thirteen independent chiefs appointed by the British. Moreover, a British Resident was to be appointed to serve as the 'eyes and ears' of the British government: he would not involve himself in the internal affairs of the chiefdoms unless the chiefs violated the terms of their appointment.

The appointed chiefs then signed separate treaties, which contained clauses that bound them to respect their new boundaries, to abolish the Zulu military system, and not to hinder any of their people from working in neighbouring territories.

On 3 September, Wolseley reported to Hicks Beach:

In the redistribution of territory ... I have given a place to the representatives [of the clans subjugated by Shaka] who, though to a large extent amalgamated ... with the Zulus, are I am assured, mindful of their ... independent origin, and proud of their distinct traditions. Such breaking up of the cohesion of the country will, I firmly believe, preclude for the future all, or almost all, possibility of any reunion of its inhabitants under one rule.

In the event, however, most of the appointees did not reflect the pre-Shakan system. Dunn is the most conspicuous example. He had secured Wolseley's admiration and was thus granted the largest chieftainship, located between the Mhlatuze and Tugela Rivers and comprising about one-fifth of the former kingdom. Wolseley viewed it as a buffer-zone. Another appointee was likewise an alien. This was Hlubi, a Sotho who had distinguished himself on the British side during the recent war. He was granted a chiefdom along the border in the west, consisting of the area hitherto dominated by Sihayo. Two members of the Zulu royal house, Hamu, the chief of the Ngenetsheni, and Zibhebhu kaMaphitha, the chief of the Mandlakazi, were similarly chosen. They were granted territory north of the Black Mfolozi. Mnyamana, most of whose adherents had been assigned to Hamu's territory, was also offered a chiefdom but declined to accept it partly because he did not wish to be split from his people. It was therefore granted to Ntshingwayo.

The boundaries of the chiefdoms, and the borders of Zululand itself, were determined by a boundary commission established by Wolseley. The general had promised the Zulus that they would be left in full possession of their land but this proved not to be the case, for Zululand was reduced in size. For instance, the commission moved the western border with the Transvaal eastward, in contravention of the findings of the 1878 boundary commission, thereby excluding people who had long been viewed as part of the Zulu nation.

Wolseley's settlement was flawed in other respects. It took little or no account of the existing state of affairs in Zululand. Members of groups with long-standing antipathy for one another, for example, found themselves as a single entity under the same appointed chief. Wolseley instructed the boundary commission to declare that Zulus owing allegiance to a chief whom they viewed as unacceptable should simply move to that of another they deemed more agreeable; but this was both impractical and insensitive. For one thing, strong emotional and religious links bound Zulus to their ancestral territories which they were loath to leave. Another problem with the settlement was that throughout Zululand there were men of great status and authority who were excluded by it, and whose position and power were now undermined by the appointment of rivals.

It was not just in Zululand that the settlement had its critics. Natal's white community, for example, was far from happy. Residents vociferously maintained that Zululand should have been annexed and opened up to white settlement, or that arrangements should be made to ease the colony's land shortage by transferring blacks from Natal to Cetshwayo's former kingdom.

Sir Theophilus Shepstone, who had been asked to comment on Wolseley's settlement plan and who naturally favoured annexation, was also condemnatory, writing, on 14 October:

We cannot rid ourselves of the responsibilities ... of the war ... by the simple device of practically leaving [the Zulus] to themselves, after we have taken away their head, and advising them not to hurt each other.

Nevertheless, Hicks Beach duly confirmed Wolseley's settlement, for as Jeff Guy has commented:

The British government, under attack for reckless expansionism, [did not believe] that direct control over Zululand was in Britain's interests [now that] the military strength of the Zulu had been terminated, and as long as the Zulu people remained divided and powerless, there was no need for Zululand to be included within the formal boundaries of the Empire; the Zulu served imperial interests sufficiently merely by occupying their territory, thereby blocking Boer expansion to the south-east, and possible foreign occupation of the coast.

Imperial policy, nevertheless, was to change. It would not be long before the Colonial Office would assume a stance more in line with the sentiments expressed by Shepstone and the settlement's other critics.

In March 1880, Melmoth Osborn, an experienced Natal civil servant and a close friend of Shepstone (whose outlook he shared), became the British Resident in Zululand, a post that had been briefly held by another Natal official. Osborn was to retain the position through the 1880s and was thus to play a central role in the affairs of Zululand. He was initially responsible to the High Commissioner, and later to the Governor of Natal, who was also the Special Commissioner for Zululand; and they in turn were directly responsible to the Secretary of State for the Colonies. With the exception of Wolseley, who left South Africa in April 1880, the high commissioners and governors depended heavily on Shepstone for advice concerning Zululand. Moreover, until 1884, the Acting Secretary for Native Affairs was Shepstone's brother, John, who was succeeded by Theophilus's son, Henrique. They, too, exerted influence on the Special Commissioner for Zululand, who consequently tended to incline towards the colonial point of view concerning Zulu affairs, an attitude that led to conflict with London.

Meanwhile, during the course of September 1879, Wolseley and the remaining British troops left Zululand. Hamu, Zibhebhu and Dunn promptly set to work exploiting their new status and augmenting their wealth, for they were avaricious and ambitious men. Hamu's people, for instance, are said to have looted the property of fellow Zulus, while one of the steps taken by Dunn was to demand a £25 licence fee from any trader wishing to enter his territory.

Most of the Zulu royal family were living in the region north of the Black Mfolozi granted to Hamu and Zibhebhu by the settlement. As a result of the war and Wolseley's plan for the future administration of Zululand, their status was greatly diminished; and salt was now rubbed into the wound when the chiefs began to round up their cattle, seize other property and impose fines on them for not having handed it over voluntarily. The seizure of the royal cattle was in accord with the wishes of Wolseley,

Utimuni, a nephew of Shaka, by George Angas (MuseumAfrica)

Above: *Mpande reviewing his warriors at Nodwengu*, by George Angas. (MuseumAfrica)
Below: A Zulu chief and his Indunas in the 1860s. (MuseumAfrica)

Above: *Isandlwana, The Graphic*, 15 March 1879. (Philip J. Haythornthwaite)
Below: *Lieutenant Coghill at bay beside the body of Lieutenant Melvill*, by C. E. Fripps. (MuseumAfrica)
Top right: Rorke's Drift, looking west towards the burning hospital. Print after H. Dupray. (Philip J. Haythornthwaite)
Bottom right: *The 1/13th and scouts of the Natal Native Horse on the march*, by Orlando Norie. (Somerset Military Museum Trust)

Above: *Major Hackett and his men driving back Zulus at Khambula*, by Orlando Norie. (Somerset Military Museum Trust)

Left: Lieutenant Colonel Northey, 60th, who was killed at Gingindlovu. (Philip Haythornthwaite)

Top right: Reconnaissance: 17th Lancers and local forces. (Philip Haythornthwaite)

Right: *The Battle of Ulundi*, by Orlando Norie. (Somerset Military Museum Trust)

Left: *17th Lancers at Ulundi.* Print after H. Dupray. (Philip Haythornthwaite)

Below: Surrender of Cetshwayo. (Philip Haythornthwaite)

Right: *Mzilikazi in the 1830s*, a sketch by William Cornwallis Harris. (MuseumAfrica)

Left: *A Matabele warrior in the 1830s*, by William Cornwallis Harris. (MuseumAfrica)

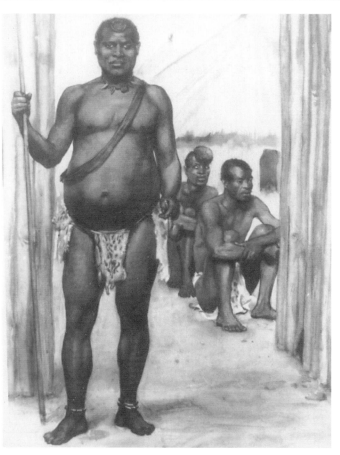

Left: *The Battle of Vechtkop,* by Heinrich Egersdörfer. (MuseumAfrica)

Opposite page, bottom: *Lobengula,* by Ralph Peacock and based on a sketch by E. A. Maund. (National Archives of Zimbabwe)

Right: Matabele spearheads and battleaxe, c.1880. (National Archives of Zimbabwe)

Below: Members of the Pioneer Column crossing the Tuli River in 1890, from the *Graphic,* 28 February 1891. (National Archives of Zimbabwe)

Frederick Courtney Selous. (National Archives of Zimbabwe)

Above: A Matabele warrior in the 1890s wearing an unusual black ostrich feather headdress. (National Archives of Zimbabwe)
Above right: A young Matabele warrior in the 1890s. (National Archives of Zimbabwe)
Below: Matabele attacking a laager during the Matabele War.

Opposite page, top: Major Allan Wilson. (National Archives of Zimbabwe)
Left: The last stand of Major Allan Wilson's patrol. (National Archives of Zimbabwe)
Above: Depiction of fighting near Gwelo on 9 May 1896 during the Matabele Rebellion. (National Archives of Zimbabwe)

Above: *Matabele on the warpath in 1896*, by S. L. Wood and based on a sketch by Major Baden-Powell. (National Archives of Zimbabwe)

Below: Sikombo's stronghold: the cross near the summit of the kopje indicates the spot where Major Kershaw was killed on 5 August 1896. (National Archives of Zimbabwe)

who had ordered Osborn to encourage the rounding up of livestock. But as Shula Marks comments, the policy 'of confiscating the royal herd was particularly misguided, as most of the cattle in the hands of the uSuthu [supporters of the royal house] was royal cattle that had been "sisa-ed" [lent] to them and from which they drew their sustenance.'

After the battle of Ulundi, Cetshwayo had placed his heir, Dinuzulu (who had been born in 1868), in the care of Zibhebhu. But the boy quickly developed a strong aversion to Zibhebhu, who, to use the words of one of James Stuart's informants, Mpatshana kaSodondo, wished 'to set himself up as practically king in place of Cetshwayo'. Dinuzulu therefore managed to escape and came under the protection of one of Cetshwayo's full-brothers, Ndabuko, a rather morbid but tenacious individual whose homesteads were located in the territory assigned to Zibhebhu by Wolseley's settlement.

Rising tension

Tension mounted between Zibhebhu and Hamu on the one hand, and Ndabuko and fellow members of the uSuthu faction. The former pair, as beneficiaries of Wolseley's settlement, were confident and assertive, and resolute to retain their ascendancy. Ndabuko and his associates, angered by their loss of status and influence and by the high-handed behaviour of Zibhebhu and Hamu, were equally determined to uphold their own authority and promote their personal interests, as well as those of their exiled king and Dinuzulu.

The uSuthu faction sent two messengers south to the residence of the Bishop of Natal, John Colenso, at Bishopstowe just outside Pietermaritzburg. The bishop was sympathetic to the plight of the Zulu nation, which he believed – and it was an unfashionable belief in white colonial circles – to be the victim of an iniquitous war and an unjust settlement.

On 9 February 1880, the messengers arrived to announce that they had been sent by an impressive array of notables, including Ndabuko, three of his brothers and Mnyamana. Zibhebhu was oppressing the house of Mpande and seemed intent on destroying Cetshwayo's family. The messengers asked Colenso if he thought it possible for them to request that Mpande's children be freed from such pressure by being allowed to occupy a territory of their own. Colenso suggested that they visit the Acting Secretary for Native Affairs, John Shepstone, and sent a letter of introduction to him on their behalf.

The next day the messengers met Shepstone, who informed them that the house of Cetshwayo had been destroyed, that it was out of the question that Ndabuko would receive any official recognition, and that any complaints against appointed chiefs should be made to the British Resident in Zululand.

Meanwhile, events far from South Africa were to fill Colenso with optimism that the lot of the Zulu nation could be improved. In April 1880, Disraeli and the Conservatives were ousted from power by Gladstone and the Liberals, partly as a result of a backlash in Britain against the Zulu War. On 24 April Colenso wrote enthusiastically:

> Now ... something will be done, I presume, to rectify the enormous wrongs of the Zulu War & (so-called) Settlement.... The heart of England, I trust, is still beating rightly, & will expect that ... the Liberals ... shall do what can be done under existing circumstances to rectify the past.

A week later, Ndabuko appeared before Osborn and requested permission to visit the Governor of Natal to pay his respects. He received authorisation, and with Shingana kaMpande (one of Cetshwayo's half-brothers and the second most senior figure in the uSuthu party) proceeded to lead more than 200 men into Natal, including twenty men of rank, most of whom came from the chiefdoms of Hamu and Zibhebhu.

The arrival in the colony of the deputation under Ndabuko at this juncture may have been entirely coincidental, but it has been plausibly suggested that the uSuthu had received word from Colenso of Gladstone's victory and that circumstances were thus more favourable for petitioning Cetshwayo's return.

In Pietermaritzburg, the Zulus had two frustrating meetings with officialdom, failing to obtain their objectives, and began to traipse home on 5 June. Yet their long trek had not been entirely futile. They had gained the firm support of the Colenso family and had learned from them that Britain had not sought war with the Zulus, and that the conflict had been brought about through the actions of officials in South Africa.

Well aware that they enjoyed official sanction, Zibhebhu and Hamu continued their high-handed activities. Indeed, as 1880 progressed, they became increasingly belligerent towards the uSuthu in their chiefdoms.

For his part, Ndabuko sent messengers secretly to Colenso. Consequently, on 3 December, the bishop (who had just visited Cetshwayo at Cape Town for the first time), wrote to F. W. Chesson, Secretary of the Aborigines' Protection Society, stating, 'It is clear that an unpleasant state of things exists in Zululand that some day or other may end in fighting & revolution.'

By late 1880, the situation was such that Osborn felt compelled to intervene after many of Mnyamana's Buthelezi had been forced to flee their homesteads, following an attack by Hamu. Osborn told Hamu and Mnyamana that he would investigate matters and pass his findings to the High

Commissioner for a decision, ordering Hamu 'to stop seizing cattle and property' while the inquiry was underway. He adopted the same approach with Zibhebhu, who had fined many uSuthu in his district, and with Ndabuko and Ziwedu (a son of Mpande). Osborn had thus raised the hopes of the supporters of the Zulu royal house. Perhaps at last their grievances would be dealt with seriously.

The inquiries appear to have been conducted in December 1880 and January 1881. The uSuthu went into great detail in presenting their evidence to Osborn. Ndabuko and Ziwedu, for instance, brought 60 witnesses to testify against Zibhebhu, whom they accused, among other things, of seizing 1140 head of cattle, mostly on the grounds that they were royal livestock. Zibhebhu responded bluntly: 'I am Chief of my territory and give notice plainly here today, as these people are in arms against me ... I will drive them out of my territory, I will eat them up.'

In April 1881, Osborn met Sir Evelyn Wood, the newly appointed Governor of Natal, to discuss the situation in Zululand. As a result, Wood sought authorisation from London for Osborn to 'inquire judicially' into matters. This was duly granted, although of course Osborn had already acted of his own volition.

It would be a mistake to conclude that Osborn's stance was impartial. His sympathies were with the two appointed chiefs. Indeed, he informed Wood, at their meeting, that when the time came to announce the findings Wood should 'support Usibebu and give modified support to Uhamu'. Moreover, on 1 June, Osborn sent word to the High Commissioner that certain Zulus in the northern districts were becoming defiant as a result of the actions of uSuthu leaders. He recommended that when Wood announced the conclusions of the inquiries, Ndabuko and Ziwedu should be forced from their homes and ordered to move to Dunn's southern chiefdom.

On 31 August, the moment the uSuthu leaders had been expectantly awaiting finally came. They formed part of a large gathering that assembled at Osborn's residence at Nhlazatshe to hear what had been concluded following their complaints. Wood arrived with Redvers Buller (now a general) and an escort consisting of squadrons of the 14th and 15th Hussars, as well as a military band.

The high hopes of the uSuthu soon turned to despair. Ndabuko, Ziwedu and Dinuzulu were informed that they had to leave their kraals and move to the territory of Dunn. Moreover, although Mnyamana was told that Hamu would have to return some of the cattle that had been taken from him, he was likewise treated curtly.

The meeting raised the political temperature. The uSuthu felt humiliated and betrayed – justice had not been done. Violence resulted. Within a couple of days of the assembly, clashes occurred when Zibhebhu's forces moved against Ndabuko's people. Together with Ziwedu's followers, they fled across the Vuna River to Mnyamana, who gave them sanctuary.

Shortly thereafter, skirmishes ensued between Hamu and the fiercely royalist Qulusi, and on 1 October Hamu gave orders for the Qulusi to be driven from his territory. Early on the morning of the 2nd, Hamu's impi, which numbered about 3200 warriors supported by a band of mounted men with rifles, clashed with the Qulusi, whom they greatly outnumbered. For a while Hamu's men were held at bay, but when the horsemen intervened, the 1000 or so Qulusi broke and, as they fled, most of them were cut down.

Northern Zululand seemed to be sliding inexorably into full-scale civil war. On 7 October, Osborn informed Wood that the 'country from within a mile or two of [Nhlazatshe] right on, is in such a disturbed state, that even native messengers have to make large circuits round to avoid contact with those within the pale of disturbance'.

Yet all-out conflict did not materialise, for neither side evidently wished the situation to degenerate that far. Instead of trying to bring about change through rebellion, the uSuthu leaders hoped that at last Cetshwayo would be allowed to return and play a role in the administration of his former kingdom.

Cetshwayo visits England

By this date the king had been a prisoner for two years, though no longer incarcerated in the castle at Cape Town. Early in 1881 he had been moved a short distance to Oude Moulen, a farm on the Cape Flats where he was not held in close confinement.

Since being exiled, Cetshwayo had impressed many of the people with whom he had come into contact by the nobility of his bearing and conduct, and had endeavoured to secure permission to return home. But although he enjoyed a significant degree of sympathy both in southern Africa and Britain, his requests had been turned down. Nonetheless, at Oude Moulen – where he enjoyed the services of a trusted young interpreter and secretary named Robert Samuelson – he spent much of his time continuing to seek a pardon by composing petitions and letters that were sent to people who could further his cause. He declared that the documents were 'now his only assegais'. On 2 May 1881, for instance, acting on a suggestion by Colenso, he formally requested that he be allowed to journey to England to state his case before Queen Victoria.

Subsequently, on 14 September, the Colonial Secretary, Lord Kimberley, sent a telegraph to the High Commissioner in South Africa, Sir Hercules Robinson, stating that 'Her Majesty's government was disposed to entertain [Cetshwayo's] request to visit England'.

Yet it was not until 12 July 1882 that Cetshwayo set sail for London, partly because the Governor of Natal, Sir Henry Bulwer, less sympathetic to the king, had persuaded Kimberley to postpone the visit. Nor was Bulwer enthusiastic, any more than were many Natal whites, at the idea of allowing Cetshwayo to return to Zululand. He believed that the requests of the uSuthu (notably from a large delegation which had arrived at Pietermaritzburg in April) that Cetshwayo should be allowed to do so did not represent the views of the Zulu nation as a whole.

Cetshwayo landed in England in early August, and in London found himself fêted and the subject of intense public interest. Cheering crowds, for example, gathered outside the Kensington house in which he was resident.

On 15 August – the day after Cetshwayo had visited Queen Victoria at Osborne House on the Isle of Wight – he met Kimberley and other senior figures. He was told that the government had 'determined to consider the possibility of making arrangements for his return to Zululand' on certain conditions. The foremost was that a portion of the country, to be defined by the government, would not be placed under his rule but would be reserved for other purposes. Cetshwayo found the condition objectionable. At another meeting two days later, the king (who suspected that the section of land in question was that which had been given to Dunn under the settlement) told Kimberley that the land which had belonged to his father 'is now very small ... and the idea of another piece ... being taken from that little country' had 'buried him up to his knees again'. On 1 September, Cetshwayo sailed for Cape Town to await the announcement of the details of the conditions under which he could return to Zululand.

This was conveyed to the former king at Cape Town on 7 December. Cetshwayo was shocked by what Sir Hercules Robinson told him, for the conditions differed from those mentioned in London. It had been decided that two vast tracts of territory would not be returned to him. One, consisting of the former chiefdoms granted to Dunn and Hlubi, was henceforth to be known as the Zulu Native Reserve, where Zulus unwilling to live under Cetshwayo could reside under a Resident Commissioner. Moreover, as recommended by Bulwer with Osborn's strong backing, Kimberley had accepted that Zibhebhu, unlike the rest of the chiefs appointed in 1879, should retain his chiefdom. The governor had a high opinion of Zibhebhu, who had told him that he could 'never come again' under Cetshwayo's rule, and believed that he would act as a 'check' on the king.

On 11 December, Cetshwayo reluctantly signed the conditions. Consequently, on 10 January 1883, he came ashore at Port Durnford and was met by Sir Theophilus Shepstone, who had been brought out of retirement to supervise the king's restoration to a tract of land between the Mhlatuze, the upper reaches of the Pongola, and the lower reaches of the Black

Mfolozi. Cetshwayo was then taken inland by Shepstone and a detachment of British soldiers up on to the Mthonjaneni Heights. The journey took a week.

On 29 January, Ndabuko, Ziwedu and Mnyamana arrived at the camp at Mthonjaneni, along with many other notable Zulus sympathetic to their king. That afternoon Cetshwayo was installed as the chief of the central territory, and during the proceedings he once again acknowledged, reluctantly, that he agreed to abide by the conditions he had first heard at Cape Town. Some 5000 to 6000 Zulus were present – to limit the number Shepstone had ordered that only married men should attend – and, in a planned protest that Cetshwayo and the uSuthu leaders had organised after his arrival on the coast, more than 40 individuals, including some of the leading men in the Zulu nation such as Mnyamana and Dabulamanzi, took it in turns to voice their grievances about the conditions under which their ruler had returned.

That evening, Shepstone, angered by what he had heard, left for Natal, leaving Henry Fynn, a son of the famous settler of the same name, to serve as Cetshwayo's new British Resident. Sir Theophilus subsequently sent a distorted report to London. For one thing, he maintained that almost all the inhabitants of the Zulu Native Reserve were pleased that they had not been placed under Cetshwayo.

After the installation ceremony, the king moved on to the Mahlabathini Plain, accompanied by his wives, attendants and a large number of supporters who included many men of the highest rank, with the aim of rebuilding oNdini.

Violence soon erupted. Shepstone had informed London that if this were to occur, Cetshwayo and his supporters would be responsible. But the deep-rooted antagonisms present in Zululand and the manner of the country's partition meant that future conflict was well-nigh inevitable. For instance, although Zibhebhu's borders had been modified, many uSuthu homesteads were still in his territory and this ensured the outbreak of clashes.

The situation was also tense in the Reserve. Here, much to the embarrassment of the authorities, it had become apparent even before the installation ceremony that there was much loyalty to Cetshwayo. The official stance was that the Zulus in question were reluctant to accept the authority of the Resident Commissioner, John Shepstone, because of uSuthu intimidation. Hence the Colonial Office, at Bulwer's request, sanctioned Shepstone to exercise 'paramount authority' in the Reserve and to impose a hut tax as an indication of white power. In February, Shepstone (who had been provided with a detachment of British troops) toured the Reserve to coerce chiefs and headmen into accepting his authority. Their choice was stark. Continued adherence to Cetshwayo would result in eviction while submission would enable them to retain possession of their lands.

The most serious violence since 1879 broke out in late March when Zibhebhu's forces plundered growing crops in an area that had just come under his authority as a result of the modified borders. The region in question was between the Mkuze and Pongola Rivers – staunch uSuthu country.

The battle of Msebe

This incident was the final straw. Ndabuko and other uSuthu leaders such as Mnyamana raised an impi to deal with Zibhebhu once and for all. The authorities would maintain that Cetshwayo was responsible for their actions. This is not certain. Cetshwayo asserted, probably correctly, that they acted on their own accord, for since his return to Zululand he had sent letters and petitions in the hope of redressing his grievances on the partition issue, without shedding blood.

The uSuthu eagerly gathered in the vicinity of Mnyamana's homesteads along the Sikhwebezi River on the afternoon of 28 March 1883. The impi numbered some 5000 warriors, significantly more than the force Zibhebhu could muster, which may not have exceeded 1500 men. The following day it set off. The army crossed the Vuna River, climbed the Nongoma Heights, and moved north-east until well within enemy territory. Adherents of Zibhebhu fled with their cattle, leaving behind their homesteads and grain stores which were burnt and plundered by the invaders. Late in the afternoon, the uSuthu halted and encamped.

The following morning, small groups of horsemen were sighted – some of Zibhebhu's men had been trained by a European to fight while mounted – and the uSuthu set off in pursuit. The horsemen fled towards the valley of the Msebe stream where Zibhebhu had laid an ambush. In the broken and eroded sides of the valley, his infantry were lying in wait. As the disorderly uSuthu swarmed into the valley, they were attacked by the concealed warriors, while Zibhebhu and his squad of horsemen, equipped with firearms, moved against the emGazini, who were on the left of the invading force. They broke, as did the Buthelezi, and soon the shaken uSuthu were in retreat, pursued by Zibhebhu's infantry, supported by rifle fire from his mounted troops who scattered any groups that endeavoured to rally.

As the uSuthu fled across the open ground, they suffered severe losses, with Zibhebhu himself, a skilled marksman, accounting for some of the dead. Eventually, as the day drew to a close, the survivors reached Nongoma, leaving scattered behind them the bodies of hundreds, indeed thousands, of their comrades. In his book, *The Story of the Zulus*, J. Y. Gibson, who worked in the vicinity several years later, commented that 'probably in no battle had the Zulus ever suffered greater loss of life'.

Among those who perished were five sons of Ndabuko and ten of Mnya-mana's. In contrast, only ten of Zibhebhu's followers were killed.

Word of what had happened reached Hamu that night, and he rose to arms. Many of his followers made their way towards the Black Mfolozi, attacking uSuthu en route. Other warriors headed north against Buthelezi living, or retiring in the direction of the Pongola. The uSuthu who had set out so confidently to deal with Zibhebhu had suffered an immense reverse. Thousands of their number had been killed, homesteads had been burnt, livestock seized and grain stores and growing crops destroyed, leaving many of them homeless and facing starvation.

The Buthelezi and other uSuthu from northern Zululand, such as the Qulusi, sought sanctuary in the Ngome Forest or in mountainous terrain such as the Hlobane range, while other fugitives quit Zululand or moved south towards oNdini or the Reserve. Hamu followed up his initial success by attacking them on a number of occasions, with the aim of dislodging them or seizing livestock. Then, in mid-April, the forces of Zibhebhu and Hamu swept through the northern districts once again, burning and plundering whatever had eluded them previously. On 30 April, an editorial in the *Natal Mercury* sang Zibhebhu's praises: he was the Napoleon of the North who was 'really fighting the battle of South Africa, and championing the cause of civilisation and order, in the stubborn and so far successful resistance he has offered to the hostility and intrigues of Cetshwayo.'

Following Msebe, Cetshwayo informed the authorities that he would no longer endeavour to abide by the conditions under which he had been allowed to return to Zululand. Moreover, he called upon Zulus to rally to his side, and from the end of April thousands of warriors could be seen at oNdini training and undergoing military ceremonies. Other uSuthu warriors were massed around Mnyamana's homesteads on the upper reaches of the Sikhwebezi.

The uSuthu leadership devised a strategy that they hoped would enable them to reverse the situation. Central to their plans was to ensure that Zibhebhu and Hamu, both of whom were receiving supplies of modern rifles and ammunition, could not launch a combined assault. It was decided to strike against Hamu first, before dealing with his more formidable ally. In early May, the uSuthu attacked. Hamu and his followers were thrown on to the defensive and forced to shelter in fortified caves, leaving their kraals and stock to be plundered. Nonetheless, things did not go all the uSuthus' way. They failed to dislodge their opponents from their fastnesses and, furthermore, suffered from retaliatory attacks and raids by the Ngenetsheni.

June proved a disappointing time for Cetshwayo. In the middle of the month, Mnyamana, whose warriors included men from oNdini, attempted

136

to finish off Hamu. However, Hamu's men – said to have been supported by about ten companies of Mandlakazi who had managed to make their way through the uSuthu cordon to assist their allies – inflicted such casualties on their opponents that the assault was abandoned. Then, as June drew to a close, Cetshwayo's half-brother Dabulamanzi attempted to relieve the pressure on Mnyamana by advancing from oNdini against Zibhebhu. But when Dabulamanzi's impi of three regiments was confronted by the armed force of the redoubtable chief, they refused to fight and withdrew.

It was now midwinter and both sides were eager to settle matters before preparing their lands for the spring rains. The uSuthu decided to concentrate their forces in a major offensive against Zibhebhu, compelling him to fight on several fronts against vastly superior numbers.

Zibhebhu attacks oNdini
Zibhebhu's intelligence network nevertheless alerted him to what was afoot and he prepared a counter-stroke. On 20 July (several days after a group of Buthelezi had raided his territory and killed a number of his supporters), he met with his allies in the south-west of his chiefdom. Some 3000 warriors were present, of whom about a quarter were followers of Hamu. That evening, Zibhebhu set off towards oNdini. After crossing the Black Mfolozi, he marched through the night and arrived around dawn on the low hills to the east of Cetshwayo's homestead.

The moment it was known that Zibhebhu was near at hand, oNdini was thrown into confusion and the disconcerted uSuthu hurriedly prepared to fight. As Cetshwayo himself was to recall, warriors began moving out to meet the oncoming enemy 'in a most disorganised state, they were only just awake, and in no state for fighting'. The uSuthu were soon running for their lives. 'There was no real fighting,' stated Cetshwayo, 'for my men at once began to run.' Most fled past oNdini before heading southward towards the White Mfolozi. They left behind them in the royal homestead Cetshwayo, his most senior officers, the women of the royal household, and a small number of warriors. Just in time, however, Cetshwayo was persuaded to flee. He escaped through a gate at the rear, mounted on a small horse led by Sihayo. oNdini was soon well alight.

The Mahlabathini Plain became a killing field. Fleeing uSuthu were cut down, including three of Cetshwayo's wives and his youngest son, who was speared in his mother's arms. The number who perished was high – though a number of the young warriors managed to escape – and many of those who died were men of rank, including Ntshingwayo and Sihayo. On 23 August, the British Resident, Fynn, was to send Bulwer a list of the names of 59 'important men' who had been slain. Moreover, when subsequently questioned on the matter, Cetshwayo (who had himself

137

had a narrow escape), was stopped after naming 52 such individuals. 'Every name I have given you,' he said, 'is that of a man of influence, a man with a following; men who say let it be so, Zulu, and it is so in accordance.' The heart had been ripped out of the uSuthu faction, signalling the end of an era.

History now repeated itself. The Mandlakazi and their allies plundered and burnt uSuthu territory, this time right up to the borders of the Reserve which sheltered most of the force that had fled from oNdini. Other uSuthu sought sanctuary elsewhere, in the Hlobane range, the Ngome Forest and the Transvaal. Cetshwayo himself, after hiding in a cave near the White Mfolozi, moved south into the Reserve. A few of his supporters then accompanied him into the Nkandla Forest, between the Mhlatuze and Tugela Rivers, and built him a homestead where he could shelter in nearby caves beside a waterfall.

From here Cetshwayo contacted the authorities, appealing for British intervention on his behalf. In response, Osborn – who had replaced John Shepstone as Resident Commissioner of the Reserve – demanded that the king place himself under his protection at Eshowe, where he had established his Residency. Initially Cetshwayo refused to do so. But on 15 October (as Hamu and Zibhebhu continued to kill his supporters) he arrived at Eshowe, realising that he needed the support of local officials if he were to protect his people or reassert himself in Zululand.

While Cetshwayo was at Eshowe, bloodshed persisted, although the uSuthu were not always the victims. On 14 December, for example, beside the Black Mfolozi, a band of uSuthu fell upon Mfanawendlela kaThangana (one of the chiefs appointed in 1879) and his followers and slaughtered them. The victorious uSuthu were led by two young members of the essentially new uSuthu leadership that had emerged after 21 July, Mankulumana kaSomaphunga of the Ndwandwe, a grandson of Zwide, and Ndabazimbi kaTokotoko, a relation of Zibhebhu.

In December 1883, Mnyamana appealed to the authorities to intervene, begging the government to establish order. Bulwer and Osborn were in favour of extending colonial rule over the whole of Zululand. Lord Derby, the Colonial Secretary, felt otherwise. When asked to consider establishing a protectorate he tartly replied: 'I don't want more niggers.'

On the afternoon of 8 February 1884, Cetshwayo died at Eshowe shortly after eating a meal. It was the view of the medical officer who examined the body that he had been killed by a heart attack. But Zulus present believed that he had been poisoned on Zibhebhu's instructions. 'The true cause of Cetshwayo's death must remain a matter of doubt,' comments Laband, 'though poisoning seems more than likely, especially since at much the same time [an] attempt was made on Mnyamana's life.' Although rendered very ill, Mnyamana pulled through, and together with

Ndabuko served as the official guardians of Cetshwayo's fifteen-year-old son, Dinuzulu.

Of Cetshwayo, Charles Ballard aptly comments:

> Cetshwayo's memory is still revered by the Zulu people. He is perhaps the most beloved of the Zulu monarchs. His entire life was devoted to maintaining the sovereignty and social system of the Zulu kingdom. His valiant stand against the British during the Anglo-Zulu War and his subsequent exile and successful campaign to be restored as king exemplifies the nobler human qualities of tolerance, statesmanship and courage.

When Cetshwayo died, the position of many uSuthu was truly desperate, and their suffering was to continue. In April, for instance, a trader described seeing Mnyamana's followers who were living in rocks and caves:

> They were in a most deplorable state, dying in dozens from deprivation and dysentery, children perishing at their mother's breast for want of nourishment, and each person covered with the itch and otherwise emaciated, and if nothing is done to relieve them before the winter sets in there will be scarcely a soul alive, for all their crops were then cut and trodden by [Zibhebhu's] forces.

The battle of Tshaneni

The tide, nevertheless, was soon to turn. Early in 1884 some of the new uSuthu leaders contacted a number of Boers living in the Transvaal and secured their support in return for the promise of land. uSuthu morale was therefore boosted in late April as word of a combined move against their enemies spread through the country.

At the beginning of May, a force of white volunteers, mostly Boers, entered Zululand from the Transvaal, accompanied by Dinuzulu, who had left the Nkandla Forest and made his way to the Transvaal in April. They established a laager in the north-west, whereupon Hamu and Zibhebhu withdrew to their strongholds. Yet not all the uSuthu welcomed Boer involvement. Mnyamana opposed the alliance and reportedly told the Boers, 'Go back to your homes. You have come to spoil our land.' However, he failed to persuade the majority of the uSuthu to fight on alone.

On 21 May, Dinuzulu was proclaimed king of the Zulus by the Boers, having been installed with traditional ritual the previous day by Ndabuko and other senior uSuthu. Two days later he is said to have put his mark on a document in which the Afrikaners bound themselves to restore 'peace, law and order' to Zululand in return for a parcel of land as large as they deemed necessary 'for establishing an independent self-government'.

Zibhebhu justly felt alarmed. Indeed, shortly after the entry of the Boers into Zululand, he appealed to Osborn, declaring that he now feared defeat and that he prayed that the English would help him. Consequently, on 6 May, Bulwer urged London to respond positively. Derby was told that if Zibhebhu were attacked by the Boers and uSuthu, he would be destroyed and that such a fate would not only be 'wholly undeserved', but would also result in 'the greatest misfortune to the Zulu country. A great portion of the country will pass away from the Zulu people, and the remainder, with the exception of the Reserve, will, under the [Zulu royal dynasty] come sooner or later under the domination of the Boers.' But the British government reacted negatively. In May, Gladstone declared in the House of Commons that military intervention would not occur outside the Reserve.

As May drew to a close, the Boer–uSuthu force moved against Zibhebhu. The chief of the Mandlakazi was well and truly at bay and decided on flight. With his people, he moved east down into thorn country, heading for Tshaneni where the Mkuze River makes its way through a narrow gap in the Lubombo Mountains. Zibhebhu's warriors, numbering some 3000, took up a position here in bush on the southern side of the river – terrain where the Boers would find it difficult to operate on horseback. The women, children and elderly were hidden among caves, boulders and bushes on the far bank.

Battle was joined on 5 June. At about 4 p.m., the uSuthu – perhaps 6000 strong – arrived on the scene with their 120 or so Boer allies. The uSuthu attacked, using the chest and horns formation. Initially it seemed that the Mandlakazi might prevail, but supporting fire from the Boers proved telling, and Zibhebhu's warriors were forced back; the majority of their losses occurred as they endeavoured to cross to the northern bank.

Zibhebhu managed to escape, and from high ground looked down on the battle site where the victors were rounding up tens of thousands of Mandlakazi cattle and driving the non-combatants from their places of refuge. He remarked to one of his men, John Eckersley, a white trader and mercenary: 'I have had my day ... but oh, my poor children.'

Following his defeat, Zibhebhu made his way to Eshowe in a last-ditch attempt to gain British assistance. On 13 June he told Osborn, 'All our cattle and property have been taken from us, and the people have nothing to subsist on.'

Three days later, Bulwer informed Derby that it was 'impossible to regard without feelings of the greatest pain and concern' the downfall of loyal Zibhebhu who had demonstrated that he had 'as chivalrous and

140

gallant a nature as the history of the Zulu nation can show'. The Secretary of State was less moved and told Bulwer that as the British had never pledged to assist the Mandlakazi chief militarily, all he was entitled to was asylum.

In September, Zibhebhu duly appeared in the Reserve with about 5000 of his people. General Smyth, who witnessed their arrival, reported:

> The men were as lean as greyhounds; sleeping mats and blankets on their heads; all fully armed with assegais and shields, but with few guns; the women with enormous loads on their heads, weary and tired; children of all ages to the infant at the back. They had also a great many cattle. How such a host could have managed to pass through a large extent of hostile territory unmolested is a mystery.

By this date, traders were settling in the Reserve and gold prospectors were beginning to exploit the gold-bearing strata in the Tugela Valley and elsewhere. More significant, though, was white settlement in northern Zululand where the band of Boers who had fought alongside the uSuthu had been joined by fellow land-hungry Afrikaners and by a hotchpotch of colonial speculators and adventurers.

On 16 August 1884, Dinuzulu had reluctantly put his mark to a proclamation that awarded the Boers 2,710,000 acres and the right to establish an independent republic. Furthermore, he conceded that the remaining portion of Zululand north of the Reserve, and its inhabitants, would be subject to the new Boer state. 'This was the worst, the most debasing moment ever suffered by the Zulu people,' comments Laband.

The boundaries of the New Republic, as it was called, were broad. Indeed, Natal officials estimated that five-sixths of Zulu territory outside the Reserve was declared part of the republic. London thus responded by formally warning the Boers in January 1886 that their claim to such a large slice of territory in the region was prejudicial to British interests. As a result, the Boers vented their anger on the uSuthu, who had appealed for British intervention. Furthermore, fines were imposed on leading uSuthu and hostages were taken. Hence the uSuthu again appealed for help. In February, messengers were sent to Osborn imploring the British 'to come at once' and save them, 'the Queen's people and land from the Boers'.

In March, Sir Arthur Havelock, who had recently taken over from Bulwer as governor, told the uSuthu that the British government would perhaps bring about an agreement with the New Republicans in which 'a portion of land' might be secured for the Zulus and that if it did so they should be grateful.

Later in the year, an agreement was reached between the British and the Boers. The latter did well in the negotiations, at the expense of the Zulus.

True, the Boers dropped their claim to a protectorate over Dinuzulu. Nevertheless, the Zulus lost a very high proportion of their best lands – most of the highland grazing and the important mixed veld in the upper reaches of the principal river systems. Much of what was left to them was tsetse territory where malaria was endemic.

Then, on 19 May 1887, the lands granted to the Zulus were joined with the Zulu Native Reserve, both areas henceforth to be known as the British Colony of Zululand. Revenue would be raised by a hut tax which, as noted above, had hitherto only been raised in the Reserve. The Governor of Natal was given the additional responsibility of serving as governor of the new crown colony. In November 1887, Havelock visited Zululand and told the uSuthu leaders:

> The rule of the House of Chaka is a thing of the past... It is like water spilt on the ground. The Queen rules now in Zululand and no one else... It is to save the Zulus from the misery that must fall upon them if they were left to themselves that the Queen has assumed the Government of the country.

But this was not all. Havelock announced that Zibhebhu should be permitted to return to his 'old tribal lands'.

Within a fortnight, Zibhebhu was homeward bound, and it was soon reported that he was taking possession of his former land by force, expelling uSuthu from their homesteads. Consequently, on 23 June 1888, between 3000 and 4000 uSuthu under Dinuzulu (who was now viewed by the authorities as merely a chief) surprised and routed Zibhebhu and his outnumbered followers in northern Zululand on the Nongoma Heights near Ivuna, the headquarters of a magistrate whose partisanship of Zibhebhu had angered Dinuzulu. Zibhebhu fled and was to live near Eshowe for a number of years before returning to his hereditary territory, where he died in 1905.

Following the battle, the British moved to quell growing resistance and, on 2 July 1888, a force consisting of regular soldiers, Zulu policemen and black levies defeated an uSuthu force under Shingana at Hlophekhulu Mountain near oNdini. Resistance began to collapse. Ndabuko surrendered to the colonial police, while Shingana and Dinuzulu fled to the Transvaal. They soon returned to Zululand, however, where Shingana was arrested. Dinuzulu instead made for Natal to surrender himself to the authorities. In 1889 the three men were tried for high treason, sentenced to long terms of imprisonment and exiled to St Helena. Here Dinuzulu was to learn to read and write and to play the piano tolerably well. Moreover, he sported European clothing, including military uniforms, and fathered several children (by two women he had been allowed to take into exile with him),

142

including his future successor, who was given the biblical name of Solomon.

Dinuzulu left behind a land that was to suffer in the 1890s from unprecedented and devastating crop failures due to drought and swarms of locusts; and in 1897, the extremely virulent cattle disease, rinderpest, virtually annihilated Zulu herds. Smallpox, introduced from the newly discovered gold mines of the Witwatersrand in the Transvaal, where Zulus had sought employment, wrought additional suffering.

A substantial number of Zulus worked in the mines. In fact, in 1894, Zululand was said to be one of their principal sources of native labour. Yet Zulu labourers were attracted not only to the Transvaal, but also to Natal and the diamond fields of Kimberley.

In 1897, Zululand was formally incorporated into Natal, which had been granted self-government in 1893, and in the following year Dinuzulu, Ndabuko and Shingana were permitted to return from exile. However, the government – in contrast to most Zulus – only recognised Dinuzulu as one of its indunas, from whom it could seek advice on matters of Zulu custom. He was also to be the chief of uSuthu Locations Nos. 1 and 2, small tracts of land beyond the Black Mfolozi.

One of the main reasons for incorporating Zululand into Natal was in order to open it up to further white settlement. Consequently, in 1904, the Zululand Delimitation Commission recommended that 2,613,000 acres (40.2 per cent) of the land should be set aside for white ownership and exploitation. Hence the territory occupied by Zulus living to the north of the Tugela was reduced to just 3,887,000 acres. As Stephen Taylor comments:

> The Zulus were watching the extinction of their pastoralist heritage. After locusts, drought and disease, they were now being squeezed between wattle and sugar plantations arising suddenly on the coast, and the white farmers' herds that roamed the hills of the north.

The 1906 rebellion

Further cause for dismay came in August 1905. This witnessed the passing of a bill at Pietermaritzburg imposing a poll tax of £1 on every adult male not already paying the hut tax: a measure intended to enhance the government's revenue by drawing young men who had hitherto eluded paying taxation into the colony's revenue net. However, as Shula Marks comments:

> Although married men who paid the Hut Tax were exempt from the Poll Tax it was the younger men who provided the money for their fathers' tax. The kraalhead was responsible for the paying of the tax,

but it was levied on all huts in his kraal, including those of bachelors, unmarried girls and widows.

Inevitably, then, and especially in view of the general impoverishment of blacks, largely due to natural disasters (which had continued into the early twentieth century), the passing of the poll tax was widely viewed by Africans as oppressive.

For some, it was the final straw. Late 1905 witnessed mounting tension not just among Zulus in Zululand, but among other Zulus and Africans living south of the Tugela. This included individuals who had espoused Christianity, the number of Zulu converts having become fairly substantial in the last decade of the nineteenth century. Small-scale violence erupted below the Tugela in February 1906, and soon occurred in Zululand itself under the leadership of Chief Bambatha of the Zondi clan. The chief, who was in his mid-40s, lived in a spectacular valley on the Natal side of the Tugela. He crossed the river in March to consult with Dinuzulu at the latter's homestead at Nongoma after hearing that police had been sent to arrest him following his refusal to pay the tax.

Secretly, perhaps, Dinuzulu found the idea of revolt appealing; and although he told Bambatha that he would not countenance rebellion, he did nonetheless allow the chief to leave his family at the royal homestead. Bambatha, presumably encouraged by what he took as tacit approval, made his way back to Natal, gathered his warriors and attacked a police patrol on 5 April, killing four of its members. He then crossed into Zululand, withdrew into the difficult terrain of the Nkandla and sent out appeals to other chiefs for support. One of those who responded was Sigananda kaSokufa of the Chube, who was in his late 90s and a stalwart supporter of the Zulu royal house.

In response, Colonel Duncan McKenzie and the newly formed Zululand Field Force – which was soon to number over 4000 whites and was assisted by some 3000 African levies – was sent against Bambatha and his associates. On 5 May, while descending Bobe Ridge, a contingent of troops came under attack from about 1000 rebels who were wearing a distinctive badge, a stiff piece of white cowhide or cowtail worn upright on the headdress, which the uSuthu had used in the 1880s. The warriors burst out from behind cover and charged. Some had guns, but most were armed with spears and small shields. Bambatha's witchdoctors had said that the troops' bullets would turn to water. The transformation failed to happen, and the Zulus were driven off with heavy loss.

The rebellion dragged on, however, and for several weeks McKenzie scoured the countryside, hunting down the rebels who were essentially conducting guerrilla warfare. The decisive battle, which McKenzie was itching for, finally came on 10 June after he had received reports that several rebel impis, including Bambatha's, were converging on Sigananda's stronghold, the deep and narrow Mome Gorge in Nkandla, and were encamped at the entrance. McKenzie promptly issued orders for his own scattered forces to advance towards the gorge.

The Zulus were in a relaxed mood and their sentries failed to notice McKenzie's approach. Hence, at dawn, the rebels, who perhaps numbered 1500, found themselves overlooked by soldiers on the surrounding heights. Immediately, the Zulus formed into a circle to receive instructions, whereupon the troops opened fire. In addition to normal firearms, McKenzie's force had 15-pounder artillery and Colt machine-guns. They caused devastation. Zulus were cut down in large numbers as shot and shell tore into them from all sides. Desperately, the survivors dashed into the gorge, which for many was to prove a fatal trap, and for several hours the soldiers added to the death toll. They then descended, and flushed out survivors. Officially, it was said that 600 rebels had been killed. Bambatha was said to be among the slain, having died in a mêlée with Natal levies at the bottom of the gorge. It was some days before his body was recognised. The head was then cut off and taken to Natal as proof of his demise. (In the 1960s a number of Zulus were to maintain that Bambatha had been among the warriors who had escaped from the gorge.)

Although further violence was to occur in Natal, the rebellion was over in Zululand, and in Natal itself, on 11 July, the situation was such that the Colonial Office was informed, 'Resistance is more or less over, rebels for the most part cowed and in hiding.'

Fatalities during the rebellion had been distinctly one-sided. Whereas around two dozen whites and six loyal blacks had perished in the five months or so of desultory fighting, the number of Zulus who died on either side of the Tugela ran into four figures. A contemporary, James Stuart, put the figure at 2300, while in *Reluctant Rebellion: The 1906–8 Disturbances in Natal*, Shula Marks estimates that up to 4000 Africans lost their lives.

One of those singled out for retribution by the authorities was Dinuzulu, who was widely believed in colonial society to have been behind the rising. Consequently, in November 1908, he found himself on trial in Greytown, a prosperous little community to the north of Pietermaritzburg, charged with high treason. He was found not guilty of the bulk of the charges, but guilty of sheltering Bambatha and his family, along with other leading rebels. On 3 March 1909, he was sentenced to four years' imprisonment and hauled off to gaol in Pietermaritzburg. He did not serve the entire sentence, for in the following year, a member of the Boer commando that had assisted the uSuthu in overthrowing Zibhebhu in 1884 became Prime Minister of the newly constituted Union of South Africa – Britain's newest dominion. His name was Louis Botha, and he soon ordered Dinuzulu's release. Nonetheless, Dinuzulu was not allowed to return to his homeland. Instead, he ended his days living comfortably on a farm in the Transvaal. He died. still only in his mid-40s, on 18 October 1913.

Dinuzulu was the last of the Zulu kings to lead his people into battle. His successors were left to reconcile themselves to white domination, a demoralising and humiliating experience which Dinuzulu himself had been compelled to learn.

PART TWO

CHAPTER 8
'MZILIKAZI –
THE MATABELE HAIL YOU'

'From all I could learn from friends and foes, he is brave, and in seasons of real danger possesses great deliberation.' *Robert Moffat*

Mzilikazi kaMashobane began life in relative obscurity and ended his days as the ruler of one of the most powerful nations in southern Africa, the Ndebele, or, as they are more commonly known, the Matabele. It was the remarkable achievement of a remarkable man.

In several respects, Mzilikazi's life paralleled that of his most famous African contemporary, Shaka. For one thing, it began in the same area – today's Zululand or KwaZulu – for in the 1790s Mzilikazi was born into the Khumalo clan, part of the Nguni cultural and linguistic group, whose territory lay in what is now central Zululand.

In about 1800, Mzilikazi's father, Mashobane, moved north with a subsection of the Khumalos and established his own minor chiefdom beside the Mkuze River in the vicinity of the Ngome Forest and to the west of the Ndwandwe clan. Mzilikazi's mother was a Ndwandwe, for she was a daughter of their formidable chief, Zwide, though whether she was biologically Zwide's child is uncertain.

Mzilikazi was his father's heir, and thus it would have been customary for him to be raised among his mother's people to avoid potential intrigues at his father's court. Traditional evidence states that Mzilikazi did go with his mother to live with his maternal grandfather. Mzilikazi therefore grew to manhood in an exciting environment, for under Zwide the Ndwandwe emerged in the opening decades of the nineteenth century as one of the most powerful forces in the region. In about 1810, Zwide drove one of his principal adversaries, Sobhuza of the Ngwane, northwards across the Pongola River, where Sobhuza proceeded to found the Swazi kingdom. Zwide then waged war against Dingiswayo of the Mthethwa, whose territory lay to the south-east of his kingdom and whom he succeeded in killing in 1817.

As noted in Chapter 1, however, Zwide soon found himself confronted by a more formidable opponent, the Zulu chief Shaka, whom Dingiswayo had taken under his wing. Zwide was to clash with Shaka in wars fought in 1818 and 1819, but before doing so he killed Mzilikazi's father (the circumstances surrounding Mashobane's death are uncertain) and installed Mzilikazi as a vassal chief in Mashobane's stead. Mzilikazi's chiefdom was a small one, no doubt numbering hundreds rather than thousands of people.

Mzilikazi did not stay long in Zwide's fold. He soon deserted to Shaka's side, apparently taking his entire chiefdom. The evidence surrounding this event strikes a discordant note, but it seems most likely that after supporting Zwide in the first war, Mzilikazi swopped sides before the decisive campaign that resulted in Zwide having to flee north. Mzilikazi was an ambitious man with an eye to the main chance, and perhaps seeing which way the wind was blowing, threw in his lot with Shaka in a desire to be on the victorious side.

At this date, Shaka was in the early stages of building the Zulu nation by conquering or accepting as allies neighbouring Nguni clans. Mzilikazi and his people were among the latter and were allowed to retain their corporate identity. Apparently, following their flight, they were billeted in the centre of Shaka's kingdom, but shortly after Zwide's defeat, Mzilikazi and his followers returned to the homeland they had abandoned.

Mzilikazi's precise relationship with Shaka is uncertain. It is sometimes maintained that he became one of Shaka's closest friends and senior generals. On this point R. Kent Rasmussen, whose book *Migrant Kingdom: Mzilikazi's Ndebele in South Africa* is essential reading, comments:

> The idea that Mzilikazi was somehow a great 'favourite' of Shaka was being expressed at least as early as the 1860s and it is a popular theme in modern literature.... Unfortunately, the claim that Mzilikazi was Shaka's favourite and that he held an especially high position in the Zulu hierarchy exists without any details to support it.

What is certain is that Mzilikazi and Shaka soon reached the parting of the ways. Things came to a head after Mzilikazi conducted a raid against the territory of a wealthy chief to the north or north-west of Zululand in or about 1821. He returned to his homestead beside the Insikwebezi River with a very large herd of plundered cattle. As Shaka's subject, he was expected to hand the livestock over to his king, who would customarily have granted many of the cattle back to the Khumalo chief. But Mzilikazi kept almost all the cattle for himself and sent Shaka an insultingly small fraction of the herd.

In response, Shaka reportedly sent several messengers to remind Mzilikazi of his duty. According to a dramatic account of events recorded in the early twentieth century by a Rhodesian Native Commissioner, A. A. Campbell (who used the pseudonym, Mziki), the messengers were first humiliated by Mzilikazi, who plucked the crests from off their heads before declaring:

> 'Messengers, take these words to [Shaka] ... say that ... Mzilikazi has no king. In peace he will meet [Shaka] as a brother, and in war he will

150

find in him an enemy whom he cannot and will not despise....
Depart! and tell your king it rests with him whether it be peace or
war.'

Mzilikazi may have hoped that Shaka would simply let him go his own
way, and perhaps acted in the way he did out of alarm at increasing
centralisation in the Zulu state. If so, he soon learned otherwise. An impi
was sent against him and evidently came to blows with the Khumalos
somewhere along the lower Insikwebezi, where Mzilikazi and his followers
successfully defended a hilltop stronghold. The Khumalos then moved
upstream to another defensive position on a hill called Nthumbane. Here,
too, they were attacked, for Shaka sent a larger force against Mzilikazi. This
apparently occurred weeks or months later, and it has been suggested that
the delay was possibly due to many of Shaka's forces being engaged in
campaigns to the south. On this occasion, the Khumalos were overcome
and the survivors scattered. They left behind many dead (especially
women and elderly men), and their cattle to be rounded up by the victors.

Mzilikazi escaped and proceeded to regroup the survivors. Then, at the
head of some 300 followers, most of whom were warriors (the figure is that
of Henry Francis Fynn, who arrived in Zululand in 1824), Mzilikazi headed
westward into the territory of a chief named Nyoka who lived beside the
headwaters of the Mkuze River, about a day's march from Nthumbane.
Mzilikazi attacked Nyoka's people, seized the chief's cattle and grain, and
soon moved on.

Evidently he took a northerly direction, and thus either entered
Sobhuza's territory beyond the Pongola or skirted the western fringes of his
domain, for some of Mzilikazi's followers are said to have deserted to the
Swazi.

Mzilikazi then turned west and crossed the Drakensberg Mountains,
intent on reaching the interior. He probably crossed somewhere just to the
west of the Usutu River and (likely in 1821) came out on the vast expanse
to the west of the magnificent mountain range: land occupied by Sotho
peoples who were not as warlike as the Khumalos. The first to suffer at his
hands were a branch of the Phuthing people living on the Vaal–Olifants
watershed, whom Mzilikazi scattered. Here the Khumalos stayed for a
while, resting and gathering up livestock and provisions, before moving on
once again.

The Sotho and their world

The Sotho were concentrated in the area stretching southward from the
Limpopo River in the north to the Orange, and west from the Drakensberg
towards the Kalahari Desert (the westernmost Sotho being generally
known as the Tswana). Their forebears had evidently begun settling in the

region centuries earlier, perhaps as early as the beginning of the second millennium AD, and in so doing had mingled with the previous inhabitants.

The Sotho were divided into many chiefdoms, and the office of chief was hereditary. In a number of respects, the Sotho differed from the Nguni. Although likewise Bantu-speaking, their speech differed markedly from that of the Nguni. Moreover, unlike the exogamous Nguni, they practised cousin marriage, and generally lived in large settlements rather than in the scattered homesteads favoured by the Nguni. Furthermore, although economically the Sotho resembled the Nguni, in the sense that they were also mixed farmers, cattle featured less prominently in their scheme of things. Finally, in contrast to the Nguni, the Sotho were notable craftsmen – many of their goods were made of metal – and carried on an extensive trade in such objects.

When Sotho boys reached their late teens, they were assembled with others of their age belonging to the same chiefdom and were circumcised and subjected to a period of hardship and rigorous discipline, initiating them into manhood. In times of war, males who had jointly experienced initiation formed age-regiments that functioned as loosely organised tactical units. Unlike the Nguni, however, Sotho regiments did not wear ornate uniforms. Standard male dress consisted of a knotted breech-hide, although hide cloaks pinned on the right shoulder were sometimes also worn. Headdresses were formed of a dense mass of ostrich feathers. Men of rank were also allowed to wear V-shaped gorgets of flattened brass that protected the throat and upper chest, as well as leopard skin cloaks. For protection, warriors carried small hide shields with distinctive projecting wings. The shields were intended to ward off light throwing spears, of which each warrior would normally possess several, and the spears were carried in a leather quiver over the shoulder. Wooden clubs and battleaxes were also sometimes employed.

Mzilikazi's further movements
From Phuthing territory Mzilikazi headed north to the middle reaches of the Steelpoort River, where he attacked the Ndzundza people of Chief Magodongo. In origin the Ndzundza were Nguni; but their forebears had crossed the Drakensberg generations earlier and had settled among the Sotho with whom they had intermarried and become largely Sothoised.

Magodongo is said to have allied himself with a neighbouring chief of comparable origin, and to have used a stratagem to repel Mzilikazi. According to Matabele tradition:

The impis of the allied chiefs came out to give ... battle, driving before them a large herd of white cattle, so that they might conceal them-

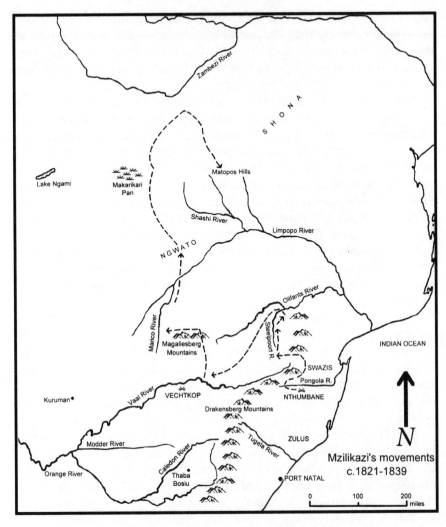

selves among the dust it raised.... [Mzilikazi] discerning the purpose
for which they came, sent ahead a posse clattering their shields,
which frightened back the cattle to their owners. In the stampede we
charged them home, inflicting serious loss. We then marched on to
the kraals, which we found deserted. Of cattle, sheep, and goats, there
were plenty and we took them for ourselves. The grain, too, in much
abundance was taken to supply our wants.

Ndzundza traditions record that Magodongo was killed and that the tribe
lost all its property.

Mzilikazi is claimed to have established a homestead called ekuPumu-
leni shortly after his arrival in the Transvaal, and is usually said to have

153

done so in the territory of his first victims, the Phuthing. But Rasmussen has argued cogently that the settlement was most probably founded in Magodongo's former territory. If so, Mzilikazi evidently did not stay long in the area – he probably pressed on in 1822 – and drought was in all likelihood one of the contributory factors.

He headed north again, having added some of the defeated to his following, and soon entered the territory of the Pedi, a Sotho people who had just been weakened by factionalism. Mzilikazi first attacked a newly established Pedi state north-east of the middle Steelpoort. He killed the chief and many of his followers before pursuing most of the survivors north-west into the Pedi heartland, where he virtually eliminated the royal family and, in a series of engagements with localised groups, made himself master of Pediland. The occupation of Pediland is said to have lasted about a year and during this period some of the Pedi were incorporated into Mzilikazi's following, albeit as second-class citizens (as was probably the case with the earlier such recruits), and were evidently encouraged to learn to speak Zulu and to adopt northern Nguni customs.

It has been frequently asserted that far from conquering the Pedi in about 1822, Mzilikazi was actually defeated, and only succeeded in overcoming them several years later after adventures conducted elsewhere. This view originated among French missionaries and is sometimes said to have been supported by Matabele tradition. But this is not the case, for the information in question was actually derived from non-Matabele sources.

From Pediland, Mzilikazi is normally held to have headed west towards modern Pretoria. He certainly did settle in that region, but only after first moving south-west towards the middle reaches of the Vaal River – a fact alluded to by A. A. Campbell and more recently clarified by Rasmussen. Another Sotho group, the Khudu, was living in the region and upon Mzilikazi's approach many of them fled, although some remained and offered allegiance to the Nguni warlord. Mzilikazi's followers settled on both sides of the Vaal – where they were to stay for several years – and soon recommenced raiding, mainly, it seems, against Sotho peoples to the west, many of whom fled while other survivors were probably made captive by the warriors sent against them.

This was not a happy period for the Sotho in general. Those living south of the Vaal – in an area stretching southward to the Maluti Mountains – had already suffered at the hands of Nguni groups such as the Hlubi who had recently fled into the interior; and, as we have seen, Mzilikazi and his potent little war-machine had wreaked further mayhem and disruption north of the Vaal. Many Sotho perished. Others, their crops destroyed, their livestock seized, resorted to cannibalism.

The beginnings of the Matabele nation

Mzilikazi fled Zululand with a small number of adherents and subsequently augmented this with Sotho and semi-Sotho peoples. A. T. Bryant has thus commented that Mzilikazi's following became 'a profoundly Sutuised community, not in name alone, but in numbers, habits, language and blood, for many of its men were Sutu captives, and practically all its females'.

That the Nguni element was outnumbered is clear; yet there is reason to believe that it was stronger than Bryant supposed. On this point, Rasmussen comments:

The modern Ndebele count more than sixty distinct names of clans whose members trace patrilineal descent back to the coastal Nguni. Since Mzilikazi appears to have left Zululand in the company only of members of his own Khumalo clan, the other Nguni clan names were all introduced subsequently.... The research of A. J. B. Hughes suggests that none of these new clan names was freshly created within Ndebele society, so their origins must lie in ... bands of refugees who joined Mzilikazi. Such evidence as exists on this subject further suggests that most of the Nguni refugees who joined Mzilikazi did so during the troubled 1820s.

Some of the refugees in question joined Mzilikazi after similarly fleeing from Zululand: among them were more Khumalos. Furthermore early in the twentieth century, an ethnologist named George Stow declared that according to native authority, Mzilikazi expressly recruited Nguni adherents from Zululand by sending envoys on secret missions to woo warriors to his side.

Additionally, Mzilikazi was joined by Nguni who had preceded the Khumalos into the interior – the Hlubi. They had fled on to the highveld in about 1818 after being expelled from their territory by another Nguni group, the Ngwane, who in turn followed them into the interior to escape from Shaka. In about March 1825, the two groups clashed in an epic battle on the west bank of the Caledon River and the Hlubi were soundly defeated. Some of the survivors were subsequently captured by Mzilikazi's warriors and taken under his wing, although admittedly most of them forsook him within a couple of years. The Nguni element among the nascent Matabele nation – as Mzilikazi's people were to become known – was strengthened, moreover, in late 1826 or early 1827 when Mzilikazi was joined by Ndwandwe refugees whose chief Sikhunyana, Zwide's son, had been defeated by Shaka. As Bryant himself comments:

Mzilikazi reaped a rich harvest in this final break-up of the Ndwandwe clan, for large numbers of its men and women, knowing

155

nowhere else to go, betook themselves to him and added considerable strength to his ever-growing tribe.

Then, again, following the defeat of Matiwane and the Ngwane in 1828 (see chapter 1), Mzilikazi was joined by some of the survivors.

The fact that the Zulu language, in the slightly modified form known as Sindebele, survived (it has persisted to this day as the speech of the Matabele nation), raises the possibility that the Nguni element among Mzilikazi's followers was not as numerically negligible as is sometimes supposed. Children generally learn the speech of their mothers, and if almost all the womenfolk were Sotho, it would be reasonable to suppose that Zulu would sooner or later have died out or at least been significantly modified.

Interestingly, the name 'Matabele' is an Anglicised version of a Sotho word, 'Matebele', which was evidently used as a blanket term by the Sotho peoples when referring to 'strangers from the east' such as the Khumalos who had made their way on to the highveld from the coastal belt. In due course, the nation founded by Mzilikazi adopted the name in its Nguni form of 'Amandebele', although most modern scholars use the root 'Ndebele' instead. In Mzilikazi's day, however, his people used other names to describe themselves, such as Khumalo or Zulu.

Mzilikazi migrates again
In late 1825, when many of Mzilikazi's regiments were conducting a major raid, apparently against the Ngwaketse, one of the most powerful and prosperous Tswana peoples whose territory lay about 150 miles to the north-west, Mzilikazi was himself attacked. An able Sotho chief, the Taung leader Molitsane, whose territory lay to the south-west of Mzilikazi's, allied himself with mounted raiders who possessed firearms. These were Griqua (half-breeds who lived in a twilight zone on the borders of European settlement) and Korana, from along the northern fringes of Cape Colony. Molitsane and his allies raided outlying Matabele cattle posts south of the Vaal. Upon the return of his regiments, Mzilikazi retaliated, recapturing some of the livestock and temporarily forcing Molitsane to flee. But the Matabele were shortly subjected to further cattle raiding by Molitsane and the Griqua and Korana, acting in concert or separately. Indeed, in 1835, a senior Matabele official named Mncumbathe told a British explorer, Dr Andrew Smith, that while living 'on the Liqua' (an Nguni name for the Vaal), the Matabele were subjected to at least seven such assaults.

The raids were no doubt primarily responsible for Mzilikazi's decision to leave the Vaal settlements in search of a new home. He evidently moved off in mid-1827, heading north. The Matabele crossed the Magaliesberg Mountains and entered a territory occupied by Sotho chiefdoms that had been weakened by a succession of recent invaders and factionalism. Some of the inhabitants submitted while others were killed or fled, and it was here, on and beneath the fertile northern slopes of the Magaliesberg in central Transvaal, that Mzilikazi once again put down roots.

The most important settlements were centred on the region around the upper Aaipes and upper Oori Rivers. His warriors soon recommenced raiding, and most of the operations were conducted against Sotho groups to the west. Furthermore, as a precautionary measure, Mzilikazi deliberately created a buffer-zone between the Vaal and the Magaliesberg range by clearing away all settlements, thereby rendering an assault from that direction especially difficult. 'I had to keep open veld around me,' Mzilikazi reportedly told an Afrikaner hunter in the 1860s.

Mzilikazi certainly had reason to be wary. This was brought home forcefully in July 1828 when he was subjected to a combined assault. Molitsane had begun raiding Matabele outposts once again and had provoked a major punitive response. He thus enlisted the support of a Korana leader named Jan Bloem. Bloem assembled a several hundred-strong commando comprising Griqua and Korana horsemen and Sotho–Tswana warriors, joined forces with Molitsane, and moved rapidly against Matabele cattle posts on the northern slopes of the Magaliesberg Mountains. Little resistance was encountered, for Mzilikazi's men were away conducting a raid of their own. Some 3000 cattle and a few women were seized by the raiders, who then retraced their steps.

While Molitsane and his people hurriedly returned home, his allies did so at a more leisurely pace and paid heavily for their complacency when a hastily assembled Matabele force struck back. Andrew Smith was subsequently told what happened by Haip, a Korana chief. On the third night of the return journey, the Griqua and Korana feasted well into the hours of darkness upon some of the seized cattle, before settling down for what remained of the night:

> Then, when approaching day could just be faintly discerned and the revellers were buried in sleep, the Zooloos [Matabele] rushed to the charge, and ... flight ... was immediately resorted to by the attacked. In the confusion a few shots were fired; but ... perhaps more the result of inadvertency than of any regular aim.

Haip managed to escape from the camp, only to find himself and many of the Tswana within a circle of Matabele warriors 'placed from six to ten yards apart, and ready to destroy whoever might be found flying'. Fortunately, he managed to evade the net when some of the warriors were distracted by other fugitives, but many of his colleagues did not live to tell the tale.

About a year later, Mzilikazi sent an impi to destroy Molitsane. It numbered some 4000 to 5000 warriors, most of whom were Mzilikazi's non-Nguni vassals, and headed for Molitsane's territory. Hearing of its approach, he abandoned his capital and retreated south beyond the Vaal. But the Matabele pressed on and caught up with the bulk of Molitsane's people beside the Modder River and cut them to pieces.

Years later, in 1871, an Afrikaner who had visited the site the day after the Matabele had struck, told the Bloemhof Commission that he had 'examined hundreds of bodies, all of which had been killed by assegais' and that he had seen 'no bodies of Moselikatse's [Mzilikazi's] people'. Members of the Matabele impi itself, who sat before the commission, declared that all, or almost all, of the Taung had perished and that many cattle had been recaptured. But Molitsane himself had not been present when the Matabele struck, and in due course found sanctuary with the famous Sotho leader, Moshweshwe.

Europeans visit Mzilikazi

In early August 1829, shortly after Mzilikazi's warriors had destroyed Molitsane's people, two adventurous white traders from the Cape were permitted to visit Mzilikazi's capital. He lavished gifts upon them and then, following their departure, sent envoys to make further contact with the outside world. They made their way south to Kuruman, a mission station run by a Scotsman named Robert Moffat, who enjoyed a great deal of prestige among natives in the interior. According to Moffat, the envoys 'were astonished and interested with almost everything they saw'. Moffat provided them with a wagon and accompanied them on the return journey.

They set off on 9 November and arrived at a kraal where Mzilikazi was resident in December, bad weather having hampered their progress. Moffat relates that he was enthusiastically welcomed by Mzilikazi and that much ceremony was laid on for his benefit:

> In order to make a display, the principal inhabitants of the neigh-
> bouring towns had been ordered to congregate at headquarters to
> give a public dance.... Hundreds might be seen descending to the
> town from all directions, men carrying their shields in full dress, and
> the women carrying supplies of pulse, milk and beans on their heads.
> Some thousand had collected on a smooth plain outside the town.
> The warriors were formed into a kind of circle, about three or four
> men deep. A number of war songs and national airs were sung, and
> one of these was composed for the occasion. Sometimes [Mzilikazi]
> took his stand in the centre, with a shield of lion skin, and a
> well-polished common butcher's knife, which he had from me, in

one hand, and which seemed to please him much, as its bright surface reflected the rays of the sun. He appeared to be chief musician, while all looked towards him and punctually imitated every motion he made in accordance with the music. To some of the tunes they danced manfully, while he looked on with apparent indescribable pleasure.... The air echoed with [Mzilikazi's] praises, his achievements, his power and his greatness, with the most extravagant epithets, such as King of the Heavens, King of Kings etc etc.

Moffat tells us something of Mzilikazi's appearance on this occasion. In common with all the married men, he was wearing a band of otter skin around his head. However, unlike his warriors – who mainly sported kilts of animal skins around their waists – he was adorned with small bunches of beads of different colours, while from either shoulder hung about fifteen pounds of beads (like two thick ropes), crossing over the breast and reaching to the feet. Moreover, 'His head was adorned with the finest feathers, formed into a couple of small bunches.'

Moffat stayed for eight days and had several discussions with Mzilikazi, including debates on theological matters such as the origin of man and the Resurrection. Mzilikazi declared that he wished to live on peaceful terms with Europeans and that he wanted missionaries to settle among his people, though his tone suggested that he was more interested in the secular benefits such contact might bring. Moffat records, for example, that the king 'seemed anxious to have firearms'. In short, as Richard Brown comments, Mzilikazi viewed Moffat as ' "a chief of considerable power" who would be able to supply the Ndebele with guns and ammunition'.

Of Mzilikazi's character and physique Moffat wrote:

Moselekatse is undoubtedly shrewd and observing, though in the course of conversation he often appears as if he were paying no attention whatever. From all I could learn from friends and foes, he is brave, and in seasons of real danger possesses great deliberation. He has evidently been in the wars, as some large scars give full proof.... In his person he is rather below the middle size, lusty, has rather a pleasing and soft countenance and is exceedingly affable in his manners. His voice is soft and feminine, and cheerfulness predominates in him ... he might be taken for anything but a tyrant from his appearance, but for all that, it may be truly said of him he 'dipped his sword in blood, and wrote his name on lands and cities desolate'.

Further bloodshed
One of the most famous Matabele campaigns of this period – although in reality it may have been a minor affair – probably occurred in the autumn

of 1830 or 1831. An impi was sent against Sotho living south of the Vaal. The latter included the followers of a remarkable individual in his mid-40s named Moshweshwe, who had emerged as a leader of considerable ability following the general collapse of the southern Sotho chiefdoms in the early 1820s and whose chiefdom was centred on Thaba Bosiu, an outcrop rising some 400 feet in Lesotho.

Near the top of Thaba Bosiu were sandstone cliffs with several passes that gave access to the defensible summit, a well-watered flat area of under two square miles. Thaba Bosiu had already withstood a series of attacks, the most significant of these in 1827 when Matiwane and the Ngwane were repulsed. Moshweshwe's defeat of the Nguni force had considerably increased his prestige and many survivors of the shattered Sotho chiefdoms had attached themselves to him.

Learning of the approach of the Matabele, Moshweshwe gathered his people on his stronghold, and awaited the Matabele attack. In 1861, Eugène Casalis, a French missionary who had entered Lesotho in 1833, recorded what happened:

> Accustomed to victory, the Zulus [Matabele] advanced in serried ranks, not appearing to observe the masses of basalt, which came rolling down with a tremendous noise from the top of the mountain. But soon there was a general crush – an irresistible avalanche of stones, accompanied by a shower of javelins, sent back the assailants with more rapidity than they had advanced. The chiefs might be seen rallying with fugitives; and snatching away the plumes with which their heads were decorated, and trampling them under foot in rage, would lead their men again towards the formidable rampart. This desperate attempt succeeded no better than the former one. The blow was decisive.

Casalis went on to state that as the Matabele withdrew, Moshweshwe sent them a gift of cattle as food to speed them on their way, believing that hunger had brought them into his country. Perhaps this was so, but it is worth noting that the gift is not mentioned by another source, Thomas Arbousset (who had arrived in Lesotho with Casalis) and whose account, dating from 1842, generally harmonises with that of Casalis. Arbousset has, however, a very different epilogue: the Matabele commander angrily burnt millet growing at the base of the mountain before heading off.

In June 1831, history repeated itself when Griqua–Korana horsemen and their Tswana allies moved against Mzilikazi again, led by an elderly Griqua chief named Barend Barends. Estimates of the size of the combined force vary greatly, but according to the most conservative figures, Barends had some 300 Griqua and Korana horsemen and several hundred Tswana allies. The invading force struck in mid-July, although Barends himself had decided to remain at a base camp and had thus delegated command to a trusted subordinate, perhaps a certain Gert Hooyman.

Most Matabele warriors were absent beyond the Limpopo River to the north and so the commando easily rounded up several thousand cattle and seized some women, before setting off southward. They moved slowly and succumbed to an attack shortly before dawn (having failed to appoint sentries) after Mzilikazi sent a rapidly assembled force in pursuit. Many of the raiders, including a significant number of Griqua, were killed in the confused fighting – some of the Griqua reportedly shot one another in the dark – and the captured livestock were retaken. After the battle, the Matabele killed their opponents' mounts and burned a substantial quantity of seized firearms.

In mid-1832 Mzilikazi was attacked yet again. His adversaries were those he feared the most – Zulus. A large Zulu impi under Ndlela kaSompisi was sent against him by Dingane, who was aware of how prosperous Mzilikazi had become and no doubt wished to relieve him of his large herds of cattle. It was the first time such a force had been sent against Mzilikazi since his flight from Zululand. (It is often said, erroneously, that the invasion had been preceded by one in 1830, a misapprehension partly due to a lapse of memory on the part of Henry Fynn many years later when writing up his *Diary*.) After travelling some 300 miles, the Zulus fell upon the Matabele, having been augmented en route by Sotho enemies of Mzilikazi. They took their opponents by surprise, for many of Mzilikazi's fighting men seem once again to have been occupied elsewhere.

Unfortunately, evidence relating to the campaign is largely confused and contradictory. It appears, however, that after attacking from the south-east, the Zulus swept through a number of homesteads around the upper reaches of the Oori tributaries before encountering strong resistance. A fierce battle was fought near the source of the Sand River and both sides evidently suffered severe losses. For instance, the Matabele induna Mncumbathe told Andrew Smith in 1835 that 'many were killed on both sides so that they could not number them'. On the whole, it appears that the battle ended indecisively. Certainly the Zulus headed home with fewer cattle than Dingane had expected and he thus had a number of officers executed.

Migration to the Marico Valley

In early August, almost immediately after the withdrawal of the Zulu impi, Mzilikazi sent three bodies of warriors west against Sotho–Tswana peoples such as the Rolong, killing many of them and putting the survivors to flight. Having established mastery of the Marico region, Mzilikazi then migrated with his people the hundred miles or so to the Marico Valley. He had evidently decided to move west before the Zulu assault had occurred, and it had doubtless brought the matter to a head. The majority of the new settlements and military posts thus established appear to have been located along the upper reaches of the river, as in the Mosega basin, while throughout the new Matabele domain were the homesteads of Tswana, who had elected to submit to Mzilikazi's rule.

In 1835 (a year after the Matabele had successfully dealt with another Griqua–Korana commando), Dr Andrew Smith explored the kingdom, and noted:

> Mzilikazi's posts are placed with considerable regularity. His own kraal [Gabeni] is nearly in the centre of his country, and then his principal soldiers are placed round him in posts not very distant from each other and no one of them more than an hour's walk from his kraal. At these posts his best cattle and those for breeding are kept.

The least desirable cattle were located in a ring of outposts. Smith estimated that over two-thirds of Mzilikazi's people were of Sotho–Tswana origin, the rest coastal Nguni.

After establishing themselves in their new homeland in the closing months of 1832, the Matabele recommenced raiding, although evidently on a reduced scale in comparison with previous years. They deliberately depopulated territory between themselves and the Vaal, thus once again creating a buffer zone, rightly believing that the greatest threat to their security lay to the south.

While living in the Marico Valley, Mzilikazi increased his contacts with whites. Individuals who wished to enter his kingdom were able to approach him through Moffat, who acted as an intermediary and with whom he communicated regularly through messengers. In 1835, as has been noted, Andrew Smith visited Mzilikazi's kingdom. He was the leader of a scientific party from the Cape, and Moffat, who accompanied the party, had secured permission for them to visit the king's court.

They arrived on the southern fringe of Mzilikazi's kingdom in late May and were brought before the king at Mosega in early June. Smith was allowed to explore the Matabele kingdom and country to the north, while Moffat stayed with Mzilikazi and discussed the prospect of letting American missionaries preach among the Matabele. Permission was granted, whereupon Moffat set off for Kuruman in early August.

After completing his explorations, Smith returned to Mzilikazi and then set off for the Cape, accompanied by Matabele emissaries whom Mzilikazi had delegated to represent him before the Governor of Cape Colony. They arrived at Cape Town in late January 1836 – having completed the final stage of the journey by sea from Port Elizabeth –

and were entertained for six weeks, with every effort being made by their hosts to impress upon them the full might and sophistication of Europeans.

On 3 March, the head of the delegation, Mncumbathe, and Governor Sir Benjamin D'Urban signed a treaty of general friendship. In June, the Matabele emissaries reported to Mzilikazi, having been joined on the way home at Kuruman by members of an American missionary party which, having arrived in Mzilikazi's kingdom earlier in the year, had already begun to set up a mission at Mosega.

In or about early August 1836, several parties of Boers made their way across the Vaal without having sought Mzilikazi's permission. Some of the Boers were intent on hunting, but others, led by Hendrik Potgieter and Sarel Cilliers, were migrants who had forsaken Cape Colony in search of a new homeland and were among the vanguard of a movement discussed in Chapter 2 and known to history as the Great Trek.

In mid-August, Mzilikazi responded by sending an impi of some 500 men towards the Vaal. It came across a number of undefended camps and attacked them. In a few cases, the Boers had received a few moments' warning and were able to mount a successful defence. For the most part, however, the camps were overwhelmed, so that about 50 of the whites and an unknown number of their non-white servants perished, although Matabele also figured among the slain. During the short campaign, the Matabele seized more than a thousand head of cattle, together with horses, oxen and a number of wagons.

The clashes occurred while Potgieter and Cilliers were reconnoitring country to the north-east. Upon returning, they gathered their followers together south of the Vaal beside the upper Rhenoster River and awaited developments.

On 9 October, Mzilikazi assembled an impi and ordered its commander, Kaliphi, to move against the Boers. The first major battle between members of the Great Trek and Africans was about to begin.

Mzilikazi's army

Mzilikazi's army consisted of age-based regiments commanded by indunas appointed by him, and were resident in military kraals. Every few years, youths who had reached the age of military service were called together and formed into a regiment. In due course, when the warriors were in their mid-30s, they were granted permission to marry and would henceforth serve as a reserve.

The strength of the regiments was substantially below that of their Zulu counterparts, normally numbering perhaps 200–400 warriors. Initially, only Nguni were incorporated into the *amabutho*, but during Mzilikazi's years in the Transvaal, Sotho were enrolled in the Matabele army. Moreover, when called upon, contingents of Sotho warriors were provided by their vassal chiefs to fight alongside Mzilikazi's regiments.

In 1835, Smith declared that if Mzilikazi 'were called upon to muster every man he has in his country, he could not produce 4000'. William Cornwallis Harris (who visited Mzilikazi the following year) stated: 'His standing army of warriors of his own tribe exceeds five thousand men, but numbers of the conquered nations swell his followers to a large amount.' Indeed, it is sometimes said that Mzilikazi could call upon up to 20,000 warriors if he so desired, but this is no doubt an inflated figure. For one thing, disease, most notably smallpox, had recently taken a heavy toll of the Matabele and Mzilikazi's subject peoples. The conclusion, therefore, is that Mzilikazi never commanded more than several thousand warriors, and that Matabele impis frequently numbered hundreds rather than thousands.

Of the warriors' appearance, Moffat wrote in 1829:

The appearance of his men in full dress was much like the dress of a regiment of Highlanders, colour excepted. A great number of strings or strips of skin, with the fur twisted, hung like a kilt around the middle, reaching to the knees. Similar tails adorn the arms and neck, while the head is decorated with a profusion of feathers. In the centre of the forehead a long blue feather stands, like a cockade. Each regiment has its own peculiar mode of adorning the head, as well as the colour of the shields.

The headdresses incorporated the Zulu headband, but otherwise differed in that they employed feathers of birds not found in Zululand, except that senior men, like their Zulu counterparts, sported crane feathers. Moreover, Cornwallis Harris noted in 1836 that some warriors, when fully dressed, wore capes of cows' tails around the shoulders.

Mzilikazi's warriors were armed with stabbing and throwing spears. Initially, no doubt, the stabbing spears were similar or identical to those employed by Zulu warriors but in due course a shorter variant was used. Knobkerries, too, were carried by some warriors. Shields were comparable to those of Zulu regiments. They were made of ox-hide and were oval in shape, the colour predominantly black for junior Matabele regiments, white for senior regiments.

The battle of Vechtkop
According to the American missionaries preaching in Mzilikazi's kingdom, the impi sent against the Voortrekkers on 9 October 1836 numbered some 3000 men, a third of whom were non-Nguni servants and camp followers. In marked contrast, Voortrekker estimates put the number of Matabele

higher, some 5000–6000 warriors, while a biographer of Sarel Cilliers goes even further, stating that the Matabele were 9000 strong, 'scattered over the plain like ants'. Understandably, Rasmussen favours the contemporary estimate of the missionaries, which is no doubt much closer to the truth, though perhaps slightly on the conservative side.

Milikazi may have seen the campaign as vitally important in defensive terms. Alternatively, it is possible that he was primarily interested in seizing Voortrekker livestock prior to abandoning the Marico Valley area, for Smith and the Mosega missionaries stated respectively that he was fearful of the threat of white settlement and the possibility of further Zulu aggression.

In due course (a letter published in the *Grahamstown Journal* of 29 December 1836 says that the Boers heard that the impi was approaching on 17 October), the alarm was raised in the trekker camp on hearing that the Matabele were approaching, having marched south-west some 175 miles in about a week. Subsequently, and likely on the morning of 19 October, Cilliers conducted a service in the absence of a minister, and then rode out of a hastily formed laager towards the Matabele, with a view to parleying, accompanied by Potgieter, 33 other Boers and an African interpreter.

The party reportedly received a terse reply from a Matabele spokesman: 'Mzilikazi alone issues commands, we are his servants, we do his behests, we are not here to discuss or argue, we are here to kill you.' But according to D. F. Kruger, who was present, before Potgieter could attempt to nego-tiate, a nervous Boer loosed off a shot towards the Matabele ranks. What is certain is that the Matabele eventually rose to their feet with a shout and charged. A running fight developed, lasting several hours, as the Boers fell back, stopping to fire as they went. 'I fired sixteen shots on the enemy before we reached the laager,' Cilliers recalled, 'rarely missing and killing two to three with one shot.' Back at the camp, riding through the opened gap which was quickly reclosed, they hurriedly dismounted and manned their battle stations.

The impi found their opponents drawn up in a strong defensive posi-tion beneath a low ridge that was subsequently christened by the Boers Vechtkop, 'Battle Hill'. The laager consisted of some 50 wagons tightly chained and lashed together, the gaps between filled with thornbush. Within the ring was an inner shelter, protected by ox-hides to stop flung spears, where the children and wounded could be housed. There were only about 35 adult men, but they could rely on the support of their women-folk who had spent their time casting lead balls which they had sewn into little bags to serve as buckshot. The laager was too small to accommodate the trekkers' livestock, other than their horses.

The pursuing Matabele did not immediately press home an attack. They simply sat down outside gunshot range to rest and await instructions from

Kaliphi. Minutes passed, but nothing happened. The minutes turned into hours – still no attack was launched. Instead, during this period, a detachment of Matabele was sent to round up the Boer livestock. Some beasts were brought up and slaughtered, the meat distributed to the impi and eaten raw. The warriors also occupied the time sharpening their spears on stones.

The Boer men kept busy cleaning out their guns. They also knelt in prayer with their friends and families, imploring God for deliverance. Tension mounted. After several hours had passed, the suspense became unbearable, and according to some sources, a certain Koos Potgieter tied a red kerchief to a whip and waved it at the Matabele. The warriors responded with a concerted hissing sound and then charged towards the laager in two or three groups from different directions, thunderously drumming their spears against their shields.

When the warriors were about 30 yards from the wagons, the trekkers opened fire. Many of the densely packed Matabele were cut down (one of the Voortrekkers claimed to have killed nine men with a single shot), but the rest kept on, vaulting where necessary over fallen colleagues. Within seconds, the foremost warriors had reached the laager where they began shaking and rattling the wagons, determined to find a way in.

The Boers, meanwhile, were working furiously, the men and boys capable of bearing arms firing at point-blank range into the swarming warriors, while the women loaded and reloaded the guns. An enveloping cloud of dust and smoke swirled across the laager: the noise was deafening. One woman, Mrs Abraham Swanepoel, saw a black hand groping towards her from the far side of the defences and chopped it off with an axe. No warrior managed to penetrate the laager, and the force of the Matabele attack soon began to die away as they fell back to regroup.

The attackers now decided upon a change of tactics, resuming the charge but pausing to hurl more than 1000 assegais over the wagons into the laager. It, too, proved a failure, and very soon the dispirited warriors gave up and began to return home. None of the sources written close to the date of the engagement suggests that the battle lasted longer than fifteen minutes. Indeed, the American missionaries declared that it was of even shorter duration, a mere two or three minutes, though this is hard to credit.

The withdrawing impi took the trekkers' captured livestock with them, several thousand cattle and some 40,000–50,000 sheep, as well as the wagon oxen.

Eventually, and perhaps a day or two later, mounted Voortrekkers re-emerged from the laager and set off in pursuit, intent on retaking their lost stock. Some stragglers were intercepted and killed, but none of the lost animals was recaptured.

About 150 Matabele dead were found around the laager. Others, of course, had either died in the running fight preceding the assault on the Boer position, or would subsequently have done so from wounds sustained. It is sometimes asserted that Matabele losses totalled around 500 dead, but this seems too high. In contrast, only two of the trekkers were killed, although about fourteen others, including women, had been seriously wounded.

When news of the battle spread, some reacted by blaming the Boers for what had transpired. For example, the 7 February 1837 issue of the *Commercial Advertiser* (a paper with a liberal-philanthropic stance), declared that their victory had been 'illegal violence and murder'.

The Matabele were shocked by the number of warriors who had perished during the campaign. Dr A. E. Wilson, one of the American missionaries, wrote, on 17 April 1837:

> When the army of the Zoolahs returned, there was nothing but lamentation heard in the land for weeks on account of those slain in battle. A good many of those with whom we were acquainted, from the neighbouring towns, were killed; numbers returned home wounded; some applied to me for surgical aid.

Boer and Zulu aggression

By early November 1836, Potgieter's and Cillier's party had fallen back to the Modder River where other Voortrekker groups were continuously arriving from Cape Colony.

Potgieter and one of the new arrivals, Gert Maritz, soon began planning a retaliatory strike against Mzilikazi. In January 1837, they set off from Thaba Nchu, where they had assembled a commando numbering 107 Boers, about 40 Griqua and a handful of Korana, as well as over 60 Tswana, mostly Rolong who had been dispossessed of their land by the Matabele. The Tswana were on foot, generally lacked guns, and were viewed by the Afrikaners as minor participants in the venture.

Maritz's section of the commando left Thaba Nchu on 3 January 1837, followed the next day by Potgieter. On the 13th they joined forces at a crossing of the Vaal, where they left their wagons. Then, instead of heading directly towards their target, they skirted west, moving faster than previously, before turning towards the Mosega basin and approaching the Matabele from the direction of Kuruman, intent on taking them by surprise.

Their approach went undetected and at dawn on 17 January they fell upon the southernmost Matabele settlements in the basin. The American missionaries found themselves 'in the midst of a slaughter':

> The Boers attacked and destroyed thirteen, some say fifteen, kraals. Few of the men belonging to them escaped, and many of the women

167

were either shot down or killed with assegais. We have no means of ascertaining how many lives were destroyed. We suppose from two to four hundred.

Other sources, however, indicate that perhaps as many as 500 Matabele perished.

At midday the commando headed off the way it had come, taking with it some 6000–7000 cattle, and having lost only two of its members, both of them Rolong. As they headed south, they were accompanied by the missionaries who had decided that it was prudent to leave Mzilikazi's kingdom.

Mzilikazi soon had fresh cause for concern. In mid-1837 he was hit again by a Zulu impi sent by Dingane. After searching for the Matabele in their former territory beside the Magaliesbergs, the Zulus made their way towards the Mosega basin. They arrived in about late June only to find no Matabele, for the survivors of the Boer raid had abandoned the valley and moved north towards Gabeni and the lower reaches of the Marico.

The Zulus followed the signs of flight and one section of the impi (which had divided into two sections) clashed with Mzilikazi's warriors on or near the Pilanesberg Mountains east of Gabeni. Ferocious fighting occurred and the battle's outcome seems to have been inconclusive. Meanwhile, the other section of the invading army had rounded up thousands of cattle and large numbers of sheep. The whole force then began heading back towards Zululand. Some of the livestock were recaptured when the Matabele gave chase, but even so, when the impi arrived in Zululand in early September, it was able to present Dingane with the greatest booty of his reign.

Mzilikazi's troubles were still not over. Within months he was struck by a large allied commando of Griqua, Korana and Tswana, which appears to have killed more of his people and carried off additional cattle.

In early November, Matabele fortunes deteriorated even further. They were attacked by a Boer commando numbering some 360 Afrikaners under Potgieter and a new arrival, Piet Uys, and accompanied by a small force of Rolong. The force entered the Mosega basin and pressed on north in search of the Matabele, who had concentrated their settlements around the lower Marico River. On Saturday, 4 November, the commando attacked the first Matabele settlements they came across, having once again taken Mzilikazi's people by surprise, which says little for his intelligence system. Matabele who resisted were gunned down; others fled and were pursued. One settlement after another was attacked and the inhabitants killed or ejected as the commando continued north in a running battle that is said to have lasted for nine days, ending on the 12th when the Boers halted some 25 miles north of Gabeni.

168

The trekkers claimed to have killed approximately 3000 Matabele without loss to themselves. Rasmussen, however, aptly comments:

The claim that 3000 Matabele perished is almost certainly exaggerated. The Voortrekkers probably spent more time collecting Ndebele livestock than they did actually fighting. Ndebele resolve to defend their territory must have been already shattered. By November they were on the threshold of leaving the Transvaal anyway, so it seems unlikely they would have risked further losses of men in what they must have recognised as a futile resistance.

Strong oral tradition among the Matabele credits Moffat with having previously advised Mzilikazi to abandon the Marico district and migrate northward to present-day Zimbabwe to avert conflict with the Voortrekkers. Indeed, some versions go so far as to maintain that Moffat actually guided the Matabele north, following the Boer commando of late 1837. The traditions have usually been viewed with scepticism by historians, partly because Moffat had never travelled in the area and because his son, John Smith Moffat, thought it most unlikely that his father acted in such a manner. Richard Brown, however, comments that 'it is highly likely that the oral tradition contains a core of truth'. He cites, for example, the existence among Moffat's papers of the draft of an interesting pseudonymous letter written in Moffat's own hand to a missionary journal in February 1853. It includes the observation:

It has been stated on good authority that an individual in whom M. [Mzilikazi] placed almost unbounded confidence earnestly and repeatedly warned him by every means to avoid coming into collision with the Boers and rather retire into the interior rather than commence a warfare with the white man.

Brown thus comments:

In view of the known relationship between Moffat and Mzilikazi, it can hardly be doubted that the unidentified individual who advised withdrawal was Moffat himself, while Mzilikazi's remark to the missionary in 1854 'I have not forgot the fulfilment of the warnings you gave me at Mosega' probably refers to the same incidents.

Flight beyond the Limpopo
Groups of Matabele who managed to escape from the commando fled north with whatever livestock they still possessed and joined up with individuals and other bands of Matabele who had likewise survived. On the

other hand, many Sotho–Tswana who had been incorporated into Mzilikazi's kingdom now took the opportunity to break free, while some Nguni subjects of Mzilikazi likewise abandoned him. The rest, however, proceeded further north and most or all of them reunited, after crossing the Limpopo, in what is now south-east Botswana. The number of migrants was probably in the region of 15,000 people: according to Rasmussen, the Matabele probably never numbered over 20,000 people during the 1830s.

Mzilikazi and his followers had entered the territory of the Ngwato, a Tswana-speaking people who had previously suffered from Matabele raids. The Ngwato scattered and the Matabele briefly occupied their territory, rounding up whatever cattle could be found and in due course harvesting the Ngwato's abandoned crops. They also celebrated the *inxwala*, or first fruits ceremony.

In early 1838, shortly after observing the festival, and while no doubt still in Ngwato territory, the Matabele evidently divided into two divisions of roughly equal size, probably with the aim of migrating further in an orderly manner and easing the problem of finding adequate food and water. Apparently, Mzilikazi did not intend the split to be permanent. He led one division north-west into inhospitable terrain. The other group – which included several of his wives and sons, including the heir apparent Nkulumane (who had perhaps been born in Zululand) and the hereditary Khumalo regent Mncumbathe – headed north-eastwards. It was led by an induna called Gundwane Ndiweni, apparently the individual previously referred to by the praise-name of 'Kaliphi'. It then turned north and by mid-1838 had halted just to the north-east of the Matopos Hills in modern Zimbabwe, where it began to establish settlements.

By the middle of 1839, Mzilikazi had himself arrived in the Matopos area, having covered much more ground. After reaching the Makarikari Salt Pan in Botswana, he had headed north-east, apparently with the aim of pressing further into the interior by crossing the Zambezi. But in so doing, he entered tsetse-fly country and therefore turned south-east after his herds began to be decimated. According to Moffat (who subsequently heard reports of the journey), 'The cattle died so rapidly that their carcasses were lying within sight of each other along the course they had taken, and where they halted for the night hundreds were left dead.'

When Mzilikazi linked up with the rest of the Matabele in the Matopos area, he found that they had installed Nkulumane as their king after hearing reports that Mzilikazi had been killed by a hostile tribe or had perished in inhospitable terrain. The rumours, combined with the fact that the vitally important annual *inxwala* ceremony (in which the king's role was of crucial importance) was due early in 1839, had induced them to choose young Nkulumane as Mzilikazi's successor and proceed with the festivities.

Mzilikazi arrived on the scene shortly after the ceremony had been held. The result was bloodshed, for he was determined to reassert control. Clashes between the two groups appear to have occurred and Mzilikazi had Gundwane and other senior figures involved in the installation of Nkulumane executed. And what of Nkulumane? According to some accounts, he likewise died. He is said to have been tied to a tree and strangled, as it was illegal to shed royal blood. But less convincing accounts state that he either escaped or was sent into exile. Rumours that this had happened were to persist for years and would ultimately lead to further conflict.

The Shona

The Matopos lie in the south-west of Zimbabwe in a part of the country known as Matabeleland. The local Bantu inhabitants of the Matopos area were members of the Shona group of peoples. The Shona had begun settling in Zimbabwe in about AD900 (they evidently came from the south) and formed the bulk of the population. Those living in the territory in which Mzilikazi and his people had arrived spoke the Kalanga dialect of Shona and were essentially descended from people who had occupied the area for close on a thousand years. Since the late seventeenth century, however, they had been ruled by an intrusive Shona dynasty, the Changamire, which had built up a powerful state with many client chiefdoms and which exported gold and ivory to Portuguese centres on the Zambezi and the coast, in exchange for items such as cloth and beads: a state capable of raising powerful armies when occasion demanded, equipped with spears, clubs, axes and bows and arrows.

The Rozvi state, as it is known, was not the first powerful Shona polity to have emerged. For centuries the Kalanga had, for example, been neighboured to the east by a Shona state which controlled trade between the gold-producing areas of current Matabeleland and the Indian Ocean. It enjoyed its heyday from about AD1300 to approximately 1450, and the ruins of its capital, Great Zimbabwe, are the most notable native historic monument in southern Africa.

By the opening decades of the nineteenth century, Rozvi power was in decline, partly due to internal strife. The situation deteriorated further in the 1820s and 1830s when the Rozvi were attacked by several migrating Nguni groups who were driven off, but at a cost. Moreover, discord among the Changamire dynasty increased. Even so, the Rozvi state was still in existence when the Matabele arrived on the scene. Its heartland lay to the east of the Bembesi River, while to the west was territory under a Kalanga sub-ruler named Ndumba.

The Matopos area lay in Ndumba's province and the Matabele encountered little resistance upon their arrival. Indeed, they soon made themselves masters of his territory, settling among the Kalanga. Some of the local inhabitants fled, but shortly returned to become tributaries of Mzilikazi, and sooner or later the Kalanga began to adopt Matabele speech and customs. Furthermore, Mzilikazi gained the vassalage of several senior Rozvi families. The tributaries cared for cattle which Mzilikazi gave into their charge (though he evidently retained ownership) in return for a levy of young people who were incorporated into Matabele society.

Campaigns

Mzilikazi, in time, would terminate Rozvi power; but his first campaign of expansion was launched in 1841 in another direction, north-west, against more vulnerable Shona living along, and close to, the Zambezi, a river that served as a trade route with the Indian Ocean. Mzilikazi succeeded in establishing his authority. Clashes also occurred in this direction with the Kololo people, who lived on the far side of the Zambezi, although they proved more formidable.

In the late 1840s and early 1850s, Mzilikazi engaged in sharp conflict with the Rozvi and some of his vassals broke away, at least partly motivated by resentment at having to hand over their young people to the Matabele, and joined forces with independent Rozvi. The overall leader of the Rozvi was a member of their main dynasty named Tohwechipi, whose paramountcy was accepted by some hitherto hostile senior Rozvi families. Raiders, some of them led by Tohwechipi, penetrated well into Matabele territory where they stole cattle and, so the Matabele claimed, committed atrocities against women. Mzilikazi hit back and several battles were fought to the east of his domain. Tohwechipi, for instance, was forced on to the defensive but at some point prior to 1852, he defeated the Matabele after engaging the services of 'strong people' – traders from the Zambezi who possessed guns. On the whole, however, the fighting went in Mzilikazi's favour and by 1857 Tohwechipi had been defeated.

The Matabele also waged campaigns to the south-west against the Ngwato, who were to prove themselves Mzilikazi's most formidable enemies. Both states were aiming to extend or retain authority over Kalanga and Tswana whom they deemed to be within their respective spheres of influence. At one point, the Ngwato ruler, Sekgoma, was reduced to paying Mzilikazi a tribute of skins. Relations between the Matabele and the Ngwato reached their lowest level in the early 1850s, but by the middle of the decade relations were more harmonious, with the territory north of the Shashi River accepted as definitely belonging to Mzilikazi.

By this date, Mzilikazi had concluded a peace treaty with the Transvaal Boers. In 1847 his old enemy Potgieter had conducted an unsuccessful raid into Matabeleland. He had then despatched representatives to Mzilikazi's court to open peace negotiations, and as a result, in late 1852, the Matabele king sent an embassy south to sign a treaty. The ambassadors found Potgieter dying, but nonetheless signed the agreement on 8 January 1853, as did the Transvaal Boers' new leader, Potgieter's son.

The Matabele state

The area within an approximately 40-mile radius of present-day Bulawayo formed the heart of Mzilikazi's kingdom. It lay generally at an altitude of 4000–5000 feet above sea level, situated at the south-west end of a plateau that covers most of modern Zimbabwe.

The Matabele kingdom is often said to have been surrounded by a deliberately depopulated buffer zone. Julian Cobbing, however, has emphasised that this was not so in his work, *The Ndebele under the Khumalos*, essential reading for anyone seriously interested in Matabele history. The belt of scorched earth did not exist. Rather, Mzilikazi's kingdom was surrounded by a zone (averaging about 50 miles in width) of tributary peoples in which Matabele cattle were grazed during winter months and some of whose inhabitants began to adopt Matabele speech and customs.

Cobbing has revealed another fallacy, namely that the Matabele kingdom proper contained huge regimental towns (an erroneous view based on a misunderstanding of Matabele terminology) and that the state was almost entirely organised along military lines, and economically dependent on raiding Shona and other peoples. Regimental settlements did indeed exist, but were smaller than has generally been thought, while private homesteads were far more common than has often been maintained, and accommodated the great majority of the people. Moreover, the basis of the Matabele economy was farming, with grain production being most important. Admittedly, raids did occur frequently. Some were punitive, whereas others were intended to extend Mzilikazi's authority further afield and to capture both livestock and humans.

Furthermore, it is often stated that Matabele chiefs (izinduna) were no more than royal 'officials', but this was not so. Strong aristocratic families existed and exerted great power in their respective chiefdoms, and although it was not uncommon for the king to do away with troublesome izinduna, chiefly succession itself was seldom if ever disrupted by the monarch.

Cobbing also rejects the view that the Matabele kingdom was divided into four formal administrative subdivisions, Amakanda, Amhlope, Amnyama (or Amabutho) and Igapha, with each division or province having its own complement of regiments under a senior induna. Rather, he comments that the 'slender historical evidence' available points in another direction, i.e., 'that the "divisions" were ... early *amabutho* which later "spawned" fresh *amabutho*, and in the process themselves disappeared'. On this point, Ntabeni Khumalo (who served in a regiment during the reign of Mzilikazi's successor) declared:

> All the later regiments came from the original regiments, the Amhlope, Amakanda, the Amnyama and Igapha.... Although they had their own regiments, the later people used to regard themselves as the descendants of one or other of the older regiments.

Cobbing therefore goes on to say:

> Amhlope, Amakanda, Amnyama and Igapha were collective group concepts comprising [people in settlements] descended from four original or *proto-amabutho* created in the period before the migration of the Ndebele to the Matopos region.

Instead of the non-existent provinces, it was the chiefdoms which formed the subdivisions of the nation. These came about as regiments matured. Initially, a regiment would be formed when the king called upon a number of young men from across the kingdom (or on occasion certain chiefdoms) and formed them into a new regiment. Then, as noted above, after several years had passed, the warriors would be granted permission to marry and would disperse to do so. Some of them would then return to the regimental base to settle with their wives, and their offspring would either remain in the settlement in question or would found private villages in its vicinity: a chiefdom would thus develop, with the former head of the regiment or his son as chief, and the men would still be liable, if need be, to military service. A proportion of their male offspring would in due course be drafted to form new regiments while others would remain behind and, if necessary, fight alongside their fathers.

Matabele society in Matabeleland is generally held to have consisted of a rigid three-tier caste system: the Zansi (meaning 'those from downstream'), the Enhla ('the people who came from upstream'), and the Holi (apparently a term of contempt). These castes consisted respectively of people of Nguni, Sotho and Shona descent, with the Zansi being socially and politically the most important group, and the Holi, the most numerous caste, being the least significant.

Cobbing believes that the idea that there was a rigid caste system 'is at best only a half truth', and states that Sotho blood flowed in the veins of a significant percentage of Matabele aristocrats north of the Limpopo, and that people of Shona descent were capable of rising to positions of importance in the state. Nonetheless, Hughes comments that the 'Zansi were very definitely the rulers of the nation.... Apart from the king's family, most of the Chiefs (izinduna) were of this caste', and adds that Enhla in

174

the mid-twentieth century frequently spoke 'strongly about the contemptuous way in which they were treated by the Zansi in the old days'.

Thomas Morgan Thomas, the missionary who settled in Matabeleland in 1859, tells us that if a Holi murdered 'a real' Matabele, he would be punished with death, whereas in the opposite circumstance, the perpetrator would most likely have to pay a fine of cattle to Mzilikazi. Furthermore, the offspring of mixed marriages were referred to as half-castes. In short, it seems reasonable to conclude that Cobbing understates the degree of stratification that existed.

Renewed contact with Moffat

In mid-1853, three white hunters from the Transvaal entered Mzilikazi's territory. They were received courteously and were granted permission to hunt elephants. Furthermore, Mzilikazi made it clear that he was anxious to see Robert Moffat once again, partly no doubt to receive medical treatment (he was afflicted by gout) and perhaps to secure the services of a trusted intermediary with the outside world. So when the hunters returned south, they were accompanied by messengers charged with contacting the missionary. They failed to do so, owing to an erroneous report that took them to Durban instead of Kuruman, where Moffat was still resident.

In May 1854, however, unknown to Mzilikazi, Moffat set out to visit him, accompanied by two white traders. He was partly motivated by a desire to hear something of his son-in-law, the famous missionary and explorer, David Livingstone, who had wandered off into the interior the previous year.

On 9 July, some days after crossing the Shashi River, Moffat and his companions were met by one of Mzilikazi's indunas who was stationed in subject Shona territory and who sent word of their arrival to Mzilikazi.

On the 13th, Moffat's party continued their journey. The terrain, he wrote, was

... exceedingly picturesque, mountains and hills of all shapes without number. Wherever the eye is directed, nothing but hills rise in endless succession, most of them covered with enormous blocks of granite and trees.... Thousands of blocks ... are perched on the pinnacles of others, which the slightest shake would send thundering down to the base.

On 22 July, after descending to lower and less hilly country, Moffat and his companions were greeted by the overjoyed Mzilikazi at a homestead called Matlokotloko. Moffat was taken aback by the king's appearance. 'There he sat – how changed! – the vigorous active and nimble monarch of the Matabele, now aged, sitting on a skin, with feet lame, unable to walk or even stand.' Mzilikazi drank beer in large quantities and may well have been suffering from cirrhosis of the liver. Moffat treated the king, whom he advised to abstain from beer, and within days he was on his feet again.

Of his relationship with the king, Moffat wrote:

> He is dotingly fond of me, and would trust his life in my hands before he would do so to any of his own subjects. He listens to my judgement without the shadow of ... suspicion ... yet, if I introduce the subject of religion ... he turns away the conversation on to something else.

During his visit, Moffat heard something about Matabele military exploits. He was told that an impi had recently conducted a punitive expedition against Shona raiders. The mission had not been an unqualified success for the Shona had had the benefit of elevated rocky fastnesses, from where they had shot arrows and hurled stones at the Matabele. On other occasions the Matabele had encountered the same problem. Hence Moffat declared that if it had not been for their mountain strongholds, the Shona 'would have been long since subdued'. Moreover, Moffat heard of a disastrous expedition that had occurred several years earlier against Sebitwane and the Kololo people. Many of the Matabele involved had been left to starve on an island in the middle of the Zambezi by local natives, who had ferried them there before slipping away, leaving the warriors to their fate.

Moffat tells us that Mzilikazi had obtained firearms from traders on the Zambezi who had made their way up the river. Of the weapons he wrote: 'All the guns I have seen are English soldiers' muskets, besides others, with Dutch stocks of beech-tree, manufactured in Birmingham.'

During his visit, Moffat declared that he was intent on pressing on to the upper Zambezi to obtain news of his son-in-law. He set off on 24 August, taking provisions for Livingstone. Much to his surprise, Mzilikazi joined him. The king travelled in Moffat's wagon, escorted by a party of warriors. They slowly headed north-west and in due course crossed the Nata River (which flows westward into Botswana) and entered countryside which became increasingly inhospitable due to lack of water. On 11 September, therefore, Mzilikazi ordered an officer and some twenty men to carry on the provisions and a packet of letters by the quickest route, while he and the rest of the party would travel back the way they had come.

On 23 September, having arrived back in the vicinity of Matlokotloko, Mzilikazi permitted Moffat to preach to his people, no doubt motivated by a desire to prolong the missionary's stay in his kingdom. At Mzilikazi's word, a sizeable assembly gathered the next day, with Mzilikazi sitting beside Moffat, who noted:

Profound silence and the most marked attention was maintained the whole time. There was something startling to my own senses to look on a congregation of fine looking men, with intelligent countenances, from youth to old age, listening for the first time to the voice of Jehovah, the only living God, their creator and preserver, who loved them and sent his son to save them from the wrath to come.

Moffat repeated the exercise on the following days before returning to Matlokotloko with Mzilikazi on 2 October. Then, on the 9th, after leaving Mzilikazi a supply of medicine, he set off for Kuruman. En route he wrote:

On reviewing the past, nothing surprises me more than the unwavering kindness of [Mzilikazi].... It may easily be supposed that I must have been extremely liberal in gifts. This however has not been the case, and of gunpowder I did not give him one grain nor a single ounce of lead.

In late 1857, Moffat revisited Mzilikazi, hoping to persuade him to accept the establishment of a permanent mission of the London Missionary Society in his territory. Mzilikazi was agreeable – though some of his councillors had serious misgivings – and so Moffat returned to Kuruman to organise the venture. In October 1859, he arrived back in Matabeleland with three missionaries, including one of his own sons. In the interim, Mzilikazi had become reluctant to permit the establishment of a mission, having heard unfavourable reports of missionary activity in Tswana country. Nonetheless, on 15 December, out of gratitude to Moffat, he announced that the missionaries could settle in a pleasant upland area called Inyathi; here they would labour fruitlessly, their missionary endeavours falling on stony ground.

Hardship, war and European involvement

Moffat left for Kuruman on 17 June 1860. He was never to see Mzilikazi again. 1859 had been a year of drought, and Moffat left behind a land that was to experience further suffering, for drought recurred in 1860 and 1861. Matabele misfortune was also compounded in 1861 by the outbreak of lung-sickness which decimated their herds, while smallpox appeared late the following year.

The 1860s also witnessed further conflict. Relations with the Shona in the late 1850s were relatively peaceful, but according to D. N. Beach, for over a decade from 1860 the Matabele 'made what was probably their greatest concerted effort to dominate the Shona', with Mzilikazi's impis operating over a wide area. For example, the Matabele moved against Tohwechipi and his followers, who had moved eastwards in 1857 into hill country such as the Mavangwe range on the upper Sabi. It is said that three major attacks were launched against them, and in 1866 Tohwechipi was forced to surrender after a lengthy siege. He was taken to Mzilikazi, who spared his life and subsequently allowed him his freedom. Vestiges of Rozvi power appear to have remained, but their great days were over.

Among other Shona attacked were Hwata and his people. The chiefdom of Hwata was centred at the head of the Mazoe Valley, a short distance to the north of present-day Harare. Although fairly small, it was economically significant, for it dominated much of the trade in ivory and gold occurring in the region. In 1864, Hwata finally surrendered and became a tributary ruler, though in 1868 a Matabele impi was sent against him again, indicating that he had attempted to throw off Matabele dominance.

During the same decade there was renewed conflict, too, with the Ngwato. At the end of February 1863, a Matabele army attacked outlying Ngwato cattle posts before making for Shoshong, the Ngwato capital. On 6 March, a battle was fought outside Shoshong and although the Ngwato had horses and possessed muskets, they were nevertheless routed, whereupon the victors proceeded to plunder and seize captives in the neighbourhood, and further conflict occurred during the course of the year.

Mzilikazi also determined to strengthen his hold to the north-west, and sent impis towards the Victoria Falls area of the Zambezi, where he was able to exploit the fact that the Kololo state had disintegrated in the early 1860s. In 1869 (shortly after Mzilikazi's death) a European hunter named Thomas Leask wrote, with some exaggeration, given the Zambezi's vast length, that 'all the people along the Zambezi are terribly afraid of the Matabele'.

Leask was just one of an increasing number of Europeans whom Mzilikazi permitted to enter his kingdom in the 1860s either to hunt or trade – activities for which they had to obtain permits. One such was a young man named William Finaughty. In 1864 he saw Mzilikazi, whom he described as 'a physical wreck', whose 'lower limbs were paralysed', so that he had to be carried about in an armchair. Another European visitor was Henry Hartley, who had first entered Matabeleland in 1859. In 1865, after receiving permission to hunt in the territory of Shona tributaries, he came across ancient disused gold workings some 70 miles south-west of Harare and returned to his farm in the Transvaal excited by what he had found. In due course, the find aroused eager white interest in the financial prospects offered by Matabeleland.

In 1868, Mzilikazi's health finally collapsed entirely. For several months he lay on the verge of death, before expiring in September, surrounded by his councillors. For a month the news was kept a secret, and his wives kept a watch over his body, which was wrapped in blankets in his hut while the nation's senior men made preparations for the transition of power.

Mzilikazi's death was then announced, and the nation summoned to a homestead called Mhlahlandlela, the Matabele capital since 1863. His body was placed in a wagon, along with his possessions, and taken to the Matopos, accompanied by the regiments in all their paraphernalia. At the foot of a hill called Nthumbane the procession halted and the corpse was carried up and laid in a granite cave whose entrance was sealed with a mass of stones. The wagon was then dismantled and placed with its former contents in another cave that was likewise sealed. So was buried Mzilikazi kaMashobane, the Great Bull Elephant of the Matabele, the father of the nation.

As Ian Knight comments:

Mzilikazi's journeys were at last at an end. His history had been extraordinary. He had witnessed the rise of the great Shaka, defied him, and survived. He had seen the coming of the Boers, and survived them too. He had conquered, lost almost everything, then conquered again, and his legacy was his nation. The Ndebele mourned him: '*Intaba seyidilike* – the Mountain has fallen.'

CHAPTER 9
THE GATHERING STORM –
THE REIGN OF LOBENGULA

'Insolent Matabele swaggered through the streets of the town with
their bloody spears and rattling shields.' *Melina Rorke*

Mzilikazi's death was followed by a marked period of uncertainty in which the elderly and highly respected Mncumbathe acted as regent. The question of who would succeed Mzilikazi was sharply contested. The majority of senior indunas supported one of Mzilikazi's sons named Lobengula, an intelligent, shrewd and perceptive individual who had been born in the Transvaal in 1829 (his mother was the daughter of a Swazi chief) and had been high in Mzilikazi's affections in the closing years of his father's reign.

Others, headed by Mbigo Masuku, the rather elderly chief of Zwangendaba, favoured the claim of Lobengula's older brother, Nkulumane, the son of Mzilikazi's principal wife. It will be remembered that Nkulumane had been installed as king of part of the Matabele nation after their arrival in Matabeleland, only for Mzilikazi to appear on the scene and ruthlessly reassert his authority. But some of the Matabele believed that Nkulumane's life had been spared and that he had been sent into exile. Now, following Mzilikazi's death, they championed Nkulumane's right to the throne.

Steps were thus taken to locate Nkulumane. According to one rumour, he had been sent back to Zululand and was now working for the Natal Administrator, Sir Theophilus Shepstone, using the pseudonym 'Kanda'. A mission was therefore sent to Natal to ascertain the report's accuracy. The man was found and identified as Nkulumane by the embassy. When questioned before Shepstone, however, he strongly denied the identification and so the emissaries returned home without him in mid-1869. A second mission, sent to corroborate the report of the first, duly returned without achieving anything concrete.

It is highly unlikely that Nkulumane was still alive. Julian Cobbing has pointed out that 'there is no single contemporary reference to his existence' between Mzilikazi's reestablishment of his authority and the events following the king's death, and concludes: 'The evidence that Kanda was not Nkulumane is circumstantial but overwhelming.'

In early 1870, Lobengula was installed as king by his supporters at Mhlahlandlela. In a letter written on his behalf on 19 August 1871, he subsequently informed the Lieutenant-Governor of Natal: 'In February of 1870, I was installed in the place of my father as chief and king of the

180

Matabele nation.... 10,000 warriors were present ... and many more had paid their homage and departed.'

The installation ceremonies lasted until 17 March. On that date, states Thomas Morgan Thomas, following a final ceremony, Lobengula was told by the 'high priest' Umtamjana: 'There is the country of your father, his cattle, and his people – take them, and be careful of them. Those who sin, punish; but those who obey, reward.'

The most notable sinners were adherents of Nkulumane who, unlike the majority of the Matabele, refused to acknowledge Lobengula as king. Matters came to a head in June 1870, by which time work on a new capital (which was soon to be called Bulawayo) was underway two miles east of Mhlahlandlela. Battle was joined after Lobengula moved against the base of his principal opponent, Mbigo of Zwangendaba, located beside the Bembesi River, on Sunday, 5 June. He is said to have attempted to parley, hoping to draw Mbigo into a debate, only to have his overtures met with contempt. Lobengula was fired upon, and William Sykes, a missionary at Inyathi, tells us that 'even the girls and women of the rebels ... insulted him with gross and indecent gestures'.

Armed with muskets and traditional weapons, Lobengula's warriors promptly moved to the attack. The first two assaults against the rebels, who were deployed in the base, were repelled by heavy musket fire from behind the palisades, but on the third assault the perimeter was breached and hand-to-hand fighting raged, in which Mbigo was among those who died. In all, hostilities lasted about two and a half hours before the surviving rebels surrendered, while others fled, some of them south-west to Ngwato territory.

Two years after the battle, a young English hunter named Frederick Courtney Selous arrived in Matabeleland and heard about the battle from two Europeans who had tended many of the wounded. One of them was Sykes. The other was a hunter and trader called Philips, who told Selous that 'although [Lobengula's warriors] had many guns, nearly all the killed had been stabbed at close quarters with assegais', and that in 'many instances he [had] found two men lying dead together, each with the other's assegai through his heart.'

In respect of the battle of Zwangendaba, Lobengula declared in the letter mentioned above that as soon as victory had been attained, he ordered that no one else should be killed because his 'heart was not for blood'. Further-more, he stated that he freely forgave the survivors and incorporated them into other regiments. Selous states much the same thing, declaring that Lobengula acted very magnanimously towards the vanquished, allowing all those who had escaped to return home and become his subjects.

Lobengula also had trouble during this period with the Ngwato king, an interesting character named Macheng. He had spent much of his life in

Matabeleland, after being seized as a youth by a raiding party, but in 1857 Mzilikazi had allowed him to return home, hoping that he would supplant Sekgoma and prove a loyal client of the Matabele state. Macheng did indeed become the Ngwato king, but as Mzilikazi lay dying he had begun to flex his muscles, for Ngwato strength had increased significantly over the years. As a result of the growth of inland trade, Shoshong had become the largest, most prosperous and best-armed town in the interior. Macheng had thus claimed sovereignty over the Tati Valley on the edge of Matabeleland, where gold had recently been discovered.

Then, during the subsequent Matabele interregnum, he began issuing permits to Europeans to work the goldfields. Lobengula regarded the Tati area as being within greater Matabeleland and in April 1870 he granted the right to mine the goldfields to the London and Limpopo Mining Company. On 2 May 1870 (a month prior to the battle of Zwangendaba), he sent a warning to the troublesome Ngwato ruler, whom he reminded of his tributary status. Among other things, he declared:

> Whilst I open my roads and my country to all traders, travellers and hunters, you on the contrary endeavour to levy tax on wagons and on gold-seekers who pass through your district, the district that you held from my father, Moselikatze, and which you now hold from me.... It is then my wish, that you desist from levying any such Taxes whereby you hinder people from coming into the Matabele and increase the prices of goods to my injury and the injury of my people.

Macheng, however, was to remain a thorn in Lobengula's side, and in June 1871 Matabele warriors attacked Ngwato who were stationed near Tati to block Matabele trade travelling southward along the Tati road. Macheng subsequently gave succour to Lobengula's enemies such as Kanda.

Lobengula's letter of 19 August 1871 was just one of many he sent to British officials during this period in an attempt to obtain their recognition of his legitimacy as Matabele king. One of the recipients was Shepstone, who nonetheless gave limited support to 'Nkulumane', for Kanda had begun singing a different tune and was readily being used by Shepstone to undermine the Matabele king. For instance, Shepstone provided him with a wagon and sent him north with an escort to Macheng, from whom he received sanctuary late in 1871.

To add to Lobengula's problems, one of his own brothers, Mangwane (who had fled Matabeleland following Mzilikazi's death), was likewise in Ngwato territory and had designs on the Matabele throne. In January 1872, he moved against Lobengula, accompanied not only by fellow Matabele dissidents but by Kanda – whom he was using as a front for his own ends – and a force of Ngwato placed at Mangwane's disposal by Macheng. Although the Ngwato soon deserted, Mangwane pressed on and set up camp in Matabeleland where messengers were sent far and wide, calling for people to rebel. The summons did not fall entirely on deaf ears. A significant number of people responded positively throughout the kingdom, but the majority of the chiefs who had previously aligned themselves with Lobengula stood firm, and he was thus able to crush the revolt. For example, a force of warriors en route to join Mangwane was intercepted and defeated. When Mangwane and Kanda realised that the cause was lost, they withdrew.

Kanda was subsequently granted asylum in the Transvaal by President Kruger and his base there became a haven for fugitives and dissidents from Matabeleland. Moreover, in 1876, he unsuccessfully attempted to gain the support of a party of discontented Transvaal Boers by offering them 'land to their hearts' content' if they would render him military assistance. 'Kuruman [another name by which he was known] is assured,' he told them, 'that if, by your aid he could reach his friends, such a number of them would immediately rally round him as to render further service from you unnecessary'. Lobengula duly received word of this proposal and one of his closest and most influential white friends, Thomas Morgan Thomas, noted in his diary on 23 August 1876, that he 'wept tears ... and said he had not yet turned his back from fear of Kuruman'.

The following year Shepstone became the British Administrator of the Transvaal, and on 2 April 1878 he wrote to the British High Commissioner at Cape Town, Sir Bartle Frere, stating, 'The possession of the person of Kuruman gives Her Majesty's Government the means of exercising great influence over the reigning Matabele king.' Shepstone wished Lobengula to allow a British Resident to be stationed in his kingdom. The monarch was not inclined to do so. Thomas Morgan Thomas acted as interpreter and recorded in his journal:

> But ultimately, when it had been suggested to his Majesty that in view of the possibility of the Transvaal Boers leaving their country for these parts and bringing with them the supposed uKurumana it would be well for him to be on friendly terms with his next-door neighbour ... Shepstone he seemed to approve of the idea of a British Consul's being placed at Gubulawayo, [being motivated by fear rather than] any good principle.

In the event, the diplomatic presence proved short-lived. The British Resident, Captain R. R. Patterson, arrived at Bulawayo in late August 1878 and soon set off on a trip to the Victoria Falls accompanied by a colleague, Lieutenant T. G. Sergeaunt, two servants, twenty bearers and one of

Thomas's sons to act as an interpreter. At the end of September, most of the party, including Patterson and the two other Europeans, met a fatal end, reputedly after drinking the poisoned water of a pool. Rumours spread that Lobengula had ordered their deaths. Some historians have doubted this, partly influenced by Thomas's view that Lobengula was induced by fear into accepting a British Resident, but the balance of the evidence does indeed indicate that the king had Patterson and his party murdered. No doubt Lobengula felt anxious in the wake of what had happened, fearing British retribution, but events elsewhere, such as the commencement of the Zulu War in 1879, diverted attention away from Matabeleland.

Raiding and the Bechuanaland Protectorate

Under Lobengula, the Matabele continued regularly to raid neighbouring black peoples. For example, they strengthened their hold on an area stretching as far east as the upper Lundi near present Gweru, and habitually raided Shona living further afield. Armies also headed west against the Tawana people, living beside Lake Ngami in Botswana. In 1883 (the year in which Kanda died in South Africa), the Matabele carried out one such attack. 'This was a very bold enterprise,' comments Selous, 'as the marauders had to traverse nearly four hundred miles of desert country, entirely uninhabited except by Bushmen; a country in which game too was very scarce, and throughout which water was only to be found in pools, often widely separated one from another.' The Matabele nevertheless succeeded in capturing a considerable number of cattle. But another attack against the Tawana in 1885 proved disastrous. The Matabele were forced to retire after being subjected to heavy rifle fire in marshy ground beside a river, and the emaciated and demoralised survivors trudged into Bulawayo in June without their shields and spears: in 1881, the Bulawayo founded at the commencement of Lobengula's reign had been abandoned in favour of a new site some miles to the north, which is now part of today's city of Bulawayo.

A number of Europeans witnessed their return. One of them, Lieutenant Edward Maund, wrote as follows:

> There can be little doubt that the [Matabele] army has much degenerated since the incorporation of the Maholi [Shona] element. They have lost the dash of the old Zulu warriors, and there is not the same discipline.

Most writers echo Maund's sentiments and portray the army of Lobengula's day as a shadow of its former self. Reverses other than the disastrous Lake Ngami campaign did occur, but so too did Matabele successes; and in the 1880s, Lobengula in fact extended his authority into areas seldom if ever subjected to previous Matabele military activity.

In 1885 Britain declared a substantial tract of country the Protectorate of British Bechuanaland, and Maund was in Bulawayo as part of a mission charged with informing Lobengula of this fact. The protectorate extended north from the Molopo River as far as the twenty-second parallel of latitude. In the north-east, the territory (which is now part of Botswana) encompassed the Ngwato kingdom, which was now ruled by a man named Khama, and had enjoyed peaceful relations with the Matabele since 1875.

The establishment of the protectorate ended Lobengula's freedom to send impis on raids against the Ngwato and the Tawana, and in the late 1880s Matabele raids occurred instead across the Zambezi to the north. Indeed, it was rumoured that Lobengula was intending to abandon Matabeleland and migrate with his people beyond the Zambezi further into the interior.

Raids in the same direction occurred into the 1890s, and led to the formation of a formidable alliance against the Matabele, consisting of a number of polities on both sides of the river. As a result, in 1892, a Matabele impi was totally routed.

The formation of the trans-Zambezian alliance was inevitably a cause of concern to Lobengula. So, too, was Portuguese involvement in Shona territory to the east, which added to his fears of encirclement. The Portuguese were the first Europeans to enter what is now Zimbabwe: they had been intermittently present since the early sixteenth century, having entered the region from their colony of Mozambique to the east. Now, in the wake of the establishment of the British protectorate of Bechuanaland, they made limited attempts to make good their historic claims over Shona territory, fearing British encroachment north of the Limpopo. Efforts were thus made to woo Shona chiefs, and in 1889 several of them were granted guns and ammunition in return for acknowledging the Portuguese. But the threat posed to Lobengula by the Portuguese proved short-lived: it was the British he really had to fear.

Cecil Rhodes and the Rudd Concession
In 1870, a remarkable young Englishman set foot in South Africa, a man possessed of intelligence, ambition, charm and ruthlessness. His name was Cecil Rhodes. He had been born in 1853 in Bishop's Stortford, Hertfordshire, the son of a clergyman.

In 1871, Rhodes made his way to Kimberley and became engaged in the diamond industry. He soon went into partnership with a fellow Englishman named Charles Rudd and then returned to England to study at Oxford. He gained a degree in 1881, by which time he was a millionaire – a millionaire eager to advance imperial interests by uniting southern

Africa under the British flag. Indeed, he wished to create a broad swathe of British territory as far as the Nile Valley itself.

Inevitably, this meant outmanoeuvring real or potential rivals, such as the South African Republic or the Transvaal. In 1887, Rhodes was alarmed to hear a report that in July of that year Lobengula had signed a treaty of friendship with the Transvaal, a treaty that made the king an ally of the Boer state and provided for the establishment of a South African Republic consulate at Bulawayo.

At Rhodes's urging, Sir Hercules Robinson, the British High Commissioner for South Africa, sent John Moffat, the son of the famous missionary and a member of the British administration in Bechuanaland, to negotiate with Lobengula. He knew the Matabele and their country well, for he himself had lived in Matabeleland as a missionary from 1859 until 1865.

Consequently, on 11 February 1888, Lobengula put his mark to what has become known as the Moffat Treaty. Among other things, he agreed that 'peace and amity' should always exist between the British and the Matabele, and promised to refrain from granting or selling any part of his dominions (which according to the treaty included the territory of the Shona) without the approval of the British High Commissioner. Furthermore, he repudiated the treaty of the previous year with the Transvaal, and the British government soon let it be known that Lobengula's domain now lay exclusively within the British sphere of influence.

Within months of the Moffat Treaty, Rhodes sent three men (one of whom was Rudd) to obtain a concession from Lobengula, whose domain he believed contained valuable gold deposits comparable to those of the Witwatersrand in the Transvaal. They arrived at Bulawayo on 20 September 1888, only to learn that Lobengula was resident at a smaller homestead called Umvutcha seven miles to the north. There they found other speculators and concession-seekers already on the scene, while Maund was shortly to appear representing a rival concern.

At noon on 30 October, following two days of discussions with his indunas at which Rudd and his colleagues, James Rochfort Maguire and F. R. ('Matabele') Thompson were present, Lobengula set his seal on a document known as the Rudd Concession.

Lobengula granted Rhodes's agents permission to dig 'one hole' near Tati. This, at least, was his belief, for in fact the document to which he put his mark stated something entirely different. Under the Rudd Concession, Lobengula supposedly bestowed upon the grantees 'complete and exclusive charge over all metals and minerals situated and contained in my kingdom's principalities and dominions, [with the exception of the Tati area], together with full power to do all things that they may deem necessary to win and procure the same.' In return, the grantees agreed, among other things, to pay Lobengula and his successors a hundred pounds ster-

186

ling on the first day of every month and to deliver 1000 Martini-Henry rifles and 100,000 rounds of suitable ammunition to Bulawayo.

Lobengula was subsequently told by anti-Rhodes traders at Bulawayo what the Rudd Concession stipulated and hence repudiated it in January 1889. Moreover, when cross-examined by Lobengula the following March, a missionary named Charles Helm (who had acted as interpreter during the concession proceedings) confirmed that the king had indeed been greatly deceived.

Meanwhile, after Lobengula put his mark to the concession, Rudd had hurried off to Kimberley, taking the document with him. Rhodes was overjoyed by what had transpired and sent Rudd on to Cape Town with a copy of the document for Sir Hercules Robinson. On 15 December, the latter forwarded the copy to the Colonial Office, declaring that he hoped that 'the effect of the concession to a gentleman of character and financial standing will be to check the inroad of adventurers as well as to secure the cautious development of the country with a proper consideration for the feelings and prejudices of the natives'.

The formation of a company to exploit the concession was now Rhodes's priority. He wished it to be a Chartered Company, in other words, one authorised by the British government to operate and enjoy governmental powers in territory deemed to be within the British sphere of influence: in recent years two such companies had been chartered to operate elsewhere in Africa. For Rhodes, obtaining such a charter would reduce the likelihood of Lobengula revoking the Rudd Concession, while for the British government the granting of a charter would enable British interests in Lobengula's territory to be furthered without expense to the British taxpayer.

In early February 1889, Rhodes became concerned by reports that Lobengula had suspended the concession. He therefore persuaded two Kimberley doctors to visit the Matabele king on his behalf. One of them was Dr Leander Jameson, an ambitious, charming and unscrupulous character, who was to play a major role in subsequent developments, a man of whom Stafford Glass has aptly commented that he 'disregarded truth if it stood in his way'.

On 2 April, the doctors arrived at Bulawayo, accompanied by a contractor bringing the first half of the consignment of arms and ammunition promised under the concession. The king, however, was troubled about the best course of action to take. Instead of formally accepting the consignment, he placed it in charge of a guard of his warriors, an action that nevertheless led Maguire and Thompson to claim that he had ratified the concession. Lobengula probably also refused to accept the money promised him in the treaty. On 12 April, Jameson set off for Kimberley – accompanied by Maguire – having made a strong and favourable impression on Lobengula, partly because he had been able to alleviate a condition from which the king was suffering – gout.

In August two senior indunas reappeared at Bulawayo. Lobengula had sent them to Britain the previous November as personal emissaries, accompanied by Maund. They returned with a letter written on Queen Victoria's behalf on 26 March by the Colonial Secretary, Lord Knutsford. The letter declared that Englishmen who asked permission to dig in Matabeleland were not authorised to do so by Her Majesty, and that it was 'not wise to put too much power into the hands of the men who come first, and to exclude other deserving men. A King gives a stranger an ox, not his whole herd of cattle, otherwise what would other strangers have to eat?'

Knutsford's letter was read out before Lobengula and an assembly that included the two indunas and all the white men in Bulawayo. Shortly thereafter, in early September, Lobengula summoned a council of indunas and proceeded to denounce one of them, a rich, elderly and highly influential figure named Lotshe Hlabangana, who had been instrumental in persuading him to sign the Rudd Concession. The exact details of what subsequently befell Lotshe differ, but it is certain he was executed, either by being strangled or by having his skull smashed in by a knobkerry. His wives, offspring and dependents, some 300 people in all, according to one version, were likewise slaughtered.

'Matabele' Thompson reappeared at Bulawayo the day after the killings, following a visit to Helm's mission station; but when informed, 'Tomoson, the King says the killing of yesterday is not over', and having simultaneously caught sight of a body of menacing warriors, he left rapidly, galloping off southward as fast as his horse could carry him.

Rhodes reacted swiftly upon hearing of Thompson's flight – Jameson was persuaded to undertake another visit to Bulawayo to renegotiate the concession. He arrived on 17 October, accompanied by an interpreter and Thompson (who had been cajoled into returning), and in December Lobengula evidently decided to honour his decision to permit Rudd and his men to mine near Tati.

By this date Rhodes had finally obtained his charter, for on 29 October 1889, Queen Victoria granted a Royal Charter of Incorporation to the British South Africa Company. Among other things, Rhodes's new company (which is often simply referred to as the Chartered Company) was authorised to 'preserve peace and order in such ways and manners' it considered necessary over a vast area, which included Lobengula's kingdom. To that end, it could make ordinances and raise its own police force, although if the company failed to respect the customs, religion and laws of peoples brought under its jurisdiction, the word of the Colonial Secretary was to prevail.

The authorisation to administer and govern granted to the company by the charter, furthermore, was conditional: the Rudd Concession did not include any such delegation of power by Lobengula. Hence as Claire Palley comments:

> While the Charter gave the Company legal capacity and conditional permission from the Crown to exercise governing powers that it might in the future acquire, the Company could only seek the source of its actual administration in the grant of governing powers by the sovereign of the country, King Lobengula.

Such powers, of course, had so far not been granted.

In late January 1890, Jameson told Lobengula that digging operations near Tati had proved a waste of time. Lobengula thus agreed to allow mining to take place on the extreme south-eastern border of his kingdom, near where the Tuli joins the Limpopo. According to Jameson, he also agreed to supply a hundred men to cut a road for the wagons. Having received permission to continue operating, Jameson headed south with Thompson, falsely maintaining that Lobengula had also agreed for mining to be undertaken to the north, in Mashonaland, i.e., territory to the east and north-east of Matabeleland over whose Shona inhabitants Lobengula of course claimed sovereignty, and which Rhodes was already preparing to occupy.

The Pioneer Column

A key figure in the plans was an energetic, ambitious and egotistical young man named Frank Johnson, who began recruiting men for the task in South Africa on behalf of the Chartered Company. At Rhodes's insistence, a cross-section of Europeans was chosen, including artisans and Afrikaners – and hence the Pioneer Corps was established. It numbered about 196 men and was divided into three troops. The force was to set out from British Bechuanaland and skirt around the southern and eastern fringes of Lobengula's kingdom in order to avoid conflict.

Frederick Courtney Selous, who was by now a celebrated hunter, was also involved in the plans to occupy Mashonaland, territory with which he was familiar. On 17 March 1890, he appeared at Bulawayo to see Lobengula. Selous describes what occurred:

> When I told him that I had been sent by Mr Rhodes to make the road round the outskirts of his land to Mashonaland, and wanted him to give me men to open up a waggon track, as he had promised Dr Jameson he would do, he denied ever having given any such promises, and then said plainly that he would not allow such a road to be made.

Selous therefore left Matabeleland to report what had happened and on 27 April Jameson once again took centre stage, having been persuaded by Rhodes to revisit Bulawayo. After discussions with Lobengula, he then left for the south on 2 May. Later in the same month, as Cobbing comments:

> Despite all the evidence to the contrary ... the Company issued the following laconic and mendacious statement: 'Lobengula still remains friendly and cordial to our representatives, and [has not withdrawn] his permission for us to enter Mashonaland.'

By this date, in fact, Lobengula and his people were preparing for war.

On 27 May, Jameson arrived at Palapye in British Bechuanaland where he was joined the next day by Lieutenant-Colonel E. G. Pennefather of the 6th (Iniskilling) Dragoon Guards, whom Sir Henry Loch – Robinson's successor as High Commissioner – had persuaded Rhodes to accept as commander of the Pioneer Column.

By now Johnson and the Pioneer Corps had encamped beside the Limpopo River, while members of the British South Africa Company's Police, which had been raised to assist them in the occupation of Mashonaland, had assembled not far away beside the Macloutsie, where they were soon to be joined by Johnson and the Pioneers. Also present beside the Macloutsie were several companies of the Bechuanaland Border Police which had been moved up to the border area to support the Pioneer Column.

By 10 June, Selous had overseen the cutting of a road east from the Macloutsie to the Tuli River, and at the end of the month the Pioneer Corps and four troops of the British South Africa Company's Police advanced from Macloutsie to the Tuli: it was a well-equipped expedition whose armament included Maxim machine-guns. Beside the Tuli they were met by a delegation from Lobengula bearing a message that the king objected to what was occurring and that if they crossed the river they could expect trouble.

As Lobengula's messengers were heading back to Bulawayo, Selous obtained permission from his superiors to cross the Tuli with B troop of the Pioneers and begin creating another stretch of road. Early on 13 July, they reached the Umshabetsi River (about seventeen miles east of the Umzing-wani, a larger river they had forded), and halted after hacking part of the way through thick woodland.

On the 18th, the main column arrived, after following in their tracks (two companies of the BSACP had been left to defend a fort that had been erected beside the Tuli), and from the Umshabetsi the column then advanced, moving north-east towards the Lundi River. Selous, who was once again to the fore, this time with A troop of the Pioneer Corps and a contingent of Ngwato, tells us that 'as the entire column of over eighty waggons ... in single file, straggled out to a length of sometimes over two miles, it was decided to cut two parallel roads from this point, upon which the column moved in two divisions'.

The column continued making its arduous way across the humid lowveld, with thick mopane bush rendering the going difficult and restricting visibility, thereby offering would-be Matabele assailants cover. At night the column laagered and employed the services of a 10,000 candle-power naval searchlight charged by a steam engine, capable of engendering superstitious awe among any of Lobengula's scouts watching the column's progress.

On 1 August, the column encamped beside the Lundi River, while Selous scouted ahead and found a narrow winding pass by which the men could ascend over a thousand feet on to the south-western portion of the high plateau of Mashonaland. Late on 13 August, the column finally reached the plateau (en route from the Lundi, Pennefather received another ultimatum from Lobengula ordering him to retrace his steps at once or risk being attacked). Captain Hoste, the commander of B Company of the Pioneers states: 'Our relief on leaving the hot steamy low veld, where ... we had seldom been able to see more than two hundred yards round us and arriving on the open veld with a cool invigorating breeze blowing may be imagined.'

Within days they were joined by Sir John Willoughby and a company of the BSACP, who had come up from Tuli, escorting a number of wagons and livestock. Then, from what was to soon become Fort Victoria (in 1891 a fort was built to hold the pass), the column pressed on without incident. As Selous comments: 'On the open downs, with our force of 500 mounted men, we would most certainly have cut up any force [Lobengula] could have sent against us.' Furthermore, he aptly notes: 'Lobengula probably never wanted to fight, though it is the most absolute nonsense to talk of his ever having been friendly to the expedition.' Selous believed, moreover, that the presence of the Bechuanaland Border Police besides the Macloutsie acted as a deterrent: 'Had the Matabele attacked the pioneer force on its way to Mashonaland, they knew very well that [the BBP] would have ridden [into Matabeleland] and made things lively for their king in the neighbourhood of Bulawayo.'

On the morning of 11 September, while the column was crossing the Hunyani River, Pennefather and two other officers went ahead to find a suitable site for establishing a fort and future settlement. They found it near the Makabusi River, and the following day the column was directed to the chosen location, which henceforth was to be known as Fort Salisbury. (It is now part of Zimbabwe's capital, Harare.)

At 10 a.m. on the 13th, the column paraded dismounted in full dress and witnessed the raising of the Union Flag. That afternoon, work on the

191

fort began and by the end of the month it was completed. On 30 September, with no opposition having been encountered from the Shona, the Pioneer Corps was disbanded and the men scattered to search for gold and stake out farms.

The company had appointed an ex-Indian civil servant, Archibald Colquhoun, as its first 'Administrator' of Mashonaland, and he set to work forming a rudimentary administration to deal with such matters as the establishment of roads and postal communications. Moreover, on 28 September 1890, he declared that the Company's 'Mining Laws' were in force in Mashonaland – a ruling that exceeded anything authorised by Lobengula. As Palley comments: 'These went far beyond regulations for mining or for the grant of licences to persons to mine: they purported to set up courts with civil and criminal jurisdiction and laid down penalties for offenders.' They were thus modified following the intervention of the Colonial Secretary.

On 20 November 1890, Loch, a staunch imperialist, urged the British government to assume jurisdiction in Mashonaland and to delegate it to the Chartered Company, maintaining that there were 400 miners in the country 'not subject to any lawful authority' and that the place would become 'a disgrace to civilisation'.

Partly as a result of a fear of Boer encroachment beyond the Limpopo, on 9 May 1891, an Order in Council was issued by the British government. It alleged that 'by treaty ... sufferance [on the part of Lobengula] and other lawful means', Queen Victoria possessed power and jurisdiction in a vast area of the African interior, including Matabeleland and Mashonaland, and declared the area to be a British protectorate. The powers previously granted to the Chartered Company were not abridged by the Order, for the imperial authorities did not wish to become involved in the administration of the area and, to quote Palley, the company was thus to act 'as the instrument of administration under the protection of the Crown'.

At this date, of course, the company was only in effective occupation of Shona territory, over which Lobengula still claimed sovereignty. Even after November 1891, when Lobengula granted land and legal rights to a German named Edward Lippert who, unknown to him, had agreed to sell the so-called Lippert Concession to the Chartered Company, this claim remained in force. Hence a clash of interests was inevitable, with both Matabele monarch and British company viewing the Shona as their subjects.

The problem was demonstrated in late 1891, for on 1 December, Jameson received word that a party of Lobengula's warriors had killed a Shona chief called Nemakonde or Lomaghundi, whose kraals were located some 70 miles or so north-west of Salisbury. Emboldened by the presence of the whites in Mashonaland, the chief, who had been one of Lobengula's tributaries, had sent Lobengula word that he was no longer the king's 'slave', a declaration that had led the Matabele monarch to reiterate that as far as he was concerned nothing had changed: rightful sovereignty over Mashonaland belonged to him and no one else. Jameson responded by informing Lobengula that 'in the event of any subsidiary chief not paying his tribute as formerly', the king should 'appeal to the white man in Mashonaland' whose laws were 'framed for black as well as white'.

Subsequently, both Jameson and Lobengula trod carefully. The latter certainly did not wish to go to war with the whites (he was well aware of Cetshwayo's downfall in 1879), while Jameson, despite accusations sometimes levelled to the contrary, had no wish to precipitate a conflict. For instance, on 22 May 1893, he wrote as follows to the Civil Commissioner at Fort Victoria:

> Make the residents of your district understand that they are not to go into Matabeleland; if people persist in doing so and get into trouble, the Company will take no steps whatsoever to assist them, but will severely punish anyone caught on the border.

The 'border' to which Jameson referred lay, according to him, between Matabeleland and Mashonaland, roughly on the line of the Umniati and Shashe Rivers.

Nor does Jameson appear to have been hell-bent on war. Glass comments that control of 'Matabeleland was the goal of the Company'. This is of course true; but as he also notes, Jameson appears to have entertained the possibility that this could perhaps be achieved peacefully. Matabele were already coming to work in Mashonaland, and in a letter to his brother of 4 October 1893, Jameson was to write that he had thought it possible that 'a policy of gradual absorption of the Matabele amongst our black labourers ... would have been better than war'. But instead of Lobengula's kingdom being gradually undermined, it was to meet its end in bloodshed.

Descent into war

1893 was to witness a major transformation in relations between the Matabele on the one hand and the Chartered Company and the settlers, whom Jameson described at the commencement of that year as a 'fair sized pauper community'.

Tension had begun to mount the previous year and worsened in 1893. A number of incidents contributed to the descent into war. The most notable occurred in June 1893, after a Shona chief called Bere, who lived near Fort Victoria, a small town 165 miles due east of Bulawayo in whose vicinity many whites had settled, stole some of Lobengula's cattle. In response, the king sent a small punitive impi across Jameson's 'border' between Matabeleland and Mashonaland. However, the impi was met by a young officer named Captain Lendy, who had been appointed Magistrate of Fort Victoria in March, and was persuaded to return. But as June drew to an end, Lobengula decided to send a much larger impi across the 'border', perhaps to recover the stolen cattle and bring errant Shona chiefs such as Bere back into line: whites were not to be molested and Lobengula sent word to Jameson and Lendy (respectively at Salisbury and Fort Victoria) to this effect.

On Sunday, 9 July, the impi set to work in the Fort Victoria area without warning, for it struck before Lobengula's correspondence had been delivered. Of the day's events John Meikle, a resident of Fort Victoria, recalled years later:

> I was lying in bed with a bad attack of fever. From early morning I seemed to hear what appeared to be a hum of many voices and I could not think what it meant. It turned out that the noise was caused by hundreds of Mashonas coming in from outside for protection.

Meikle subsequently saw Matabele warriors coming down on either side of the town, and closing in at the lower end of Fort Victoria, killing any Shona unfortunate enough to be within stabbing reach. Another eye-witness, an Anglican minister, Reverend A. D. Sylvester, wrote within weeks of the raid:

> About 3 o'clock in the afternoon, whilst I was holding my Sunday school, I found my church and parsonage surrounded by ... Matabele, who were on all sides massacring the Mashonas without mercy, simply out of thirst for blood.

Melina Rorke, who was likewise present in Fort Victoria, comments that 'insolent Matabele swaggered through the streets of the town with their bloody spears and rattling shields'.

On the morning of the following day (and not the 14th, as is often said), the commander of the impi, Manyao, entered the town with a dozen or so followers and handed over a letter to the senior figure present – Lendy was out conducting a patrol – written on Lobengula's behalf on 28 June by a European called James Dawson, whom the king had known since 1884. Among other things, the letter stated that Shona who took shelter with the whites were to be handed over for punishment. At 4 p.m., Lendy appeared on the scene and was asked by Manyao to hand over the Shona men, women and children huddled in the town who, he said considerately, would be taken off and killed in the bush away from the vicinity of Fort Victoria. Lendy refused, and the induna and his attendants withdrew.

Meanwhile, elsewhere on the 10th, Manyao's warriors had moved against kraals in the neighbourhood which had escaped their attention the previous day, killing Shona and seizing livestock. The days that followed witnessed more of the same. Meikle comments: 'For fifty miles the country was laid waste and not a kraal left standing. The inmates for the most part took refuge with their flocks and herds in inaccessible places. Their greatest loss was their granaries.' Just how many Shona perished is uncertain. Selous put the figure at over 400, while the Reverend Sylvester said that hundreds were 'murdered wholesale'. Both are perhaps exaggerations.

As Robert Blake comments:

The raid symbolised the whole dispute about jurisdiction over the Shona. Lobengula and the senior induna... who represented him, were acting legitimately by their own lights. The Shona were their 'dogs'. What business had the white men to interfere? Equally, the representatives of the company could not tolerate an incursion that made a mockery of British rule and the *Pax Britannica*.

Meanwhile, on the 9th, Jameson had received a telegram from Lendy reporting the raid and word from Lobengula that the impi would not harm whites. He was not unduly perturbed. Indeed, on the following day, he sent a telegram to Rutherford Harris, the Company's secretary in South Africa, stating that 'really this little trouble might be quoted by you as proof of Loben's friendliness vide his wire [from Palapye] on the trouble he takes to prevent raiding parties interfering with whites'.

On the 13th, Jameson set out to cover the 188 miles from Salisbury to Fort Victoria. He arrived on the 17th to find the settlers in militant mood, the raid having been a more serious affair than he had thought. It had not only resulted in the deaths of Shona but had also alarmed whites in the district and brought economic activity such as mining to a standstill. Moreover, he discovered that in the preceding days Lendy and the settlers of the district, who had gathered for safety, had hurriedly turned Fort Victoria into an armed camp. A laager had been formed under the south wall of the fort to accommodate those unable to enjoy its security. Lendy had overseen matters, and was busy training a force of 400 settlers for action.

Jameson therefore telegraphed Cape Town, giving the plight of the Shona as a reason for driving the impi off and received the following reply: 'Yours just received. Mr Rhodes understands that you may find it necessary in the interests of the Mashonas ... to drive the Matabele away ... but he says if you do strike, strike hard.'

At about midday on the 18th, Jameson met with Manyao and the Matabele indunas, one of whom, Manyao's second-in-command, Umgandan, was a cocksure young man of striking appearance, 'the handsomest African native I have ever seen,' recalled Hans Sauer, one of the Europeans present. The indaba (meeting) took place just outside the gates of the fort and Jameson treated the Matabele in a blunt manner, ordering them out of the country. 'I told them I would give them an hour to retire,' reported Jameson to Loch later the same day, no doubt meaning that the impi must start heading towards what Jameson claimed was the border (some 30 miles away), rather than cross it within that time period, as is sometimes maintained.

The following May, Lord Henry Paulet, one of those present at the indaba, told a Commission of Inquiry, headed by Francis Newton CMG: 'I did not conceive that he meant [Manyao] to cross the border in an hour, because it was an impossibility.' Others said the same thing, and it was a view accepted by the commission. Nevertheless, as Glass comments:

> While clearly an hour was given, the argument becomes somewhat academic when we realise ... that the Matabele had no such measurement of time. They would not have understood what was meant by an 'hour', and all [the interpreter] could do was to point at the sun, and then lower down in the western sky.

At about 2.15 p.m., an hour and three-quarters or so after the indaba had ended, Jameson sent Lendy with orders to drive the Matabele off if they had not commenced their withdrawal. Lendy promptly rode off at the head of a patrol almost entirely consisting of volunteers – only a handful of the men were policemen. Its strength is uncertain, but about 50 men seems the most probable figure.

The patrol cantered very briefly before slowing down to a walking pace, heading a little west of north. After riding a short distance, a small advance guard was sent 600 yards or so ahead, while flanking parties were likewise detached.

Soon the advance guard caught sight of about 70 Matabele 'moving slowly, in disjointed lots and groups', states the Newton Report, 'from the S.W to the N.E. in the direction of Magomoli's kraal', a homestead belonging to a Shona chief ten miles due north of Fort Victoria which Manyao had made his headquarters. They were carrying grain and driving stolen cattle.

The Matabele in question were led by Umgandan, who had quarrelled with Manyao as the impi had headed towards Magomoli's kraal after the indaba. While Manyao and most of the impi were in favour of withdrawal, in accord with Jameson's ultimatum, Umgandan and some of the young warriors were in defiant mood. Newton was to record that all the witnesses at the subsequent inquiry agreed that the young induna had been 'insolent in voice and manner' at the indaba, giving the impression that he meant to defy Jameson. Hence, instead of pressing on towards Magomoli's kraal to prepare for departure, Umgandan and his followers had broken off to attack a kraal west of Fort Victoria, while a second wayward party proceeded to invest another Shona settlement, Makoombi's, roughly halfway between Fort Victoria and Magomoli's kraal.

About an hour after leaving Fort Victoria, receiving word of the sighting of Umgandan's party, Lendy and the rest of the patrol rode up, and he gave the order to open fire. The surprised warriors fled and were pursued by the patrol, now in extended formation. From time to time the pursuers dismounted, fired and then continued what, to use Newton's words, 'became a mere chase', for 'the Matabele practically offered no resistance'. After about ten minutes, Lendy gave orders to cease firing. But some members of the patrol pressed on and in so doing came across the Matabele force threatening Makoombi's kraal. They fired a few shots at long range, whereupon the warriors ran off.

In all, little execution was done by the patrol. Lendy told Jameson upon his return to Fort Victoria later in the afternoon that about 30 Matabele had been killed, but the subsequent Newton Report did not accept this figure, stating, 'The Induna Manyao and his colleague Umgengwan say – and they should know best – that eleven men were missing of whom nine are believed to have been killed, and two to have run away.' Newton thus concluded 'that in the pursuit of the Matabele there was no wholesale slaughter of the natives nor deliberate shooting of men already shot'.

Umgandan was among the Matabele who died, having been 'shot at by several men', reported Newton. An account of his death is to be found in Meikle's *Reminiscences*. He states that upon moving against the induna's party, the patrol dismounted 'and began firing at the fleeing Matabele'. He continues:

One of the first to fall was the king's nephew [Umgandan].... He was a fine, big specimen of a Zulu who was too proud to run [Newton concluded that he was suffering from the after-effects of an attack of colic] and he followed the others until he fell. He was on my right front about one hundred and fifty yards away. Somehow I could not bring myself to open fire on him although he was nearest to me.

'I have declared war on the Matabele!'

The victorious patrol, as has been noted, returned to Fort Victoria late on the afternoon of the 18th and Lendy reported what had happened to Jameson, falsely maintaining that the Matabele had been the first to open fire. No doubt encouraged by the fact that the patrol had routed the Matabele without loss to themselves, Jameson was determined to prosecute matters to a finish, a stance in line with general settler opinion in Fort Victoria. One of those present, Ivon Fry, tells us that upon hearing Lendy, Jameson turned to people lining the fort's walls and announced: 'I hereby declare war on the Matabele!'

Jameson spent much of the evening of the 18th in the telegraph office in Fort Victoria, communicating with both Sir Henry Loch and Rhodes, telling them what had happened and arguing in favour of war.

The following morning found him on the wire once again, this time sending word north to Major Forbes of the BSACP in Salisbury. According to Forbes, Jameson declared 'that the events of the previous day had shown him clearly that if we wished to remain in Mashonaland, and not to sacrifice all that we had gained in the previous three years, we must settle the Matabele question once and for all'. Jameson had a plan. Three columns, each of 250 mounted men, were to advance respectively on Bulawayo from Salisbury, Fort Victoria and Tuli, with Forbes leading the men from Salisbury before assuming command of all the company's combined forces.

It is sometimes maintained that the primary motivation for deciding to wage war against the Matabele was a desire to boost the value of the Chartered Company's shares on the Stock Exchange. The company was undoubtedly in monetary difficulties and Jameson was aware that the conquest of Matabeleland could prove financially advantageous. On 19 July, he telegraphed to a colleague in Kimberley that 'Rhodes might consider the advisability of completing the thing ... as we have an excuse for the row over murdered women and children now and the getting [of] Matabeleland open would give us a tremendous lift in shares and everything else.' Nonetheless, as Glass comments, 'If the Company had been thinking of a war to boost share prices why should Jameson need to mention it at that particular moment?' The war, he correctly states, 'was not brought about for this purpose – it was the result of a chain of events in Mashonaland and of Jameson's decision of 18 July 1893.'

Some argue that the events which culminated in Jameson taking that decision were deliberately manufactured by Chartered Company officials anxious for war, a central facet of the plot being an invitation to Lobengula to send warriors across the 'border' to punish wayward Shona, such as the cattle thieves, so that Jameson would have an excuse to launch hostilities against the king guilty of ill-treating Shona. The evidence, however, does not warrant such a conclusion.

On the evening of the 19th, Jameson contacted the sympathetic Loch once again, stating, 'Surely we are justified in punishing the murderers more severely – in fact, in getting rid of them altogether.' The time was right to strike, he declared, it was the best season of the year for campaigning (which would be hindered by summer rains if delayed) and, what was more, much of Lobengula's army was known to be absent, having departed, on 11 June, on a campaign against members of the trans-Zambezian alliance, such as the Lozi in what is now western Zambia.

As noted above, Jameson's stance was in line with general settler senti-ment. On the following day, 20 July, a public meeting in Salisbury expressed its hope that advantage would be taken 'of the present position of affairs to settle, once and for all, the supremacy of British power and civilisation in this territory'.

Loch was likewise keen to see this occur, but on 24 July, following further contact from Jameson, he declared:

I could not with the great interests at stake sanction any forward movement until preparations [which Jameson had already initiated] were sufficiently advanced so that, humanly speaking, success would be assured.... I fully appreciate the readiness expressed by the Euro-peans in Mashonaland to respond to the call of the Chartered Company, but a question of such paramount importance as making war upon the Matabele must be left to the decision of the authorities as to the policy to be pursued, the time to be selected, should the necessity arise, and the manner in which it is to be conducted. But they may rest assured the authorities are fully alive to the urgency of the situation and will not be backward in taking action that will secure not only the present but the future safety of the country.

The following day, Lord Ripon, the Colonial Secretary, with whom Loch had been in contact, reminded the High Commissioner that the British government's policy concerning developments in the Chartered Company's area of operation had always been to leave it to fend for itself: no imperial military assistance would be forthcoming.

On 26 July, Loch informed Ripon that the company was 'fully aware' that it was 'solely responsible for providing both men and money for any war' against Lobengula. On the other hand, Loch declared that such a war would probably have an impact on the neighbouring Bechuanaland Protectorate: the imperial forces there, he maintained, thus needed to be strengthened, something that he had begun doing by recruiting more men to serve in the Bechuanaland Border Police – a force which, under instruc-tion from Loch, proceeded to concentrate at Macloutsie, the northerly base of the BBP.

On 27 July, meanwhile, runners arrived at Bulawayo to report the clash on the 18th that had resulted in Umgandan's death. Lobengula reacted angrily to the news that Lendy's men had opened fire first. On the king's behalf, a European at his court named Johann Colenbrander wrote a letter to Loch, complaining about the fact that the Matabele had been attacked and that wayward Shona had been afforded protection in Fort Victoria. Furthermore, while anxious to avoid war, the king embarked upon acrimonious correspondence with Jameson, for he was determined not to relinquish his claims over the Shona and rejected the existence of the Umniati–Shashe border, to which he had never conceded.

It was in August that Lobengula sent envoys on a peace mission (the most senior of whom, Umshete, had visited England on diplomatic business in 1889), initially to see Loch at the Cape, then to travel on to see Queen Victoria. Hearing of the embassy, Jameson and other Chartered Company officials threw a spanner in the works, informing Loch that Lobengula was not really interested in peace: he was trying to buy time to prepare for war. Umshete's party arrived in Cape Town on 23 September and a number of futile interviews followed with Loch, in which Lobengula's representatives refused to discuss the issues of the border and the Shona: the country, and the Shona, belonged to the Matabele king. It was as simple as that.

By the time of Umshete's arrival at the Cape, Jameson's military preparations were well advanced. In July he had sent Captain Pieter Raaff, Resident Magistrate of Tuli since March 1892 and a veteran of the Zulu War of 1879 (who had commanded Raaff's Transvaal Rangers and had been awarded the CMG), south to Johannesburg to procure 750 horses and recruit soldiers, although Jameson did not inform Loch of the recruitment campaign.

Jameson intended Lendy to lead one of the columns – the one that would set out from Fort Victoria – but Lendy declined to take charge and so, on 31 August, Major Allan Wilson, a Scotsman by birth, was confirmed as commander of the Victoria Column, which was still being prepared for action.

By this date, it had been decided that Forbes, who had been able to arm and equip 250 men from the company's stores in Salisbury, should move south to Fort Charter (55 miles closer to Fort Victoria than Salisbury) and await the arrival of mounts. By 10 September, Forbes's men were at Charter, by which time some horses had already arrived and others were to do so as the month progressed.

Furthermore, by late September, Raaff was back at Tuli – he arrived on the 23rd – after successfully recruiting men in the Transvaal and procuring horses for them and members of the other columns. They, and the other men who had volunteered to serve on behalf of the company, would not receive regular pay. But upon the campaign's successful conclusion there would be rewards in Matabeleland: loot, land and gold claims.

Late August and September also witnessed a strong anti-Matabele propaganda campaign by the Chartered Company, which falsely reported that swarms of Lobengula's warriors were menacing Europeans in both Mashonaland and Tati (the latter having come under the direct administration of Loch the previous year). As Glass comments: 'It was necessary to create a war atmosphere, to establish a picture of Matabele aggressiveness, so that when the columns were ready to advance the request for them to do so would not be without strong support.'

Finally, on the morning of 5 October, things came to a head when Loch authorised Jameson to proceed against Lobengula. He did so after hearing that on 30 September Matabele warriors had fired at members of one of the Chartered Company's patrols, and that thousands of Matabele warriors were massing on the Mashonaland border. Later on the 5th, Loch received a report that a patrol of Bechuanaland Border Police had been fired on that very morning.

Contrary to the wishes of the British government, the High Commissioner had long wanted to commit imperial forces to the impending conflict. He was not motivated by a spirit of altruistic support for the Chartered Company. Rather he hoped that imperial troops would play the dominant role in the conflict, thereby paving the way for him to exercise a greater say in the company's administration of Mashonaland and Lobengula's soon-to-be conquered domain.

Indeed, later in the month, he was to suggest to Ripon that political control of the company's territories be taken away, albeit temporarily, and vested in government officials responsible to himself and to the home authorities. The report that members of the BBP had been fired on gave him an excuse to involve imperial forces in the war – Loch had been authorised by the Colonial Secretary on 23 September to sanction prompt action if circumstances required.

On the 5th, therefore, with the Matabele 'taking the offensive', the High Commissioner ordered the Bechuanaland Border Police massed at Macloutsie to act in concert with the forces of the Chartered Company against Lobengula. Although there is good reason to reject the veracity of the reports received by Loch, upon the basis of which he authorised the commencement of hostilities, the Matabele War had begun.

CHAPTER 10

'THEIR STORY IS IMMORTAL' – THE MATABELE WAR

'I believe that no civilised army could have withstood the terrific fire they did for at most half as long.' *Sir John Willoughby*

On 5 October, when Jameson received authorisation from Loch to move against Lobengula, Forbes and the Salisbury Column had already begun edging closer to Matabeleland from Charter. Indeed, he had begun doing so on the 2nd. Then, on the morning of 7 October, the order to advance was received and the column began moving in earnest. The following day it crossed the 'border', the Umniati River, and headed south-west to a small kopje covered with old mine workings, Iron Mine Hill, 25 miles east of present-day Gweru. Forbes arrived on the 14th and awaited the Victoria Column, with whose commander he had agreed to rendezvous at the site.

Meanwhile, Allan Wilson and the Victoria Column had set off on the 4th. After initially moving north towards Charter, they headed west upon reaching an old post station at Makori. After travelling in that direction for eight miles, they halted and remained stationary for three days. On the 9th they were joined by Jameson and Sir John Willoughby (who was acting as Jameson's military adviser), who rode up from Fort Victoria. Then, on the 10th, Lendy appeared on the scene with an Artillery Troop and 56 dismounted men from Tuli. Probably on the following day, the strengthened column crossed the Shashe River, bound for Iron Mine Hill.

On the morning of the 16th, the Victoria Column made its rendezvous with Forbes. It also met up with Jameson and Willoughby, for they had pressed on ahead of the column to see Forbes. As Glass pertinently comments: 'One doubts whether they would have been quite so intrepid – even foolhardy – had Jameson himself credited any of the hair-raising reports with which the High Commissioner had [recently] been assailed.'

So far no major Matabele forces had been encountered. Contact, however, had been made the previous day with small parties of Matabele. On the 15th, Forbes and some of his command had rounded up Matabele cattle and while doing so, one of his men, Captain John Campbell, an ex-Artillery officer, was shot and wounded by a warrior sheltering behind a rock. Moreover, Forbes and some of his men came across about twelve warriors, with whose young leader Forbes parleyed before deeming it wise to retire. More significantly, on the 15th, members of the Victoria Column briefly clashed with a number of Matabele, members of the Insuga regiment.

Within hours of the arrival of the Victoria Column at Iron Mine Hill, Campbell died of his injuries. He was buried at dusk that evening with full military honours. 'All the Salisbury and a great many of the Victoria Column attended the funeral,' states Forbes in one of the chapters he contributed to W.A. Wills's and L. T. Collingridge's book, *The Downfall of Lobengula.* 'I think there were a good many standing round the grave that evening who realised for the first time that what we had undertaken was no child's play, but stern reality, and that poor Campbell's fate might at any time be the fate of one or all of us.'

At 5.30 a.m. on 17 October, the combined force left Iron Mine Hill, heading south-westward towards Bulawayo, 135 miles away. The two columns marched parallel to each other and approximately 300 yards apart, where the ground permitted, and were guided by a Matabele defector called Mnyenyezi Khumalo.

The strength of the combined force is uncertain, for the sources are far from unanimous on this point. Nonetheless, it totalled fewer than 700 Europeans, about 155 Cape boys and other non-white ancillaries, as well as a force of about 400 Shona recruited in the vicinity of Fort Victoria.

Among its weaponry were five Maxim guns hoisted on to cavalry carriages. The Maxim was a machine gun that had been introduced to the British Army in 1889, and had first been employed in action in Uganda. It was fed with cartridges from belts, had a range of up to 2730 yards, and was capable of firing 600 rounds a minute.

On the 22nd, the columns entered the southern fringe of the vast Somabula Forest. Forbes states:

We found that we had to go through a narrow strip of thick bush with a good deal of cutting to be done. To make things worse a fog came on, and it was a very anxious time. We got through the bush safely however, and after crossing a nasty little stream, got up into the high open ground again.

The forest was an ideal place for the Matabele to conduct an ambush. Lobengula had heard his first reports of the invasion on the morning of 12 October, and an impi was indeed present in the forest, but failed to make contact.

It is believed that the number of Matabele warriors in 1893 probably numbered about 15,000, some of whom had just returned from the trans-Zambezian campaign and had been placed in isolation after contracting smallpox while they were away. Summers and Pagden have estimated that about 12,500 warriors were at the king's disposal to defend his kingdom against the invaders, and this is likely more or less correct. His principal regiment was Imbizo (sometimes spelt Imbezu) which had been formed in 1871, numbered about a thousand warriors – making it stronger than most or all of the other regiments – and contained a high proportion of Zansi. It had a fearsome reputation. Zansi were also found in other regiments, but the majority of Lobengula's warriors were either Enhla or Holi.

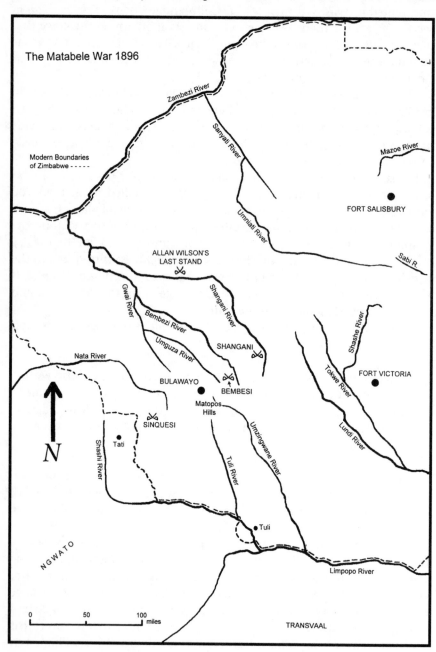

The Matabele War 1896

Modern Boundaries
of Zimbabwe - - - - -

Zambezi River

Sanyati River

Mazoe River

Umniati River

FORT SALISBURY

Sabi R.

ALLAN WILSON'S
LAST STAND

Gwai River

Bembezi River

Shangani River

Shashe River

Umguza River

SHANGANI

Nata River

FORT VICTORIA

BULAWAYO

Tokwe River

BEMBESI

Matopos
Hills

SINQUESI

Lundi River

Tati

Shashi River

N

Umzingwane River

Tuli River

Tuli

NGWATO

Limpopo River

0   50   100
|___|___| miles

TRANSVAAL

Indeed, some regiments were entirely composed of Matabele of Shona descent.

Lobengula's warriors were armed with traditional weapons, including battleaxes of Shona origin. Some also carried multi-barbed Tonga fish spears from the banks of the Zambezi. Firearms were also employed. In March, for instance, Lobengula had finally distributed the Rudd Concession rifles.

The dress of Matabele warriors at this date differed somewhat in appearance from that of earlier days, for over the decades a transformation had occurred. New types of headdress had come into vogue, (headbands had virtually disappeared), and were usually made of black ostrich or guinea fowl feathers stitched to a string net. They differed in style (although said to have been identical among members of the same regiment) and were normally worn in conjunction with capes made from black ostrich feathers or the tails of jackals.

By 24 October, the Salisbury and Victoria Columns, were approaching the east bank of the Shangani River, having burnt kraals and seized livestock and grain en route. On the far bank could be seen a line of high bushy hills or kopjes through which ran a pass. While work on preparing drifts got underway, Forbes and Wilson crossed the river to seek a suitable place to laager and found an open ridge about 1000 yards from the river. By 3 p.m. two drifts had been prepared and the columns proceeded to cross (covered by men Forbes had sent forward on to the west bank) and made their way on to the ridge where two laagers were formed some 1000 yards from the nearest hills.

The laagers were about 150 yards apart and connected by thick fences of thorn which enclosed the majority of the draught oxen. About 80 yards or more to their rear, another enclosure was formed to hold at least 1000 captured cattle; and other seized cattle were sited further away on a slight rise some 600 yards or so behind the Salisbury laager, between it and the river, at a point where the native levies were encamped. In an account written just over a year later, Willoughby comments that with the exception of 'isolated patches of bush, the ground in the vicinity of the laagers was fairly open to a radius varying from 300 to 600 yards'.

The battle of Shangani

A Matabele impi under Mjaan Khumalo, a cousin of Lobengula, was close at hand – it was the force that had failed to make contact in the Somabula Forest – and the following morning it moved in for the kill.

According to the accounts of Willoughby and Forbes, the impi numbered approximately 5000–6000 men, but Summers and Pagden favour a more conservative figure: 'It is unlikely that more than 3500 Matabele were present.' Ntabeni Khumalo (a grandson of Lobengula who served in Imbizo and recorded his recollections of the war in 1940) declared that the impi consisted of three regiments, Insuga (also known as Insukamini), Induba and Inqobo, although other sources also mention Ihlati, Amaveni and Isiziba.

The Matabele launched their assault before 4 a.m. They intended to take the enemy by surprise, but were thwarted, for the alarm was raised as they drew near in the darkness, and one of their regiments was not yet in position. Accounts differ as to how the invaders were alerted. Willoughby, for example, relates that one of the approaching Matabele fired his gun by mistake.

The same source comments that at 3.50 a.m., the sound of heavy firing was heard coming from the direction of the encampment to the rear of the Salisbury laager. That the Shona levies encamped on the rise were the first to be attacked is confirmed elsewhere. Forbes tells us that the 'friendlies' in question woke to find Matabele 'upon them and stabbing them', but that the survivors nonetheless managed to make their way to the laager.

Following this, the force of the Matabele assault was principally directed against the rear and right faces of the Salisbury laager and the left and rear faces of the Victoria laager, though, to quote Willoughby, the Matabele soon began 'a steady and continuous fire on all sides with Martini rifles and muzzle-loaders.' Owing to the darkness, the Matabele could not be seen at first and their positions were only given away by the flashes that occurred when they discharged their firearms.

In response, the defenders fired into the bush, employing both rifles and machine guns. Unfortunately, Shona levies guarding the captured cattle located in the enclosure near the laagers panicked and ran towards the Victoria laager, and as a result some of them were accidentally killed by machine gun fire.

Despite the defenders' stiff fire, Willoughby says that in several places the Matabele managed to advance to within 150 yards of the laagers and that a small number got as close as within 80 yards and managed to stampede the captured cattle in the enclosure abandoned by the Shona levies. But most of the Matabele did not advance beyond the edge of the bushes and, after about twenty minutes of heavy enemy fire, were compelled to retire further into the bush.

Forbes then sent out some mounted men to ride around the vicinity and help bring in any levies who had failed to reach the sanctuary of the laagers. No serious resistance was encountered (a few shots were fired by Matabele lurking in the bushes) and the horsemen soon returned with a few Shona.

Forbes records that shortly after this, 'when it was getting light enough to see some distance', a body of 200–300 Matabele warriors – the Insuga regiment – began moving forward from a small rise about 350 yards to the south-east. They advanced down the slope in a casual, 'most plucky' manner, and opened fire upon reaching the bottom, while other Matabele resumed shooting from the surrounding bush. But this assault likewise ended in failure. Forbes says that Insuga were subjected to very heavy fire by two or three Maxims and about 200 rifles, and soon withdrew with much greater alacrity than they had approached.

Subsequently, Forbes sent out 40 mounted men of the Salisbury Column to check whether the enemy had withdrawn, and horsemen likewise left the Victoria laager for the same purpose. Willoughby only mentions that troopers emerged from the Salisbury laager and says that they rode out at 4.45 a.m. while the light was still poor, whereas Forbes says that the mounted men left the laagers in broad daylight, i.e., sometime after dawn, around 5 a.m. Perhaps they were referring to different incidents, but in any event, the end result was the same, for both sources report that the troopers were driven back. Forbes states that within half a mile or so of the laagers, each body of troopers made contact with the enemy and, 'after a smart skirmish', withdrew, pursued by the enemy until supported by the defenders' Maxim fire.

According to Forbes, after the return of the troopers, a large number of Matabele appeared on a small hill approximately 2000 yards to the west, apparently in the process of reforming, but were dispersed by shellfire. For his part, Willoughby records that at 5.30 a.m., following a lull, the Matabele attacked once again, though in a less determined manner, and soon fell back before being reinforced by warriors (men who had not taken part in the earlier fighting) who took up a position about 2200 yards south-west of the laagers – probably the same incident mentioned by Forbes. However, shellfire forced them to give ground.

Mounted troops subsequently re-emerged from the laager and moved against the Matabele, some of whom were now sheltering in deep dongas to the north and south. The troopers from the Victoria Column succeeded in dislodging a small number of enemy they came across and pursued them for some distance, reportedly killing many of them. On the other hand, Captain Spreckley from the Salisbury laager did not encounter any rebels in the direction he rode. This was also true, at least initially, of Captain Maurice Heany. He rode off north-west with his men for about 1000 yards without seeing any enemy; but as he was about to engage Matabele to his front, he was attacked from both sides by a large number of warriors and had to conduct a fighting withdrawal. The Matabele in question then took up a position behind a kopje and opened fire. Forbes ordered them shelled by a 7-pounder and sent Heany (who had returned to the Salisbury laager) and Captain Henry Borrow against them. They found the Matabele gone. The desultory battle was over.

According to Forbes, only one of the Europeans present lost his life, a trooper of the Victoria Column who had been shot in the groin, while he places the number of native levies killed at between 40 and 50, and says that several native women and children also died. Willoughby, on the other hand, states that 23 black levies were killed, and that the wounded totalled 38, seven of whom were European.

Matabele losses were undoubtedly heavier. A. J. de Roos, a Dutchman who served with the column, states that 'the surrounding country was strewn with dead and wounded'. Forbes put the figure of Matabele dead at minimum 500, while Willoughby estimated that perhaps as many as 600 lost their lives: both figures are almost certainly too high.

The column broke camp at 3 p.m. and confidently pressed on, shadowed by the Matabele, who harassed them during subsequent days. On the 26th, at one stage, the horse carrying Captain Gwynyth Williams, a former officer in the Royal Horse Guards, bolted and carried him off out of sight. As Forbes later learned, Williams eventually reached broken terrain where he was killed in a fire-fight with warriors who had chased him. He was 'a very great loss'.

The battle of Bembesi

1 November 1893 witnessed the major engagement of the war. It occurred when the Matabele attacked the columns again when they were near the headwaters of the Bembesi River, about seventeen miles from Lobengula's capital. The impi involved consisted of the veterans of Shangani and reinforcements from Bulawayo, most notably Imbizo, Lobengula's finest regiment. It likely numbered over 6000 men, though slightly higher figures are sometimes given.

At 11.50 a.m., before battle was joined, the columns laagered on a small hill not far from the summit of a east-west ridge. The laagers were about 100 yards apart (that of the Salisbury Column was the more northerly) and a small kraal lay between them. The countryside in the immediate vicinity was open, but there was dense thornbush on the ridge, about 350 yards or more to the north. Lunch was cooked, and some of the men began to mend clothing. Such was their confidence, moreover, that they sent all their oxen and most of the horses a mile or so off to the south to graze and water on lower ground.

The Matabele were concealed in the thornbush. According to Summers and Pagden, they were heading west through the woodland in a strung-out formation extending about three-quarters of a mile, intent on ambushing the columns beside the Umguza River near Bulawayo. At about 12.50 p.m., states Willoughby, 'a dense mass of natives were seen emerging from the bush on a high ridge to the north-west', some one and a half miles away, and immediately came under 7-pounder shellfire. The warriors, who

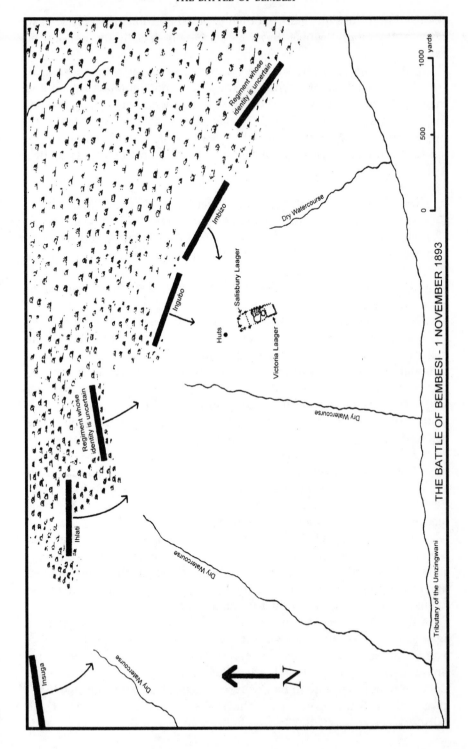

THE BATTLE OF BEMBESI - 1 NOVEMBER 1893

belonged to Insuga, hurriedly left their exposed position and took cover in a fold of the ground, where they were to remain virtually throughout the battle.

The vast majority of the Matabele, however, were still in the thornbush, and the regiments in the centre of the line – most notably Imbizo and Ingubo, which were closest to the laagers – rapidly made their way towards the edge of the bush. As a result, a lax pair of picquets were taken by surprise, one of whom was stabbed to death while the other successfully ran for his life towards the Salisbury laager, which provided covering fire. As Forbes comments:

> It was entirely owing to their own carelessness that they had been surprised, as although there were small patches of bush that were very thick, they could get a good view for 500 or 600 yards, and would have been quite safe if they had been keeping a proper look out.

Willoughby tells us that the closest Matabele rushed through the bush 'in splendid order' and almost immediately occupied its outer fringe, from where they opened fire while other regiments moved up in support.

Although some warriors unsuccessfully attacked the Victoria laager, the main Matabele thrust was against that of the Salisbury Column. Willoughby records that the assault was conducted 'with great determination and admirable pluck', but that the Matabele fire was generally ineffective for, as at Shangani, they mostly aimed too high.

Most of the defenders returned fire from behind the defences, but some behaved in a foolhardy manner by standing on the wagons, a risky stance even given the poor marksmanship of the enemy. One of those who did so was M. W. Barnard, who later recalled that the enemy came on in a disorganised manner, 'more in the shape of a lot of locusts than anything else'. Cecil Paddon, another participant, relates that small bodies of Matabele repeatedly rushed forward in an attempt to come to blows, but were repulsed. A few others took advantage of an area of dead ground between the bush and the Salisbury laager, and crawled up to some half-built huts about 100 or 150 yards to the north of the laager, from where they opened fire, inflicting some casualties on the enemy. Eventually, they were forced to withdraw, leaving two of their number dead.

Forbes goes on to say that while the main attack was in progress against the Salisbury laager's right face, several unsuccessful attempts 'were made to get around us' – attempts which were thwarted by Maxim fire. This evidently included fire by guns belonging to the Victoria Column which was able to manoeuvre its 7-pounder and four machine-guns – three Maxims and a Hotchkiss – so that they could assist the Salisbury laager.

The Maxims proved particularly deadly during the course of the battle. Imbizo suffered the most, and one of their number, Ntabeni Khumalo, later remarked that when the machine guns 'opened fire they killed such a lot of us that we were taken by surprise. The wounded and the dead lay in heaps.' For his part, Willoughby comments:

> The Maxims especially, and all the machine guns, played a most important part throughout, and, without their assistance, I think it is doubtful whether the rifle fire brought to bear could have succeeded in repelling the rush; the Matabele themselves have since stated that they did not fear our rifles so much, but that they could not stand against the Maxims.

Willoughby was impressed by the spirit of the warriors of Imbizo and Ingubo: 'I cannot speak too highly of the pluck of these two regiments. I believe that no civilised army could have withstood the terrific fire they did for at most half as long.' De Vere Stent, a journalist who was with the column, echoed his sentiments: 'The facing of the Maxims by the Ingubo regiment at a distance of a hundred and ten yards, [he no doubt underestimated the distance somewhat] was, perhaps one of the most magnificent displays of physical courage that Africa has ever seen.'

Forbes states that the Matabele assault lasted for about 40 minutes, whereupon the demoralised warriors began retiring, doing so 'in a sulky sort of way ... walking quietly back until they were out of sight.' His time-scale harmonises with that of Willoughby, who relates that at 1.30 p.m. the Matabele began to show signs of having had enough of the murderous fire to which they had been subjected and began withdrawing into the bush.

Meanwhile, when hostilities commenced, the oxen and horses had been recalled, and it was at about 1.25 p.m., shortly before the Matabele assaults ceased, that the horses reached the scene, whereupon some of them, frightened by the din of battle, stampeded. They ran off north-west in the direction of two Matabele regiments, Ihlati and Isiziba, which fired on them; they turned southward and in due course were brought back to the wagons by a few white horsemen, following an abortive attempt by Insuga to capture the animals. On the other hand, the oxen remained in the open throughout the battle, a short distance to the south of the laagers, protected by a small guard.

Firing ceased shortly before 2 p.m., at which point two parties left the laagers. About 100 dismounted men were sent to clear the enemy from the bush. They advanced in skirmishing order and drove off enemy they encountered. At the same time, a troop of horsemen headed off north-west in pursuit of Insuga. At about 2.15 p.m., however, they suddenly found

211

themselves under attack as warriors charged out of the bushes towards them on their right flank. Shell and Maxim fire forced these Matabele to retreat back into cover.

According to A. J. de Roos, at least 1000 Matabele must have died in the battle. Willoughby states that at least 800 to 1000 Matabele were either killed or wounded and that Lobengula's two finest regiments seemed to have been 'practically annihilated'. Forbes does not give an overall figure for Matabele casualties, but states that Imbizo must have had about 500 of their number (which he places at 700) either killed or wounded. A modern commentator, Julian Cobbing, rejects such figures, and calls attention to the fact that on 1 January 1894, the missionary, Helm, wrote that Imbizo and two other regiments between them only lost about 130 men in the entire campaign. It is likely that Matabele losses were over-estimated by de Roos and other contemporaries. Nevertheless, it seems reasonable to conclude that the campaign entailed more serious fighting than Cobbing maintains, though some Matabele regiments undoubtedly performed in a cautious manner.

The columns' casualties were low. No members of the Victoria Column died, while one member of the Salisbury Column was killed and eight wounded, two of whom subsequently died of their injuries. Willoughby states that the native levies sustained no casualties because they huddled together in the kraal, while Forbes notes that a 'coolie' was shot in the arm.

The following day, the victors resumed their march on Bulawayo. On 3 November, they heard a massive explosion emanating from its direction. Prior to the battle of Bembesi, Lobengula had abandoned his capital and had ordered its destruction if his warriors were defeated. Bulawayo had thus been torched: the explosion was caused by the destruction of his supplies of gunpowder and ammunition. Bulawayo was still smouldering when the column entered it on the 4th.

The advance of the Southern Column
Meanwhile, the third invasion force, the Southern Column, had likewise advanced into Matabele territory. It was commanded by Colonel Goold-Adams of the Bechuanaland Border Police and consisted of the BBP Loch had ordered to assemble at Macloutsie, as well as Raaff's force of volunteers, for on 6 October Jameson had instructed the latter to act jointly with the BBP, following a request to that effect by the High Commissioner.

The Southern Column set off from Macloutsie on 11 October, having been slowed down by Raaff's late departure from Tuli, which, much to the fury of Loch, he only left on the 10th. The delay had been ordered by Jameson who wished to retard Goold-Adams's progress so that the Salisbury and Victoria columns could arrive at Bulawayo before the imperial forces. The Southern Column numbered 450 officers and men, half of whom belonged to Raaff's contingent, and its armament included five Maxims.

On 18 October, the column was at Tati, having been reinforced en route by Khama (who had been approached by Loch to render military assistance) and nearly 2000 of his Ngwato, about half of whom possessed Martini-Henry rifles. Moreover, at Tati, Adams was joined by Selous who had expressly made his way out from England for the campaign.

The evening of the 19th witnessed the column's departure from Tati as Goold-Adams pressed eastwards. On the 29th, he arrived beside the Sinquesi River and laagered. He had left part of the column at a previous encampment, about ten miles behind on the Ramaquabane River, and the following day he ordered it to join him, aware that at least 3000 Matabele warriors under Gampo Sithole were about twelve miles ahead.

Most of the Ramaquabane force arrived on 1 November, but part of it under Captain Thomas A. Tancred halted about three miles short of Goold-Adams's camp, for their oxen were exhausted. Tancred thus outspanned and sent the stock to the nearest watering place. His command consisted of 35 members of the BBP, ten of the Chartered Company Police, and 100 Africans, while his armament included two Maxims.

Anxious to rejoin the bulk of the Southern Column, Tancred marched on early the next morning with part of his command, leaving the rest to follow in his wake. But at 8.15 a.m., when he was approximately half-way, he was attacked by about 650 Matabele. The sound of gunfire was heard by Goold-Adams, and mounted men hurriedly rode out of the laager to Tancred's aid. Selous was foremost among them, and was wounded upon his arrival. Thus assisted, Tancred's party was able to continue with the reinforcements. They came under increasing pressure, however, as more and more Matabele arrived on the scene. The warriors were finally driven off by the Maxims in Goold-Adams's laager and fell back into the surrounding hills. They were pursued by Goold-Adams's horsemen and Khama's troops, and were shelled by 7-pounders. By 11.30 that morning, hostilities were over. Gampo had not committed his entire command to the attack, which was largely undertaken by the Nyamayendlovu regiment, and of the Southern Column only two whites and a small number of natives had been killed. Selous estimated Matabele losses as about 100 men.

Goold-Adams then headed towards Bulawayo, albeit slowly, for Loch had failed to instill in him any sense of urgency. On 6 November, by which time Khama and his warriors had decided to make for home, Goold-Adams received word from Jameson that Bulawayo had been taken, that Lobengula was in flight, and that Gampo and his impi had withdrawn towards the Gwai River. The Southern Column belatedly arrived at the former Matabele capital on the 15th (although Goold-Adams had ridden ahead to see Jameson), by which time Loch had heard with dismay that the Chartered Company's forces had beaten his men to Bulawayo.

The pursuit of Lobengula

Lobengula was at Shiloh, about 30 miles north of Bulawayo, when he heard of the outcome of the battle of Bembesi. On 7 November, Jameson sent a letter calling upon him to return, for he would be 'kindly treated'. But Lobengula continued to move north, with the aim of crossing the Zambezi. As it was deemed vital to apprehend him, a strong force was despatched on the 14th, commanded by Forbes and comprising 300 Europeans (90 of whom were members of the BBP) and 200 native carriers. The armament included four Maxims and a 7-pounder.

Large Matabele forces were said to be 30–40 miles or so north of Bulawayo, such as in the vicinity of Shiloh, intent on protecting Lobengula's flight. Forbes arrived at Shiloh on the 23rd, having advanced by a circuitous route and, instead of encountering Matabele, found a force that Jameson had sent to Shiloh with fresh supplies. On the 25th, Forbes resumed his march with a reduced force of almost 300 men, together with four wagons, four Maxims and a Hotchkiss gun, and rations for twelve days. He had orders 'to push on and do his utmost to capture the King'.

The pursuit proved laborious, for heavy rains hampered progress. In three days they only covered seventeen miles. It was too slow. Forbes therefore ordered 130 of the men to head back with the wagons and continued the pursuit with the remainder, mostly Chartered Company volunteers, some of whom were on foot. He did so with two horse-drawn Maxims: supplies were carried by pack horses.

At about 3 p.m. on the afternoon of 3 December, as the column was nearing the Shangani River two envoys from Lobengula met a couple of stragglers after unsuccessfully trying to locate Forbes. They were troopers of the BBP, William Daniel and James Wilson – the latter proving to be a deserter from the 11th Hussars under an assumed name. They were handed a bag of gold sovereigns worth about £1000 and given the following message from the king: 'Take this and go back. I am beaten.' But instead of handing the money over to Forbes and delivering the message, the troopers kept the gold for themselves and withheld the message, a deception that led to their being imprisoned after the war when the truth became known.

Late on 3 December, Forbes encamped near the south bank of the Shangani. Shortly before this, at about 5 p.m., he had sent Major Allan Wilson and a small party consisting of several officers and twelve men on good mounts to reconnoitre across the river and determine the whereabouts of Lobengula, who had been joined during his flight by about 3000 warriors, some of them survivors of Shangani and Bembesi. Wilson was instructed to be back by 6.30 p.m., when darkness would fall. The time came and went: there was no sign of him. Hours passed – but still nothing. Finally, at about 9 p.m., two of Wilson's party returned, having been sent back because their horses were knocked up. Then, at 11 p.m., three others arrived. One of them told Forbes that he believed that Wilson wished Forbes to move up to join him during the night so that they could launch an attack on the Matabele at dawn. Instead, Forbes ordered Captain Borrow and twenty men of the Salisbury Column to reinforce Wilson in case he ran into trouble.

Early on the 4th, while Forbes was preparing to move off to reinforce Wilson with the rest of his command, the sound of gunfire was heard coming from across the river, which had risen significantly during the night and was now in spate. After travelling about half a mile up the Shangani, Forbes himself came under attack from warriors who had crossed the river beforehand. He managed to repel the enemy – whom he estimated as about 300 strong – at a cost of five men wounded, and sixteen horses and two mules killed.

Forbes notes that during the skirmish he and his men 'heard a considerable amount of firing where Major Wilson was'. Shortly thereafter, Forbes was joined by three of Wilson's men who swam across the flooded river, one of whom told him: 'I think I may say we are the sole survivors of that party.'

After being reinforced by Borrow, Wilson had ridden off at daylight on the 4th to capture Lobengula, having been told by a native that only a few men were with the king. After about six miles, he had come across Lobengula's wagons, but not the king, who had apparently abandoned them the previous afternoon and had continued his flight on horseback. Here Wilson came under fire from both front and flanks, and thus answered in kind. Seeing that the enemy were attempting to encircle him, he galloped back some 650 yards to a large ant-heap, dismounted his men, and fired at the oncoming warriors, before again retreating.

Wilson's party included two American scouts and he now ordered them and a trooper to ride post-haste to bring up Forbes, whom, as noted above, they located after swimming the Shangani. As the men rode off under attack by Matabele, Wilson's position became critical, for the enemy, including members of Imbizo and Ingubo, were encircling him and he was soon cut off. In a desperate final stand, Wilson and his 33 men fought to the last in a manner that won the admiration of their numerous assailants, who undoubtedly suffered heavier losses. Wilson and his colleagues were soon lionised by the white community. Of them H. Rider Haggard wrote: 'The fame of this death has spread far and wide ... their story is immortal and will be told hundreds of years hence.... Surely, it is no small thing to have gained such a death.'

The following morning, Forbes began to withdraw up the Shangani River from a laager he had hastily prepared the previous day. The journey proved a nightmare due to rain, lack of food, enemy harassment and the frequently difficult nature of the terrain. On the 8th, Matabele briefly attacked, and although they failed to harm any of their opponents, they succeeded in driving off the sole remaining pack-ox and cattle that Forbes's men had rounded up that morning. On the 10th, Matabele struck again twice, killing a member of the BBP and eight horses. After the second attack, the gun carriages were abandoned and the Maxims were carried on in blankets when the retreat resumed at 10 p.m. with a night march. On the 12th, a further clash occurred, with the Matabele concentrating their fire on the Maxims, and two of Forbes's men were wounded.

The spirits of the retreating men soared, however, on the evening of the 14th when they arrived at the camp of a well-supplied relief column that had come up from Bulawayo to meet them. Willoughby was one of those who welcomed Forbes and his men:

> The whole party, including the few wounded, five in number, had had a very severe time of it; the men had undergone considerable hardships from their clothes and boots being worn out with the rough wear, and from want of food, the last few days, having had to eat some of their horses.

Finally, on 18 December, they reached Bulawayo.

Meanwhile, in November, Goold-Adams had sent out patrols to the south and south-west of Bulawayo to induce Matabele forces there to surrender and thus follow the example of some of their colleagues who had already done so. Major S. D. Browne of the BBP led one patrol, consisting of 65 five mounted members of the BBP and 30 dismounted members of the Chartered Company's forces. He moved south into the Matopos and conducted sorties there until Christmas, meeting little resistance, burning homesteads, and receiving the surrender of some of the warriors in the area – men who had formerly belonged to the impi under Gampo. Gampo himself, with the remainder of his men, was encamped to the west on the Gwai River at this date and was only to 'come in' at the end of March the following year.

By this date the British South Africa Company had demobilised its volunteers and, on 22 December 1890, had established its new Police Force which consisted of 150 mounted men, almost all of whom had recently served in one or other of the company's columns.

In February, James Dawson, who enjoyed Lobengula's affection, set off from Bulawayo with a couple of companions to contact him. He took with him a letter in Loch's name promising Lobengula that he would be treated in an honourable manner. On 1 March, Dawson reported that they had come across the remains of Wilson and his men and had buried them, and confirmed reports (which had come in during the course of February) that Lobengula had died. According to Dawson, Lobengula had contracted smallpox and died of fever on 22 or 23 January when some 30–40 miles south of the Zambezi. Subsequently, however, some sources maintained that Lobengula had committed suicide by drinking poison, a view confirmed in 1943 by several leading Matabele.

In the meantime, the imperial forces in Matabeleland had begun to withdraw, and this process was completed in the weeks that followed the news of Lobengula's death.

CHAPTER 11

'THE MATABELE ARE COMING!' –
THE MATABELE REBELLION

'This region of turbulent savages, this last stronghold of South
African barbarism has been completely pacified.' *E. F. Knight*

Knight wrote the above in his book, *Rhodesia of Today*, published in
1895, the year in which the Chartered Company adopted the name
Rhodesia for combined territories that included Mashonaland and Matabeleland. He continued:

Very great credit indeed is due to the Administrator and other officers
of the Chartered Company who have with such admirable tact,
discretion and decision brought about this end....The natives
appeared to be unaffectedly pleased to see the white man in their
country and there is no doubt that our invasion and occupation have
been welcomed by the vast majority of the Matabele nation ... no
conquered people were ever treated with more consideration.

This was, in fact, a very complacent opinion, indeed a very inaccurate one,
and soon to be shattered. Substantial numbers of Matabele were about to
rise in revolt.

Various factors contributed to the rising; and it was the actions of the
victors of the Matabele War of 1893, such as Cecil Rhodes, which played a
decisive role in shaping the course of events. Robert Blake has commented
that as far as Rhodes was concerned, 'the important task after the war was
to keep the settlers sweet and carry out his promises to the Victoria volunteers'. Moreover, Rhodes was preoccupied by other matters – the seizure of
Matabeleland was, after all, only a means to an end. This, combined with
his mistaken belief that the Matabele were generally pleased to be free of
Lobengula's yoke, meant that he paid less attention than was required to
ensuring that the administration of the newly won territory was sound
and that the Matabele were treated with circumspection. As Terence
Ranger has aptly commented:

The most important thing about Rhodes's views and aims was that he
did not really pay much regard to Africans at all.... After 1893, for
instance, it did not occur to Rhodes that the Ndebele were any longer
a factor that had to be taken into account in adumbrating his plans
for the north.

The months that followed Lobengula's downfall witnessed the large-scale granting of Matabele grazing and agricultural land by the British South Africa Company to Europeans, not only to men who had participated in the conquest of Lobengula's domain but to other individuals as well, such as members of the British aristocracy. Well-nigh all the core territory of Lobengula's former kingdom was granted away. A Land Commission established in the latter half of 1894 (and upon which the British government was represented) reported in October that the amount of unallotted land remaining was insufficient to support the Matabele and that they should thus be relocated to proposed reserves to the north and north-east.

The reserves, however, were unsuited to settlement – for one thing, they were badly watered, 'cemeteries not homes'. Most, if not all, of the Matabele therefore remained where they were, squatting on land that was now, of course, the property of white individuals or syndicates, although in most cases the farms had no European presence at this date.

The new administration dealt in a similarly sweeping way with Matabele cattle, seizing not only livestock that had belonged to Lobengula but also animals owned by his subjects. The British government was anxious that the Matabele would be allowed to retain enough beasts for their needs. As Ripon told Loch on 13 December 1893: 'Her Majesty's government attach importance to securing to Matabele ample cattle for their requirements.' But reality fell short of this ideal. Much livestock was seized as loot in late 1893, and patrols charged with securing further cattle were frequently sent out the following year and indeed in 1895. Additionally, some whites simply helped themselves to livestock or bought it from Matabele at ridiculously low prices.

In October 1894, the Land Commission recommended that the company should immediately 'appoint officials entrusted with the duty of exercising supervision over the natives' and 'ascertaining the number of natives and cattle on the Reserves'. Consequently the Native Department in Matabeleland was established. At first it was essentially involved in collecting cattle, and a number of the commissioners were to prove themselves overbearing and at times brutal.

In June 1895, all Matabele cattle and their offspring were officially declared to belong to the company. Then, in November, the Land Commission's chairman, Judge Joseph Vintcent, declared that according to the Native Department, the number of cattle in Matabeleland still in African possession was 74,500, far short of the number estimated as belonging to the Matabele prior to the war (according to one reckoning, as many as 280,000). Of these, 40,930 were to be allotted to the Matabele: the remainder were to be sold off by the company to 'bona fide farmers', or would serve as police rations, or would be given to influential supporters such as Willoughby.

The seizure of the balance thus began in December and continued into early 1896. Compounding the resentment felt by the Matabele over the massive loss of livestock was the manner in which the 40,930 beasts allowed to remain in their hands were distributed, for Vintcent later admitted that the company gave cattle to 'the more deserving indunas and headmen'. As Ranger aptly remarks: 'It looks very much as if the share-out was used to reward "loyalty" rather than to meet the needs of the Ndebele in general.'

The Matabeleland Native Police, who numbered about 300 men by the beginning of 1896 (the force was raised in 1895 and was manned by Matabele) were involved in the seizure of cattle. They also played a major role in procuring forced labour, especially for the mining industry, and by late 1895 the force's commander, H. J. Taylor, declared that 9000 Matabele had been compulsorily recruited. Such tasks were hardly likely to make the police popular, but the harsh way in which some of them engaged in their work (there were reports of them raping a number of women while marauding around the countryside) heightened feelings even further. In short, they were widely hated by many of their own people.

To make things worse, in late February 1896, rinderpest struck and began to decimate many of the remaining cattle. To prevent the disease spreading, thousands of healthy beasts were shot by the Native Commissioners – in the view of many natives, an act of sheer malevolence. After Lobengula's downfall, a series of disastrous droughts and incessant plagues of locusts added to Matabele woes.

Nevertheless, Selous, speaking from first-hand experience, tells us that in the areas such as Filabusi where the first Matabele rose in revolt, rinderpest had not yet struck and locusts had done little damage to crops which, because of sufficient rain, 'were exceptionally good'. It would thus be a mistake to conclude that the Matabele rebellion was primarily due to hardship wrought by nature. Essentially, it was an uprising against the Chartered Company's harsh rule.

Before the revolt began, the strength of Matabele dissatisfaction was not grasped by the administration: so much so that on 29 December 1895, at Rhodes's behest, Jameson led the bulk of Rhodesia's white police (including the majority of those in Matabeleland) south in an attempt to overthrow the government in the Boer republic of the Transvaal. It was hoped that the invasion would receive support from non-Afrikaner whites in the republic, but things did not go according to plan and, on 2 January 1896, Jameson was forced to surrender.

The Matabele revolt
News of Jameson's defeat rapidly spread through Matabeleland, where preparations for revolt, partially involving the storage of grain in under-

ground granaries to sustain a campaign, had already been underway for several months. The time had come to act, and meetings were thus held by indunas to make plans, although the rising was never to be directed by a single dominant military authority. Nevertheless, the Matabele were soon to prove themselves potent adversaries. Weapons were still widely held, for measures undertaken to disarm the fighting men following the war of 1893 had been half-hearted and the regimental system had not been truly dismantled. Moreover, additional firearms had been surreptitiously procured, or were used by members of the Matabeleland Native Police, many of whom, trained as proficient marksmen, threw in their lot with the rebels at the outset. Furthermore, whereas the experiences of the Matabele War had no doubt dampened the martial enthusiasm of some warriors, this was by no means universally the case, for many regiments had either not been committed in 1893 or had not sustained significant casualties.

On 20 March, a detachment of African police was attacked at Godhlwayo and two 'boys' were killed. Three days later, the murder of isolated whites began. The first Europeans to die were probably those killed by the Godhlwayo rebels at neighbouring Filabusi, a farming and mining community about 65 miles south-east of Bulawayo, and among the murderers were former native police.

Killings soon occurred elsewhere in Matabeleland and in the main former tributary areas, and many whites fled to the sanctuary of centres such as Bulawayo, a town that had come into existence near Lobengula's former capital. Selous, for instance, who had been managing a farm on behalf of the Chartered Company at Essexvale about 25 miles to the south-east, rode to Bulawayo with his wife. Having ensured her safety, he then set off with one of a number of patrols detailed to try to quell the revolt and rescue fellow whites. In his book, *Sunshine and Storm in Rhodesia*, Selous writes that there was reason to believe that by the evening of 30 March 'not a white man was left alive in the outlying districts of Matabeleland', for while some had been saved by relief parties, many had been 'cruelly and treacherously murdered'. According to the early Rhodesian historian, Marshall Hole, 122 men, five women and three children were killed in March, and further murders were to follow, though on a reduced scale.

Among the dead were whites who had treated the Matabele decently. In 1938, Nganganyoni Mhlope (who had been involved in slaying settlers in the Inyathi area) recalled people he had helped to kill: 'They were our friends but since we were starting to fight they might have killed us too.'

On 25 March, the imperial authorities, which had imposed strict controls on military or police activity in Rhodesia following the Jameson Raid, inadequately responded to news of the rising by declaring that ammunition could be issued to 'not more than 100 volunteers'. That night panic swept Bulawayo when a false alarm circulated that hostile Matabele were approaching. 'The gallant inhabitants,' recalled a regular officer, Captain MacFarlane, 'lost their heads and scrambled and fought for what rifles were left in the Government Store. It was a disgraceful scene and the less said about it the better.'

Bulawayo went into laager the following day. According to Frank W. Sykes:

> Early in the morning, the commencement of a laager was formed round the Market buildings with empty wagons. Four machine guns were placed, one at each corner of the enclosure, and barbed wire thrown on the ground at a distance of about forty feet all round the line of wagons.

During the day, the laager – which was soon strengthened – was empty save for men on duty, but as night approached, it filled rapidly with people eager to enjoy its security; and although some preferred to remain in their own homes, they nonetheless resorted to the discomfort of the laager when alarms were raised. Then, according to Sykes, it 'would be literally covered with human beings lying on the ground packed like sardines', while others slept in the wagons or in the Market Hall. The *Matabele Times* of 6 April states that a count of people who had sheltered in the laager the previous Friday night had totalled 1547, of whom 915 were men. Defences were also provided elsewhere about the town. The *Rhodesia Review*, for instance, tells us that by 11 April, Williams's Consolidate Buildings in the west of Bulawayo had been transformed 'into a very strong fort, and the top of the second storey into an observatory, with telephone and helio-graph station'.

When the rising commenced, white military organisation was abysmally weak. There were only 48 officers and men of the Matabeleland Mounted Police in the whole of Matabeleland. Although few in number, they were at least loyal. On the other hand, members of the Native Police who had not joined the rebels were deemed suspect and thus disarmed as a precaution. About 600 whites in Matabeleland had enrolled the previous year to serve in a new volunteer unit known as the Rhodesia Horse, but as this was not a standing force, it was not available for immediate service and some of its scattered members were among those who had been murdered.

The majority of the Rhodesia Horse soon managed to make their way to Bulawayo and in April they were incorporated by the Acting Adminis-trator, A. H. F. Duncan, in a new unit, the Bulawayo Field Force, commanded by Colonel John Spreckley, composed of every white man in the town capable of lifting a rifle. It consisted of about fourteen troops (amounting to some 850 men) one of which, the Afrikander Corps, was mainly made up of Boers who had settled in Rhodesia.

On 1 April, Rutherford Harris – who was at Kimberley – was informed that 200 regulars were en route from England and that Colonel Herbert Plumer, the Assistant Military Secretary in Cape Town, would take charge of them and raise additional men in Cape Colony. (By early June Plumer's command, the Matabeleland Relief Force, was to number nearly 800 men.) Moreover, in mid-April, Sir Hercules Robinson, once again High Commissioner, offered Lord Grey – who had been appointed Jameson's successor as Administrator and was then at Mafeking – the services of 500 imperial troops stationed in Natal. The offer was made partly at the urging of Rhodes who had arrived in Rhodesia in late March and was in Mashonaland. It was accepted.

Meanwhile, several clashes had occurred between Matabele rebels and European patrols. On the afternoon of 4 April, for example, a few hundred Matabele assaulted a patrol of 169 men under the Honourable Maurice Gifford which had set out from Bulawayo that morning for Shiloh, a settlement to the north, and whose armament included a Maxim gun. The rebels were driven off and the patrol laagered for the night on open ground. The hours of darkness proved quiet, but shortly after setting off the following morning, Gifford was attacked again, this time by a larger number of Matabele. The rebels were again repulsed and Gifford crossed the Umguza and laagered on the eastern bank some twenty miles from Bulawayo.

Early on the 6th, members of the patrol who had been sent out to scout came across the rebels gathered at a kraal and opened fire, before falling back towards the laager, pursued by the enemy. An anonymous member of the patrol stated: 'Our men were hardly in laager when [the Matabele] rushed out into the open from the bush, with the evident intention of charging the laager. The steady fire from the men, however, soon checked them, and a few shots from the Maxim made them retire into the bush again', save for a few warriors who bravely took cover behind some stumps and dead trees in the open and maintained a galling fire until despatched by some of Gifford's best marksmen.

Hostilities died away at about noon. The patrol then spent the afternoon strengthening its position, while word was sent to Bulawayo asking for assistance. But before relief arrived, the patrol – which was short of ammunition and food – was attacked unsuccessfully once again on the morning of the 7th. Despite the various clashes, Gifford's losses were slight: two dead, one mortally wounded and a few others less seriously injured. Gifford himself had received an injury which led to the loss of his arm. The total number of Matabele dead – who had belonged to a force under Nyamanda, Lobengula's eldest son – was estimated as at least 200.

On 10 April, another patrol, 100 strong and again with one Maxim, was almost annihilated by warriors under an induna called Babyaan. Commanded by Captain George Brand, the patrol had left Bulawayo on 2 April to rescue whites in the Gwanda district to the south-east. It found the whites gone (they had moved to Tuli) and on the 9th the patrol duly began heading back up the road towards Bulawayo. The following day it entered very broken country where Matabele warriors were sighted on overlooking hills. Snipers then opened fire and a running fight developed as the patrol made its way through the hills.

Sunshine and Storm in Rhodesia contains a vivid account of events by Lieutenant Webb of the Afrikander Corps:

> Our route lay over successive ranges of ridges and valleys, and afforded plenty of cover for the enemy, as the grass was about three feet high, and the country thickly studded with bush and trees. The enemy [whom Webb believed were over a thousand strong] formed a half-moon round us and skirmished excellently, taking advantage of every bit of cover. They also fought with ferocious determination, and often showed pluck verging on lunacy.

Eventually, Brand occupied a huge flat rock in the Nsezi Valley, projecting about 15 feet above ground, and fighting continued, with the rebels firing from cover at a range of only 30–40 yards. Brand handed over command to a more experienced colleague, Captain van Niekerk, who decided that it would be best to charge the enemy and hopefully drive them from their vantage points. Several such sallies occurred and by 5.30 p.m. the Matabele had had enough and began to retire after having been engaged for about six hours. Five members of the patrol had been killed, two were mortally wounded and over twenty less seriously so. Van Niekerk (who was credited by many members of the patrol for its survival) was one such, having been hit twice. Moreover, 33 horses had been killed.

It was in mid-April that the authorities set to work constructing a chain of forts between Bulawayo and Mangwe to the south-west along the road to Bechuanaland, a task that was eased by the fact that the area contained a number of collaborating chieftaincies. On 11 April, for example, a certain Captain Molyneux left Bulawayo with 60 men and proceeded to establish a small fort on a hill at Figtree, about 30 miles to the south-west.

The rebels were to focus their attention on Bulawayo, which would be loosely besieged by strong impis on all sides other than the south-west. Selous states that he thought that it was on 16 April – the day a patrol from Bulawayo clashed with a rebel force beside the Umguza River, a few miles to the north-east – that the inhabitants first became aware that the Matabele had advanced to within striking distance of the town. Those involved in the clash on that day belonged to the northernmost group of rebels, whose leadership was centred on the middle Bembezi River where Nyamanda was holding court.

Although they shared the goal of driving out the whites and restoring the old order, the rebels were initially divided into two main factions, for not all of them wished Nyamanda to succeed Lobengula. The other faction, located to the south of Bulawayo, favoured the installation of a brother of Lobengula called Umfezela. A key advocate of Umfezela's cause was Umlugulu Khumalo, the Matabele 'high priest' whose official duties included organising the first fruits ceremony, a man described by Selous as 'a very gentle-mannered savage, and always most courteous and polite'.

Moreover, some senior indunas did not rebel. This was true, for instance, of Gampo, whose chiefdom lay in western Matabeleland: in the 1880s he had been the foremost induna in the kingdom and had married no less than five of Lobengula's daughters. It was also true of Mjaan, the former commander of Imbizo. As a result, the rebellion was also partly a civil war in which Matabele intent on ending white rule clashed with those who were prepared to accept or collaborate with the Europeans: such clashes occurred either entirely or principally in western Matabeleland.

On 17 April, the Colonial Secretary, Joseph Chamberlain, announced that all the forces in Rhodesia were to come under the command of General Sir Frederick Carrington, a veteran of native warfare. Carrington was instructed that once the defeat of the rebels was assured, he was to let Sir Richard Martin, the imperial Deputy Commissioner, judge what punitive measures were then necessary and effect a settlement. Nonetheless, as Ranger comments: 'Rhodes was highly unlikely to tolerate the prosecution of war or the making of peace in a manner of which he disapproved.' Hence although the British government was keen to sideline him, Rhodes was to play a key role in events.

Following the clash on the 16th, three unsuccessful attempts were made by the whites to dislodge the impi beside the Umguza. The most serious occurred on 22 April, and as a result of its failure, morale in Bulawayo reached a low ebb.

On the 25th, however, Captain Ronald MacFarlane, an ex-officer of the Ninth Lancers, led a detachment of some 120 whites and about 170 natives in another attempt to drive off the rebels. The force's armament included a Hotchkiss gun and one Maxim. Fierce fighting broke out on the far bank of the Umguza and the Matabele sustained heavy losses before MacFarlane, who had lost four of his own men, decided to fall back following the approach of enemy reinforcements from the west. The rebels were evidently disheartened somewhat by the outcome of the fighting and thus generally withdrew several miles downstream to the north-west, at some distance from Bulawayo, although a few parties remained in the neighbourhood.

On 28 April, Grey arrived in Bulawayo and found its inhabitants in ebullient mood. Indeed, he described the town 'as safe as Piccadilly'. But the murder of eight 'coolies' on its periphery earlier that very day underlines the fact that Grey's comment was only partially correct.

The new Administrator wished to follow up the success of the 25th, but it was not practical to do so given that he lacked the required number of men and supplies. Furthermore, Chamberlain and the High Commissioner had forbidden a major offensive until Carrington arrived. May proved, therefore, to be essentially a month of consolidation on both sides.

On 2 May, Gwelo (which had gone into laager at the start of the rebellion) was relieved by a column from Salisbury under Lieutenant-Colonel Robert Beal. On the 11th, Colonel William Napier set off from Bulawayo at the head of over 600 men to link up with Beal, and on the 19th they met near the Shangani River after Napier had routed a body of Matabele on the way, burnt kraals and seized corn.

Instead of then making directly for Bulawayo, Napier set off, on the 21st, down the valley of the Insiza River with the bulk of the combined force, while Colonel Spreckley and about 400 men likewise headed south by a different route, with the intention of linking up with Napier south-east of Bulawayo, near to where the road from Bulawayo to Belingwe forded the Insiza.

Selous, who was with Napier, tells us that as the main body made their way down the valley, they skirmished with Matabele, burnt native homesteads, seized or destroyed grain, and captured livestock. They also came across the grisly remains of whites, such as the Fouries, who had been murdered in March. Selous states:

> I went down to the scene of the massacre of the Fourie family. The murders had evidently been committed with knob-kerries and axes, as the skulls of all these poor people had been very much shattered. The remains had been much pulled about by dogs or jackals, but the long fair hair of the young Dutch girls was still intact.

The scene was such that both 'Englishmen and Dutchmen alike' vowed 'a pitiless vengeance against the whole Matabele race'. Napier linked up with Spreckley on the 27th and arrived back at Bulawayo on the last day of May.

Early on 3 June, General Carrington duly arrived to assume command of operations. His staff included Colonel Robert Baden-Powell, of subsequent Scout Movement fame. Carrington had at his disposal the approximately 800-strong Bulawayo Field Force and other irregular units such as

226

the Gwelo Field Force of 336 men under Captain Gibbs and Beal's Salisbury Column of 150 men. In addition, Plumer's Matabeleland Relief Force had recently arrived on the scene, soon to be followed by a 200-strong Cape Corps, which had been formed by Grey at Mafeking in late April and was now marching towards Bulawayo. It consisted of half-castes and natives from South Africa (some of whom were Zulu) and would thus add to the non-white element made up of Matabele 'friendlies' and Ngwato already sent up by Khama at Carrington's disposal. Additionally, Carrington could call upon the 500 regulars offered to Grey who had been moved to Mafeking, and 480 regular mounted infantry at Cape Town.

Carrington decided to strike at once. On 4 and 5 June, two large patrols under MacFarlane and Plumer were sent out to the north and north-west of Bulawayo to engage the enemy. They proceeded to burn kraals and destroy large quantities of grain. On 8 June, MacFarlane had a stiff clash with a rebel force about 1000 strong in the Redbank Hills, but failed to defeat them decisively.

Meanwhile, late on the 5th, a report reached Bulawayo that a large Matabele force had been sighted encamped on a ridge beside the Umguza north-east of the town, overlooking the ford on the main road to Salisbury. It is said to have consisted of 'carefully selected, picked men from eight different impis' (*Report on the Native Disturbances in Rhodesia, 1896–97*, 1898). Colonel Spreckley was charged with dealing with it and set out at about 9 a.m. on the 6th. Selous and Baden-Powell were among the 250 or so mounted men under his command.

The patrol crossed the Umguza and rode against the waiting rebels. In Selous's words:

> At this time we were hidden from the Kafirs by the slope of rising ground behind which they had retreated, but when this was crested they were seen in the bush little more than a hundred yards in front of the foremost horsemen. The order was at once given to charge, on which a whirlwind of horsemen bore down on them.

The Matabele, said by Selous to have numbered about 1000 men (Baden-Powell puts the figure at around 1200), responded by firing an ill-aimed volley. Baden-Powell comments:

> As we came up close, the niggers let us have an irregular, rackety volley, and in another moment we were among them. They did not wait, but one and all they turned to fly, dodging in among the bushes, loading as they ran. And we were close upon their heels, zigzagging through the thorns, jumping off now and then, or pulling up, to fire a shot (we had not a sword among us, worse luck!) and on again.

According to Baden-Powell, at times groups of Matabele tried to rally but were soon put to flight, while Selous says that the action was 'not a fight but only a pursuit in which the natives were killed as fast as they were overtaken'. The pursuit ceased when the rebels entered a belt of thick bush.

The above-mentioned report states that the rebels 'probably lost more heavily on this occasion than at any other action during the campaign'. In late August, the Administrator's daughter, Lady Victoria Grey, visited the site and wrote: 'All the ant-bear holes are filled with the corpses of niggers, they are only skeletons now. In several places we came across skeletons lying in the bush with the shield and assegai and sandals lying beside them.'

Following this reverse, the Matabele survivors retreated to the formidable natural stronghold of Intaba Zi Ka Mambo. This is often said to have been a centre of the Mwari cave-cult under a 'priest' called Mkwati: a cult focused on several shrines devoted to the worship of Mwari or Mlimo, the Shona high-god. Although Mwari had been worshipped by the Shona for centuries, the Mwari cave-cult was a more recent phenomenon. It had originated with Venda, who had migrated into Zimbabwe early in the nineteenth century from south of the Limpopo, where they had been subject to Shona influence, and where they had merged worship of their own high-god (associated with a cave shrine) with that of Mwari.

Some historians believe that the Matabele were strongly influenced by the Mwari cave-cult, which had a number of shrines in their territory, and that the cult's officers played a central role in inspiring and coordinating the rebellion of 1896. That members of the Mwari cave-cult were involved in the rebellion is evident; but the rising should be seen essentially as a desire by the Matabele themselves to overthrow white rule and restore the old order, and it was the royal family and aristocracy who provided the main leadership.

On 16 June, grim news for the Europeans arrived from the north-east. The supposedly docile and quiescent Shona in Mashonaland had likewise risen in revolt, killing white men, women and children, thus further undermining the Chartered Company's position.

Carrington responded by sending the Salisbury Column back to Mashonaland, and provided it with the support of other detachments, including the mounted infantry at Cape Town, whom he ordered to make their way to Salisbury via Beira, a port in Mozambique. To strengthen his hand in Matabeleland itself, he ordered up the regulars at Mafeking.

Before their arrival, he launched a major assault under Plumer on Intaba Zi Ka Mambo, where Nyamanda (who had been recognised by Umlugulu and other Matabele as their king by this date) and many other members of the royal family were present. Plumer left Bulawayo on 30 June. According to Frank Sykes, 'the numerical strength of the Column, including natives,

Cape Boys (drivers) etc., was about 1200 and was by far the largest yet concentrated in Rhodesia.'

On 3 July, Plumer arrived at a recently built fort at Inyathi, some twenty miles from the enemy. The next day a Thembu scout called John Grootboom, who spoke English and Sindebele, reported that their presence was known to the rebels. The latter intended sending their cattle and other loot northwards on 5 July, anticipating an assault later that day.

But Plumer made a night march and attacked at dawn. 'All through the night we rode,' recalled the journalist De Vere Stent, 'a stealthy band of khaki grey intruders ... on towards the mountain looming indistinct before us.' The column then divided, 'some to outflank the position, others to move into the heart of the enemy's fastness'. Battle was then joined against the rebels, who had been weakened by the departure of some of their number as Plumer had drawn near. He describes their position 'as a confused mass of kopjes with grassy hollows scattered among them; all these kopjes are full of caves and shelters formed among the interstices of the boulders and capable of containing many thousands of people.'

His force nevertheless succeeded in storming the position in a series of independent actions lasting from 6 a.m. until noon, despite stiff resistance. Most of the defeated rebels then began heading south to join fellow rebels, such as Umlugulu, who had retired into the Matopos following the reverse on 6 June. Plumer says that the number of rebel dead was estimated at about 100. In contrast, eighteen of his men were killed, nine of whom were Europeans, and their deaths deeply affected Rhodes, who had spurred on one of the assaults while himself unarmed.

Fighting in the Matopos

A number of inconclusive engagements followed with the rebels in the Matopo Hills, a region described by Oliver Ransford:

> It is difficult to imagine worse country to campaign in than the Matopo Hills ... an entire army could very easily be swallowed up and lost in this fantastically broken mass of hills measuring some thirty miles from west to east, and fifty miles across. Its innumerable kopjes are strewn with gigantic boulders, and riddled with caves, and surrounded by almost impenetrable underbrush.

In July, Plumer moved with the bulk of his command, supported by ancillaries, against Matabele rebels under Babyaan and Dhliso in the centre of the northernmost Matopo Hills. Late on the 19th, he left an encampment at 'Usher's No. 1' (a farm belonging to William Usher) just to the north of the Matopos, guided by Baden-Powell who had undertaken scouting work

229

and thus knew the country. Carrington, although ill, was with the column, as were Lord Grey and Rhodes.

Shortly after midnight, the column halted to sleep, but before dawn Plumer was on the move once again, approaching a pass through hills that led to a valley occupied by the rebels. After briefly halting, partly to jettison greatcoats and other impedimenta, the column resumed its march and entered the valley.

Baden-Powell was in command of the column's advance guard which consisted of Cape Boys, 200 friendly Matabele, twenty mounted white scouts, a Hotchkiss gun and two Maxims. He states that his telescope 'soon showed that there was a large camp [on the eastern side of the valley] with numerous fires, and crowds of natives moving among them. These presently formed into one dense brown mass, with their assegai blades glinting sharply in the rays of the morning sun.' The column's guns were rapidly brought up and opened fire, 'banging their shells with beautiful accuracy over the startled rebel camp'.

While this was happening, Baden-Powell made his way into the bottom of the valley and came to a spot where two valleys ran off from the main valley. One was merely a long narrow gorge heading off to the south, through which ran the Tuli River, while the other followed an easterly direction, forming a small open plateau surrounded by kopjes. Scanning the plain, Baden-Powell suddenly saw rebel warriors making their way across the valley, falling back from the shellfire and intent on taking up positions among the kopjes. He duly sent back word of their movements before conducting a flank attack at the head of the friendly Matabele against the unsuspecting rebels.

Of the assault he comments: 'Our friendlies went very gaily at the work at first, with any amount of firing, but very little result.' A comparable point is made by Frank Sykes, who served in the Medical Corps of the Matabeleland Relief Force. 'In this engagement the "friendlies" completely lost their heads and fired their rifles off wildly as fast as they could load without any definite object. They were a useless rabble, as well as a considerable source of danger to those near them.' Baden-Powell therefore called up the Cape Boys, who 'went to work with a will'. He also brought up the Hotchkiss and two Maxims, the fire from which helped to drive the rebels back, as the fighting gradually shifted along the eastern valley. Sykes tells us that, with the exception of the scouts, the white members of the column 'were held in reserve, and were simply spectators of the fight from the surrounding heights'. On the other hand, Baden-Powell says that Plumer moved up in support and helped to repel some of the enemy who had tried to cut him off. Certainly it was Baden-Powell's men who bore the brunt of the day's fighting against the rebels.

During the afternoon the column returned to camp. Its casualties were slight: a white sergeant (who had been attached to the scouts) and three Cape Boys had been killed, while a number of Cape Boys and 'friendlies' had been wounded. As for rebel casualties, Sykes comments: 'There are very conflicting accounts as to the number of the enemy who were killed.... Some exaggerate their loss into hundreds, whilst the rebels themselves give the equally ridiculous return of barely a dozen.'

Given the nature of the terrain, which afforded the Matabele a considerable amount of cover and the opportunity to slip away, it is unlikely that their losses were very high, though they were no doubt more than a mere handful. Baden-Powell, for instance, states that he saw about twenty dead in a particular spot and that the Cape Boys found 'numerous bodies and blood-trails' that 'spoke to the success of the morning's attack'.

Meanwhile, on the 19th, Major Tyrie Laing had entered the Matopos from the west in command of 170 mounted Europeans, 300 'friendlies' and an armament that included a couple of machine guns (one of which was a Maxim) and a 7-pounder. Laing had been given the task of storming local rebel positions and then moving east to support Plumer. He made his way up a narrow gorge before laagering for the night in more open ground beneath a prominent hill called Inungu.

At dawn on the 20th, Laing was attacked, the brunt of the assault being against the northern side of his position. Sykes states: 'So fierce and determined was the onslaught, that several of the foremost [Matabele] actually succeeded in sweeping up to within a pace or two of the rifles.' But firing from the defenders, including case-shot from the 7-pounder, compelled the Matabele to fall back, where they opened fire from cover. Baden-Powell states that at one place several of the best rebel marksmen were gathered and did 'great execution' until the 7-pounder opened up on them. He also relates that four men firing the Maxim were successively shot in turn by the Matabele.

Laing's force had been badly mauled. Sykes and Baden-Powell both confirm that three Europeans were killed. One of them was a picquet who had been chased back to the defences, only to be shot in the head on arrival by a Matabele. The 'friendlies', who had been encamped a short distance from the white element of Laing's force, suffered heavier losses. Baden-Powell, for instance, put the figure at 25, and estimated that nearly 100 of the enemy were slain.

Undaunted, Laing pressed on north-east later that morning to support Plumer, and dispersed another body of warriors, leaving him free to continue across what he aptly describes as 'most difficult and dangerous country'. But during the course of the afternoon he changed direction, after beginning to suspect his guides of treachery, and headed for Carrington's camp at 'Usher's No. 1.' Late on the 21st, he was joined by a

100-strong search party under Baden-Powell which had been sent out to find him, and immediately proceeded to Carrington's camp, arriving at about 3 a.m. on the 22nd.

Morale among Carrington and his staff was dented by recent developments, and was not improved when a strong force failed in an attempt to storm Inungu on the 25th. Bringing the Matopos rebels to heel was proving no easy task. This was demonstrated once again when Plumer conducted an assault on rebel positions in the eastern Matopos.

On 31 July, the camp at Usher's No. 1 was broken up and Plumer set up camp at Sugar Bush (later called Fort Umlugulu) near the north bank of the Nsezi River and on the north-eastern periphery of the Matopos. Across the Nsezi, in hills overlooking the encampment, were some 4000 Matabele rebels under Umlugulu and two other indunas, Sikombo and Nyanda, the majority of them being centred on a commanding feature called Tshingengoma.

Early on 5 August, Plumer advanced from Sugar Bush with 700 men, crossed the Nsezi and moved into the hills, guided once again by Baden-Powell. At dawn Plumer halted below one of the hills located at the entrance to a pass leading to a valley. The subsequent founder of the Scout Movement describes the valley as being semicircular, its back 'formed by a single high ridge of smooth granite' (Tshingengoma) from which 'five offshoots ran down into the valley like fingers from the ridge of knuckles' and at the tip of which were rocky peaks or kopjes.

At 7.30 a.m., Captain Beresford, 7th Hussars, was sent with 130 dismounted men and artillery to occupy a kopje at the far end of the valley and to cover the advance of the rest of the force. Initially Beresford headed south, but soon swung to the right, thereby disappearing from view, and proceeded to ascend the kopje. Upon reaching a small shoulder half-way up the hill, nearly an hour after setting off, he came under attack from a large number of Matabele who closed in from three sides. He rapidly formed his command into a square and a sharp fight ensued, lasting for over an hour. According to Baden-Powell, the Matabele attacked 'in great numbers', apparently confident of victory, only to be repeatedly checked by the steady destructive fire of their opponents (including Maxim fire) in what was 'a stiff and plucky fight on both sides'. Sykes comments that the Matabele 'made a desperate rush from the surrounding rocks', only to be halted by case-shot fired at point-blank range when they were within a few paces of the guns.

Realising the gravity of the situation, Plumer began advancing to Beresford's assistance, and upon swinging to the right saw the position occupied by the beleaguered officer and his men, whereupon the Matabele began falling back, making their way to take up positions on the next of the spurs or 'fingers' described by Baden-Powell, who continues:

This ridge we at once attacked, and we were at the foot of the ridge almost as soon as the enemy were on the upper part of it.... Dismounting and leaving our horses under cover of the rocks, we commenced to clamber up the hill, firing whenever we got a chance.

The Matabele return fire was generally too high and passed well overhead. Most of the warriors therefore began making for the next spur, but some who had occupied the kopje at its base stood their ground and fired in a more telling manner than had their colleagues. The task of dislodging them was given to a squadron of MRF under Major Kershaw, a popular officer noted for his gallantry: Baden-Powell, on the other hand, was ordered to lead a unit, Coope's Scouts, past Beresford's position and if possible make his way around the flank and rear of the enemy.

While he rode off, Kershaw and his men set to work, and according to Sykes they were assisted by another squadron under Captain Drury. Kershaw was well to the fore of his men when his progress abruptly halted near the summit when he was hit by enemy fire. He fell mortally wounded, as did a nearby NCO who was struck almost simultaneously.

Baden-Powell duly arrived on top of Tshingengoma, where he skirmished with a few rebels and saw others falling back across the ridge some way off. From the summit he had a 'splendid bird's eye view of the whole battlefield' and witnessed the final stages of the fighting below.

Following the clash in which Kershaw died, fighting had ensued further back up the valley, away from Beresford's position, as rebels occupied at least two of the other spurs and their associated kopjes. They were compelled to abandon them after being attacked, and by 3 p.m. the day's fighting was over. Reassembling his men, Plumer began the return to Sugar Bush; as the column was leaving the hills, it was jeered by Matabele warriors (part of Umlugulu's impi) who had arrived on the scene too late to take part in the fighting.

Five of Plumer's men had been killed and fifteen had been wounded, two of whose injuries proved mortal: the fatalities were all white. Yet although, according to Baden-Powell, 200–300 rebels had died, morale was at a low ebb. Sykes comments: 'A perceptible gloom was cast over the whole Force by the untimely deaths of these brave comrades in arms.'

Shortly before midnight on 8 August, the column set off from Sugar Bush again, hoping to surprise the Matabele in the vicinity of Tshingengoma at first light. Most of the men marched on foot, and after six arduous hours in which Baden-Powell once again guided the column, the foremost units arrived at the foot of Tshingengoma an hour before dawn and rested for a while, awaiting the arrival of the rest of the column, some of whose members had got lost en route. Throughout the 9th, intermittent skirmishing occurred with rebels in the neighbourhood, but on the 10th the column withdrew.

On 27 August, Lady Grey wrote to her children and expressed a widely held sentiment:

> The Matopos ... extend a very long distance and fighting in them is practically throwing away valuable lives for no adequate gain. The men are simply shot at from behind rocks without ever really a chance of an open fight and if they do drive the enemy back a kopje or two and kill a certain number of them very little is gained for they simply retire on other kopjes and after a time come back and re-occupy the old positions when the white force has moved some-where else.

By this date, however, Rhodes wished to negotiate and had indeed opened up contact with rebel leaders in the Matopos. Stent relates that the deaths of the Europeans at Intaba Zi Ka Mambo had affected Rhodes deeply and had turned his mind towards the idea of a compromise peace. But other considerations were also at work. Rhodes was eager to have the war concluded speedily, thereby limiting the cost of operations to the Company and removing the need for imperial forces to be in Rhodesia 'before their presence', comments Ranger, 'turned gradually but inevitably into imperial control of the administration'.

Some of the rebel leaders were likewise eager for peace and had quarrelled with others who felt differently. Their supplies of ammunition and food were running low, while for some months enemy patrols had been systematically burning kraals and destroying crops in the open country. If the struggle continued, the Matabele would face starvation.

The Indabas

On 14 August, after hearing that some of the rebel leaders wished to talk, Rhodes and a few companions boldly met several of them in the Matopos. Further contact followed and led to an indaba (meeting) at an appointed rendezvous on 21 August, where Rhodes was accompanied by Johan Colenbrander (who was to act as interpreter), Hans Sauer and De Vere Stent. They had revolvers but no guards. Rhodes's party arrived first. A group of senior indunas approached with a white flag, watched by thousands of warriors on overlooking hills.

According to Stent, their spokesman, Somabulana, related the story of their wanderings since the days of Mzilikazi and then exclaimed:

> 'The Maholi and the Mashona ... what are they? Dogs! Sneaking cattle thieves! Slaves! But we the Amandabili, the sons of Khumalo, the Izulu, Children of the Stars; we are no dogs! You came, you conquered. The strongest takes the land. We accepted your rule. We

lived under you. But not as dogs! If we are to be dogs it is better to be dead. You can never make the Amandabele dogs. You may wipe them out ... but the Children of the Stars can never be dogs.'

Somabulana and other indunas complained bitterly about how the Matabele had been treated by the company's administration, and Rhodes was profoundly affected by what he heard. The indaba ended at nightfall, after Rhodes had promised to disband the black police and clearly implied that he would reform the administration, put an end to the collection of cattle, and guarantee the lives of the senior indunas.

Another indaba occurred on 28 August. It was a heated affair, attended also by Matabele who wished to continue fighting. They interrupted indunas who were more conciliatory and some of them angrily questioned Rhodes. Stent says that a young chief scathingly retorted when told that Rhodes would provide land upon which they could settle: 'You will give us land in our own country! That's good of you!'

The negotiations were taking place despite general hostility among the settlers and other whites who wished the war to be prosecuted to a finish: 'Rhodesia demands a little more than peace,' commented the *Bulawayo Sketch*, 'they demand justice ... punishment for the dastardly crimes committed.' Sir Richard Martin, who had been sidelined by Rhodes, agreed. After the second indaba he made a strong but unsuccessful protest to his superiors, proposing that the negotiations should be taken out of Rhodes's conciliatory hands and conducted by himself in a firmer manner. But the Colonial Secretary came down in favour of Rhodes.

On 9 September, Rhodes attended another indaba, this time accompanied by Lord Grey and Martin, at which a demand for the surrender of weapons made on 28 August was repeated. Within days, Martin wrote:

I cannot say I considered the tone of the meeting satisfactory. The chiefs did not salute and at times showed a decidedly impertinent air, and spoke as though they had as much right to demand the withdrawal of troops that they complained were in their gardens, as we had to call them to lay down their arms.

On 11 September, General Carrington remarked in frustration that the war could not be ended militarily without a further campaign in the next dry season, requiring the services of an additional 2500 white troops plus appropriate support such as a detachment of engineers for blasting operations.

With no sign of the Matabele surrendering, on 18 September, Rhodes sent an ultimatum (via two senior indunas) to the minor indunas – the element least willing to yield. If no surrender happened soon, fighting would rapidly resume. It worked. On the 21st, Rhodes was able to inform Grey: We may say the matter is over as far as these hills are concerned. It was just as well.

A fourth indaba took place on 13 October, at which the leading 'loyalists', Gampo, Faku and Mjaan, were also present and were rewarded by being given salaried posts, while senior rebel indunas were promised similar positions on proof of good behaviour.

Meanwhile, operations had been conducted against what remained of the north-eastern rebel faction. On 23 September, Baden-Powell had reported to Carrington that his patrols had had a 'great effect' and that natives were surrendering: a process that gained momentum in October, by which time famine was taking its toll. Nyamanda surrendered in December.

By the close of 1896, therefore, peace had returned to Matabeleland, although fighting was to continue in Mashonaland into 1897. The struggle had not been entirely futile from the rebel viewpoint. Rhodes and others had been made acutely aware that the company's administration needed to be radically overhauled and that the Matabele should be treated more humanely, not only to prevent further trouble – there were a number of scares following the rising – but also to keep in line with public sentiment elsewhere, most notably in Britain, where the subject of native treatment in Rhodesia had become a matter of widespread general interest.

Some improvements were implemented; but the Matabele also experienced disappointments. For instance, partly owing to the company's unwillingness to pay large sums of money for the purchase of land already granted to whites, the well-intentioned Lord Grey failed to push through a programme of land reform aimed at allowing Matabele to settle on land of their own in central Matabeleland. In short, white rule had not been overthrown and the Matabele were still viewed very much as second-class citizens, a state of affairs that was to continue into the second half of the twentieth century when many Matabele and other blacks in Rhodesia would once again fight for their freedom.

CHAPTER 12
EPILOGUE

In 1979, white minority rule came to an end in Rhodesia. It did so after a bitter and prolonged war between the Rhodesian security forces and terrorist armies, principally ZANLA, the Zimbabwe African National Liberation Army (consisting essentially of Shona freedom fighters) and ZIPRA, the Zimbabwe People's Revolutionary Army, whose members were mostly Matabele. Although ZIPRA had less manpower, its men were better equipped and wore camouflaged uniforms, in contrast to those of ZANLA, many of whom wore civilian clothing.

It will be recalled that the Chartered Company's administration of Rhodesia survived the rebellions of 1896–7. In 1923, however, it ended when Rhodesia became a self-governing colony, with the British government having the right to veto legislation discriminating against non-whites. But in the 1960s armed conflict began with black nationalists who were intent on bringing white rule to an end.

In 1964, small groups of ZIPRA and ZANU guerrillas infiltrated northern Rhodesia from neighbouring Zambia, where their respective organisations were based. They had been trained in sabotage and subversion in countries such as the Soviet Union and China. But most of them were soon captured by the small but efficient Rhodesian security forces, partly acting on intelligence provided by local tribesmen.

In November of the following year, the white minority headed by Ian Smith (a great admirer of Sir Winston Churchill) made a Unilateral Declaration of Independence from Great Britain rather than accept the British government's policy of moving towards majority rule. In a population of some 4,870,000 non-whites, there were 228,000 or so Europeans most of whom were of British extraction, although there was also a marked South African presence as well as other minority groups such as the Portuguese. There was, moreover, a strong will to resist what most perceived not only as a threat to their own way of life but as an insidious communist plot to subvert Western civilisation in general.

The first serious incursion by ZANLA insurgents occurred in April 1966, and others followed, some of them by ZIPRA. In mid-1967, approximately 90 guerrillas (mostly ZIPRA) crossed the Zambezi, but their presence was reported. They were soon intercepted and 47 of them killed and 20 captured.

A further 123 guerrillas infiltrated Rhodesia in the closing days of 1967. They established base camps and tried to recruit local tribesmen for training. In March 1968, however, they were detected and the security forces struck, killing 69 of them and capturing many others.

Despite these setbacks, which indicated that large guerrilla concentrations were outclassed by an enemy enjoying greater mobility and airpower, large-scale incursions continued until this strategy was abandoned in 1969 following further reverses. As Martin Meredith comments:

> The nationalist strategy had been disastrous. They had committed a large proportion of their well-armed and well-trained forces to almost inevitable annihilation; they had failed to mobilise the African population or even reach them on a political level.

Dissension soon wracked ZIPRA and its political wing, ZAPU. In February 1970, Jason Moyo, who controlled ZAPU's military administration, published a stinging indictment of the party leadership:

> Since mid-1969, there has been a steady decline of a serious nature in our military administration and army. Military rules have been cast overboard. Planning of strategy is seriously lacking. Indiscipline is fast approaching dangerous proportions.

ZIPRA was not to pose a significant threat for years to come.

Meanwhile, ZANLA's failure to make headway had likewise resulted in demoralisation and infighting. Incursions ceased while a military reappraisal was undertaken. In the early 1970s, arms and ammunition caches were established for future operations in areas of Rhodesia where the native population had been largely won over by ZANLA agents.

In contrast, white morale had been boosted, both by the failure of the nationalists to make headway and by the failure of sanctions to bring the country to its knees – the United Nations had imposed comprehensive mandatory sanctions in 1968. Morale was also buoyed up by South African support, both economic and military, for in 1967 South Africa had committed a small number of combat police to help the Rhodesian security forces. In short, a Dunkirk spirit prevailed. White Rhodesians were generally defiant, closely knit and fiercely patriotic, steeped in the heroic endeavour of predecessors such as Allan Wilson and his ill-fated patrol, and aware of the distinguished service rendered by Rhodesians in two World Wars.

In December 1972, hostilities recommenced when ZANLA terrorists crossed into Rhodesia from bases established in Mozambique (without the blessing of Mozambique's colonial masters, the Portuguese, who were fighting their own war against black nationalists) and attacked two white farms, causing a number of injuries. Other such attacks in the north-east soon followed. In 1973, the government responded by imposing collective fines and other punitive measures on native communities suspected of aiding guerrillas – the African tribespeople thus found themselves under pressure from both sides – and extended national service to Asians and men of mixed race. Black volunteers were also serving in the Rhodesian Army, most notably in the Rhodesian African Rifles, a unit dating from 1940 whose officers (until 1979) were all white.

ZIPRA rejoined the fray in 1976, by which time the Portuguese had left Mozambique: their troops pulled out in 1974 with the result that Rhodesia's 764-mile long eastern border now bounded a hostile state. Moreover, in 1975 South Africa had withdrawn its combat police from Rhodesia. ZIPRA guerrillas entered Rhodesia from Mozambique, together with ZANLA forces, but withdrew after clashing with the latter.

ZIPRA then opened a new front by infiltrating Rhodesia from bases to the west in Botswana. Sporadic hit-and-run raids occurred in the Bulawayo area and along the main road running from Bulawayo to the Victoria Falls. Furthermore, others infiltrated from Zambia (some did so by crossing Kariba Dam in rubber dinghies) and thus the Rhodesian armed forces found themselves increasingly stretched, despite measures to meet the problem – such as the extension of the period of national service. Fear spread to more and more of the country's inhabitants, black and white. Indeed, European emigration was becoming an increasing problem. In 1976 nearly 15,000 whites left the country, many of them settling in South Africa.

By mid-1977 the war had spread right across Rhodesia, with ZIPRA's military capability greater than hitherto, for since August 1976 ZAPU had carried out a massive recruitment campaign among the Matabele and Kalanga and many men had thus made their way to Botswana en route to training in Zambia, Angola and Russia. The bulk of ZAPU's forces, however, were not committed to the struggle – they were with-held for a full-scale invasion in due course – and so ZANLA continued to spearhead the guerrilla war effort. By the middle of 1977 there were only about 150 ZIPRA at large in Rhodesia, in contrast to approximately 3000 ZANLA.

Reluctantly, on 24 November 1977, Ian Smith finally conceded to the principle of one-man one-vote, although he believed that by negotiating with moderate or pliant black leaders (whom Smith believed enjoyed the support of most blacks in Rhodesia) he would nonetheless be able to secure future significant white influence in Rhodesia's affairs, including control of the security forces. Meredith comments:

Majority rule to him meant simply a parliamentary rearrangement; the blacks would be given a majority in Parliament but be deprived of the power to interfere with constitutional provisions safeguarding white interests.

Exiled black leaders outside Rhodesia such as Joshua Nkomo, the head of ZAPU, denounced the talks as an attempt to install a 'puppet' government and the war went on.

A marked feature of the conflict was a succession of pre-emptive strikes launched against guerrilla bases in neighbouring states by the Rhodesian military, such as the SAS, a small unit that enjoyed the respect of its British counterpart. In October 1978, for instance, during Operation Gatling, the Rhodesians hit ZIPRA's bases in Zambia. The Rhodesian Air Force took control of Zambian air space (Zambia's Air Force stayed grounded) and for three days Rhodesian forces carried out assaults which claimed the lives of over 1500 guerrillas.

Operation Gatling occurred a month after ZIPRA had downed a civilian Viscount airliner, using a SAM-7 missile, and had then murdered ten survivors. In February 1979, ZIPRA brought down another Viscount, killing all aboard. The Rhodesian security forces thus retaliated by launching an air raid on a ZIPRA base in distant Angola, and by striking targets once again in Zambia.

Talks with moderate black leaders, such as Bishop Abel Muzorewa, nevertheless continued and led to an 'internal settlement', which introduced universal suffrage. In a General Election in mid-1979 Muzorewa was elected Prime Minister of what was henceforth to be known as Zimbabwe-Rhodesia, but control of the security forces remained in white hands. Needless to say, militant nationalists kept waging the armed struggle, while the 'internal settlement' was likewise rejected by the international community.

In September 1979, by which time both sides in the struggle were war weary, representatives from their respective camps met for talks at Lancaster House in London. An agreement on a new constitution was reached and a ceasefire agreement was signed on 31 December. Consequently, in 1980, a Commonwealth Monitoring Force arrived in Zimbabwe-Rhodesia to supervise the ceasefire and monitor a General Election. To the shock of many whites, in April 1980, Muzorewa and his party were swept aside and Robert Mugabe of ZANU became the first Prime Minister of what was now simply called Zimbabwe. The early years of his premiership witnessed ugly scenes in Matabeleland, as his security forces (bolstered by troops from North Korea) stamped their authority on the area, and it has been estimated that up to 30,000 Matabele perished.

During the many years of fighting which led to the establishment of Zimbabwe, the freedom fighters had consistently been bested by the highly professional Rhodesian armed forces. As Leroy Thompson, an expert in the field of counter-insurgency, comments:

> The Rhodesian Army was one of the best counter-insurgency forces ever created, a fact obviously appreciated by South Africa, which

absorbed certain elements of the Rhodesian Army almost in their entirety into the South African Army when they left Rhodesia.

The ANC and Inkatha

By 1980 South Africa was itself experiencing black unrest, with nationalists determined likewise to end white minority rule, not only in South Africa but also in its dependency of South West Africa. Here, from 1965, the South African armed forces had been engaged in a guerrilla war against local freedom fighters, a war which had led to South Africa's engagement in conflict with communist forces in Angola as well.

In South Africa, African nationalism was dominated by the ANC (African National Congress), which had come into existence in 1912. Its founding fathers included John Dube (the son of a minor Zulu chief), the ANC's first president, and another Zulu speaker called Pixley kaSeme, the husband of one of Dinuzulu's daughters, who served as treasurer. Nonetheless, in the years that followed its foundation, the ANC failed to 'awake the mass of Africans to political awareness', to use the words of a Zulu chief and member of the ANC, Albert Lutuli.

This changed during the 1950s. In 1948, hardline Afrikaners – the National Party – were elected to power, and they introduced apartheid, a policy of racial segregation more rigorous than had existed before. Consequently, during the 1950s, the ANC began to enjoy mass black appeal and engaged in civil disobedience. It enjoyed its greatest support in the Eastern Cape, for in Natal the movement had been weakened by factionalism and had lost its sense of direction.

Tension in South Africa reached new heights in 1960. On 21 March, a crowd of about 5000 blacks in the township of Sharpeville descended on the police station. A couple of months earlier, nine police had been beaten to death by a mob in Durban and when a scuffle developed, the Sharpeville police (who had been reinforced) opened fire, killing 69 of the demonstrators.

At this date the ANC's leader was Albert Lutuli, a devout Christian who had been elected the movement's president in 1952. He promptly called a day of mourning and prayer, effectively a one-day national strike. Moreover, on 26 March, he burned his passbook before the media and urged others to do likewise, for passbooks were a hated part of the apartheid system. Within days, the government responded by declaring a State of Emergency under which the police had sweeping powers of arrest. Lutuli was among those arrested, and the ANC and a more radical nationalist movement, the PAC (Pan African Congress), which objected to the ANC's policy of allowing white members, were banned.

In June 1961, by which time the State of Emergency had been lifted, the detainees freed, and Lutuli awarded the 1960 Nobel Peace Prize,

241

militant members of the ANC such as Nelson Mandela, a Xhosa and the movement's deputy president, decided on the use of violence to undermine apartheid. Consequently, in 1964, Mandela and other leading militants were sentenced to life imprisonment for terrorist offences. Lutuli, on the other hand, concentrated unsuccessfully on securing the imposition of sanctions against South Africa by the international community.

Lutuli died in July 1967, and his funeral address was delivered by a Zulu protégé, Chief Mangosuthu Gatsha Buthelezi, a paternal grandson of Mnyamana, Cetshwayo's former prime minister, and a maternal grandson of Dinuzulu, Cetshwayo's son and successor. Lutuli's hopes of living to see an end to white dominance in South Africa had thus not come to fruition. Apartheid was still very much in place and indeed had become more firmly entrenched, for in recent years the Nationalist government (which had been continually re-elected by white voters since 1948) had devoted much of its attention and resources to building up the country's armed forces to protect white minority rule from both external and internal opposition.

Part of the apartheid system was the policy of setting up tribal homelands known as Bantustans, supposedly independent black states; and in March 1972 the South African government established a self-governing territory called KwaZulu, which consisted of 44 separate blocks of land north and south of the Tugela. Its chief minister was Buthelezi, a staunch Zulu nationalist who had portrayed his great-grandfather Cetshwayo in the epic 1964 film *Zulu*, starring Stanley Baker and Michael Caine. For years he had been an outspoken critic of apartheid both at home and abroad. He was now to remain a thorn in the South African government's side. For example, he refused to accept the fiction that KwaZulu was really independent, and openly called for the release of Mandela and other imprisoned black leaders.

In March 1975, moreover, Buthelezi set up the Inkatha movement (a revival of a defunct movement first established in the 1920s) to serve as 'an instrument of liberation', albeit one eschewing armed confrontation with the South African security forces. As Buthelezi was to comment in March 1992:

In our history, Zulus went to war for spoils. It was very clear to us that any war with the South African Defence Force [the most potent military machine in Africa] would be a war without spoils, just ashes.

In June 1976, violence erupted in the vast black township of Soweto near Johannesburg, South Africa's greatest city, and spread elsewhere, only to be crushed by the government. History repeated itself on a greater scale in the mid-1980s. Nevertheless, in August 1990, with the South African economy being badly hit by sanctions imposed some years earlier by the international community to bring an end to apartheid, South Africa's moderate new president, F. W. de Klerk, released Mandela and unbanned organisations such as the ANC.

By this date, Buthelezi was finding himself increasingly marginalised, and had indeed been denounced as a stooge of the South African government by more militant nationalists, who viewed him and Inkatha (whose membership was almost entirely Zulu) with hostility and contempt. This acrimonious state of affairs had prevailed ever since members of the ANC's leadership in exile had decided to undermine him a decade earlier.

Indeed, violence between supporters of Inkatha and more radical blacks, both in Natal and elsewhere, had been occurring for a number of years. North of the Tugela, in the Zulu heartland, Buthelezi was supreme. But in the urban areas around Durban and Pietermaritzburg he had lost ground to the UDF (United Democratic Front), a surrogate for the then banned ANC. Heightened bloodshed occurred following Mandela's release, and in the years 1990–4 nearly 10,000 people were killed in KwaZulu-Natal alone as Inkatha and suppporters of the ANC fought for supremacy, and in many cases Zulu killed Zulu.

Bloodshed also occurred on the Witwatersrand, to which Zulu males had gone to work and where they lived in hostels in townships such as Soweto. A clash between Zulu migrant workers and local militants had occurred in Soweto during the disturbances of 1976, but 1990 witnessed the start of more serious conflict in the black townships of the region. In June 1992, for instance, marauding Zulu hostel dwellers killed 42 residents of Biopatong, and the world's television portrayed street battles waged between the two factions. One such occurred in the heart of Johannesburg itself in early 1994.

Then, in late April of that year, following protracted constitutional talks between the government and other parties, most notably the ANC, South Africans of all races went to the polls. Nationally, Nelson Mandela and the ANC swept to power. In KwaZulu-Natal, however it was Inkatha that topped the polls, gaining 50.3 per cent of the vote. Even allowing for electoral malpractice (of which the ANC was likewise guilty) Inkatha clearly enjoyed a higher degree of support in the province than many had anticipated. Hence it was to be the dominant party in the KwaZulu-Natal regional assembly. On the other hand, it only gained 43 seats in the national parliament, in contrast to the 82 of the National Party (which obtained significant non-white support) and the 252 of the ANC. During the election period, violence ceased in KwaZulu-Natal but it has sadly continued since then, with supporters of Inkatha and the ANC once again adding to the death toll.

And what of the Zulu monarchy? It still exists, despite various vicissitudes over the years, and 'the institution, role, authority and status' of the Zulu monarch in KwaZulu-Natal is enshrined in South Africa's new constitution. The current king is Goodwill Zwelithini, a great-grandson of Dinuzulu and a nephew of Buthelezi, who began to emerge from under his uncle's shadow in the period leading up to the 1994 elections. There is still a strong sense of Zulu nationhood in South Africa and the king enjoys the adulation and deep respect of a considerable percentage of the Zulu people.

BIBLIOGRAPHY

Abbott, P. and Botham, P., *Modern African Wars (1): Rhodesia 1965–80*, 1986.

Baden-Powell, R. S. S., *The Matabele Campaign*, 1900.

Ballard, C., *The House of Shaka: the Zulu Monarchy Illustrated*, 1988.

Barthorp, M., *The Zulu War: A Pictorial History*, 1980.

Beach, D. N., 'Ndebele raiders and Shona power', *Journal of African History*, XV, 4, 1974.

–, *The Shona and Zimbabwe 900–1850*, 1980.

Becker, P., *Rule of Fear: the Life and Times of Dingane, King of the Zulu*, 1964.

Bhebe, N. M. B., 'Aspects of Ndebele relations with the Shona in the 19th century', *Rhodesian History*, 4, 1973.

–, 'Ndebele trade in the 19th century', *Journal of African Studies*, 1, 1, 1974.

Binns, C. T., *The Last Zulu King: the Life and Death of Cetshwayo*, 1963.

Bird, J., *The Annals of Natal, 1495–1845*, 1965.

Blake, R., *A History of Rhodesia*, 1977.

Brown, R., 'The Ndebele Succession Crisis, 1868–1877 in *Historians in Tropical Africa*, 1962.

–, 'The external relations of the Ndebele kingdom in the prepartition era', in *African Societies in Southern Africa*, (ed) L. Thompson, 1969.

Bryant, A. T., *Olden Times in Zululand and Natal*, 1929.

Bulpin, T. V., *To the Banks of the Zambezi*, 1965.

Cobbing, J., 'Lobengula, Jameson and the Occupation of Mashonaland 1890', *Rhodesian History*, 4, 1973.

–, 'The Evolution of Ndebele Amabutho', *Journal of African History*, XV, 4, 1974.

–, *The Ndebele under the Khumalos, 1820–1896*, (unpublished Ph.D thesis, University of Lancaster, 1976).

Cole, B., *The Elite: the Story of the Rhodesian Special Air Service*, 1984.

Colenbrander, P., 'The Zulu Political Economy on the Eve of the War', in *The Anglo-Zulu War – New Perspectives'*, eds A. Duminy and C. Ballard, 1981.

Cooper-Chadwick, J., *Three Years with Lobengula and Experiences in South Africa*, 1894.

Davenport, T. R. H., *South Africa: A Modern History*, (4th ed.), 1991.

Du Plessis, J., *A History of Christian Missions in South Africa*, 1911.

Duminy, A., and Guest, B., (eds) *Natal and Zululand from earliest times to 1910*, 1989.

Emery, F., *The Red Soldier: Letters from the Zulu War, 1879*, 1977.

Etherington, N., 'Anglo-Zulu Relations 1856–1878' in *The Anglo-Zulu War – New Perspectives*, eds A. Duminy and C. Ballard, 1981.

Fagan, B., 'The later Iron Age in South Africa', in *African Societies in Southern Africa*, (ed) L. Thompson, 1969.

Flint, J., *Cecil Rhodes*, 1976.

Gardiner, A., *Narrative of a Journey to the Zoolu Country in South Africa*, 1836.

Gibson, J. Y., *The Story of the Zulus*, 1911.

Glass, S., *The Matabele War*, 1968.

Guest, W. R., 'The War, Natal and Confederation', in *The Anglo-Zulu War – New Perspectives*, eds A. Duminy and C. Ballard, 1981.

Guy, J., *The Destruction of the Zulu Kingdom: The Civil War in Zululand 1879–1884*, 1979.

Hamilton, C. A., 'The Character and Objects of Chaka': A Reconsideration of the Making of Shaka as 'Mfecane' Motor, *Journal of African History*, 33:1, 1992.

Hammond-Tooke, W. D., (ed) *The Bantu Speaking Peoples of Southern Africa*, 1974.

Harris, W. C. *The Wild Sports of Southern Africa*, 1839.

Haythornthwaite, P., *The Colonial Wars Source Book*, 1995.

Hole, H. M., *The Making of Rhodesia*, 1926.

Holme, N., *The Silver Wreath: Being the 24th Regiment at Isandlwana and Rorke's Drift*, 1979.

Hughes, A. J. B., *Kin, Caste and Nation among the Rhodesian Ndebele*, 1956.

Isaacs, N., (eds. L. Herman and P. Kirby) *Travels and Adventures in Eastern Africa*, vols I and II, 1970.

James, L., *The Savage Wars: British Campaigns in Africa, 1870–1920*, 1985.

Knight, E., *Rhodesia of Today*, 1895.

Knight, I., *The Zulus*, 1989.

–, *Brave Men's Blood: The Epic of the Zulu War, 1879*, 1990.

–, *Zulu: Isandlwana and Rorke's Drift 22nd–23rd January 1879*, 1992.

–, *Zulu War 1879: Twilight of a Warrior Nation*, 1992.

–, *Nothing Remains but to Fight: the Defence of Rorke's Drift, 1879*, 1993.

–, *Warrior Chiefs of Southern Africa*, 1994.

–, *The Anatomy of the Zulu Army from Shaka to Cetshwayo 1818–1879*, 1995.

Knight, I. and Castle, I., *The Zulu War Then and Now*, 1993.

Kuper, H. and Hughes, A. J. B., *The Shona and Ndebele of Southern Rhodesia*, 1954.

Laband, J., *Fight Us in the Open: the Anglo-Zulu War through Zulu Eyes*, 1985.

–, 'The Zulu army in the war of 1879: some cautionary notes', in *Kingdom and Colony at War*, eds J. Laband and P. Thompson, 1990.

–, 'The Battle of Khambula, 29 March 1879: a re-examination from the Zulu perspective', ibid.

–, 'Mbilini, Manyonyoba and the Phongolo River frontier: a neglected sector of the Anglo-Zulu War of 1879', ibid.

–, *The Rise & Fall of the Zulu Nation*, 1997.

Legassick, M., 'The Sotho-Tswana Peoples before 1800', in *African Societies in Southern Africa*, (ed) L. Thompson, 1969.

Liesegang, G., 'Nguni migrations between Delagoa Bay and the Zambezi River', in *Journal of African Historical Studies*, III, 2, 1970.

Lye. W. F., *Andrew Smith's Journal of his Expedition into the interior of South Africa*, 1975.

Marks, S., 'The Traditions of the Natal "Nguni": a second look at the work of A. T. Bryant', in *African Societies in Southern Africa*, (ed) L. Thompson, 1969.

–, *Reluctant Rebellion: The 1906–8 Disturbances in Natal*, 1970.

Mason, P., *The Birth of a Dilemma: The Conquest and Settlement of Rhodesia*, 1968.

Meikle, J., *Reminiscences* (unpublished).

Meintjes, J., *The Voortrekkers: the story of the Great Trek and the making of South Africa*, 1973.

Meredith, M., *The Past Is Another Country: Rhodesia 1890–1979*, 1979.

Mitford, B., *Through the Zulu Country: Its Battlefields and its People*, 1883.

Moffat, R., (ed. J. P. Wallis), *Matabele Journals of Robert Moffat*, 1945.

Morris, D. R., *The Washing of the Spears: A History of the Rise of the Zulu Nation under Shaka and its Fall in the Zulu War of 1879*, 1966.

Muller, C. F. J. (ed) *Five Hundred Years: A History of South Africa*, 1969.

Mziki [A. A. Campbell], *Mlimo: the Rise and Fall of the Matabele*, 1926.

Norris-Newman, C. L., *In Zululand with the British throughout the War of 1879*, 1880.

Okoye, F. N C., 'Dingane: a reappraisal', *Journal of African History*, Vol X. no.1, 1969.

Omer-Cooper, J. D., '*The Zulu Aftermath: A Nineteenth Century Revolution in Bantu Africa*, 1966.

'Aspects of political change in the nineteenth-century Mfecane', in *African Societies in Southern Africa*, (ed) L. Thompson, 1969.

Owen. F., (ed. G. Cory) *The Diary of the Rev. Francis Owen, Missionary with Dingaan in 1837–38*, 1926.

Palley, C., *The Constitutional History and Law of Southern Rhodesia 1888–1965, with Special Reference to Imperial Control*, 1966.

Phillipson, D. W., 'Early iron-using peoples of southern Africa', in *African Societies in Southern Africa*, (ed) L. Thompson, 1969

Plumer, H., *An Irregular Corps in Matabeleland*, 1897.

Preller, G., *Lobengula: the tragedy of a Matabele king*, 1963.

Ranger, T. O., *Revolt in Southern Rhodesia, 1896-97*, 1966.

Ransford, O., *Bulawayo: Historic Battleground of Rhodesia*, 1968.

Rasmussen, R. K., *Migrant Kingdom: Mzilikazi's Ndebele in South Africa*, 1978.

Ritter, E. A., *Shaka Zulu: The Rise of the Zulu Empire*, 1957.

Roberts, B., *The Zulu Kings*, 1974.

Rorke, M., *Melina Rorke*, 1939.

Samkange, S., *Origins of Rhodesia*, 1968.

Saunders, C., *Black Leaders in Southern African History*, 1979.

Selous, F. C., *A Hunter's Wanderings in Africa*, 1881.

–, *Travels and Adventures in South-East Africa*, 1893.

–, *Sunshine and Storm in Rhodesia*, 1896.

Smith, A., 'The Trade of Delagoa Bay as a factor in Nguni politics 1750–1835', in *African Societies in Southern Africa*, (ed) L. Thompson, 1969.

Smith-Dorrien, Gen. Sir H., *Memories of Forty-Eight Years Service*, 1925.

Spies, F. J. du Toit, 'Bloedrivier – "n ondersoek na die werklike feite"', in *Standpunte*, 17 (1), 1963.

Storry, G. J., *The Shattered Nation*, 1974.

Stow, G. W., *The Native Races of Southern Africa*, (ed.) G. McCall Theal.

Stuart, J., *The James Stuart Archive of Recorded Oral Evidence*, vols I, II, III and IV (eds) C. de B. Webb and J. B. Wright, 1976, 1979, 1982 and 1986.

Stuart, J. and Malcolm, D., (eds) *The Diary of Henry Francis Fynn*, 1969.

Summers, R. and Pagden, C. W., *The Warriors*, 1970.

Sykes, F. W., *With Plumer in Matabeleland*, 1897.

Taylor, S., *Shaka's Children: A History of the Zulu People*, 1994.

Thomas, T. M., *Eleven Years In Central South Africa*, 1872.

Thompson, L., *Ragged War: the Story of Unconventional and Counter-Revolutionary Warfare*, 1994.

Thompson, L., *The Political Mythology of Apartheid*, 1985 – *A History of South Africa*, 1996.

Thompson, P., 'The Natal Native Contingent at Rorke's Drift, 22 January 1879', in *Kingdom and Colony at War*, eds J. Laband and P. Thompson, 1990.

Unterhalter, E., 'Confronting Imperialism: the People of Nquthu and the Invasion of Zululand', in *The Anglo-Zulu War – New Perspectives*, eds A. Duminy and C. Ballard, 1981.

Van Jaarsveld, F. A., 'A Historical Mirror of Blood River', in *The Meaning of History*, (eds.) A. Konig and H. Keane, 1980.

Walker, E.A., *The Great Trek*, 1934.

Webb, C. de B. and Wright, J. B., (eds) *A Zulu King Speaks: Statements made by Cetshwayo kaMpande on the Customs and History of his People*, 1978.

Wills, W. A. and Collingridge, L. T., *The Downfall of Lobengula: the Cause, History and Effect of the Matabele War*, 1894.

Wilson, M. and Thompson, L., (eds.) *The Oxford History of South Africa*, vols I and II, 1971.

Wilson, M., 'Changes in social structure in southern Africa: the relevance of kinship studies to the historian', in *African Societies in Southern Africa*, (ed) L. Thompson, 1969.

INDEX

Nyezane, 102 (battle of, 103) 104,
112, 114-117
Nyoni Heights, 80, 86
Nzobo kaSobadli, 42-43, 49, 57-58

O

Ogle, John, 40
oNdini, 69, 71, 73, 78, 80, 101-102,
105-106, 111, 115-117, 119-121,
124-126, 134, 136-137
Orange River, 45, 151
Osborn, Melmoth, 128-133, 138,
140, 141
Oude Moulen, 132
Owen, Francis, 36, 47-48, 50

P

Palley, Claire, 189, 192
Patterson, Captain R. R., 183-184
Pearson, Colonel Charles, 74, 102-
105, 111-112
Pedi, 70, 72, 154
Pietermaritzburg, 57, 62, 66, 101,
129-130, 133, 143, 145, 243
Pioneer Column, 189-191
Plumer, Colonel Herbert, 223, 227-233
Pondo, 26,27, 32, 37, 40, 61
Pondoland, 40-41, 61
Pongola River, 15, 29, 33, 57-58, 133,
135, 136, 149, 151
Port Elizabeth, 32, 162
Port Natal, 28-31, 34, 37-43, 46-47,
53, 56, 59
Portuguese, 11, 15, 27, 41, 171, 185,
237-239
Potgieter, Hendrik, 46, 49-50, 163,
165, 167-168, 172-173
Pretoria, 70, 105, 154
Pretorius, Andries, 52-58, 61-62
Pulleine, Lieutenant-Colonel Henry,
83-84, 88-90, 92

Q

Qulusi, 77, 104-106, 125, 132, 136
Qwabe, 11, 14, 28-29, 35, 37,

R

Raaff, Commandant Pieter, 106, 107,
200, 212, 213
Ranger, Terence, 218, 220, 225, 234
Ransford, Oliver, 229
Rasmussen, R. Kent, 150, 154, 155,
165, 169, 170
Raw, Lieutenant, 84-86, 88
Regiments: (Matabele)
Amaveni, 206
Inqobo, 206
Ihlati, 206, 211
Imbizo (Imbezu), 203, 206, 208,
210-212, 215, 225
Induba, 206
Ingubo, 210, 211, 215
Insuga (Insukamini), 202, 206, 207,
210, 211
Isiziba, 206, 211
Regiments: Zulu
iNdlondlo, 85-86, 93
iNdluyengwe, 85, 86, 93, 94, 97, 98
iNgobamakhosi, 78, 79, 85, 86, 90-
92, 107, 108, 110, 111, 121
iSangqu, 85, 86, 89
Mbube, 85, 86, 89
uDlambedlu, 102
uDloko, 85, 86, 93
uDududu, 85, 86, 89
uKhandempemvu, see uMcijo
uMbonambi, 85, 86, 90, 91, 109,
111
uMcijo, 65, 85, 86, 88, 89, 91, 107,
109, 111, 119, 121, 122
uMxhapho, 85, 86, 89, 102, 119
ungwini 104,107, 110
uNokhenke, 85, 86, 89, 91, 109
uThulwana, 64, 67, 78, 85, 86, 93,
98
uVe, 78, 85, 86, 90-92, 121
Retief, Piet, 45-51, 57-59
Reynolds, Surgeon-Major James, 96,
98
Rhenoster River, 163
Rhodes, Cecil John, 185-190, 195,